Staying Connected How to Continue Your Relationships with Those Who Have Died

Staying Connected

How to Continue Your Relationships
with Those Who Have Died

Rudolf Steiner

Selected Talks and Meditations

1905-1924

Edited and Introduced by Christopher Bamford

☙ Anthroposophic Press

Copyright © 1999 by Anthroposophic Press.

See page 267 for the list of sources for this collection.

Published by SteinerBooks [Anthroposophic Press]
P.O. Box 749
Gt. Barrington, MA 01230

www.steinerbooks.org

LIBRARY OF CONGRESS CATALOGING IN PUBLICATION DATA

Steiner, Rudolf, 1861–1925.
    [Selections. English]
    Staying connected ; how to continue your relationships with those who have
died : selected talks and meditations, 1905–1924 / Rudolf Steiner ; edited and
introduced by Christopher Bamford.
        p. cm.
    Includes bibliographical references.
    ISBN 0-88010-462-7 (pbk.)   ISBN-13 978-0-88010-462-3
    1. Future life—Anthroposophy. 2. Anthroposophy.
    I. Bamford, Christopher. II. Title.

BP596.F85 S73713 1999
299'.935—dc21   99-048781

Printed in the United States of America

Contents

Part Three
"Experience"

This is what it comes down to: that we learn to experience that those who have passed through the gate of death have only assumed another form.

Having died, they stand before our feelings like those who, through life circumstances, have traveled to distant lands, whither we can follow them only later. We have therefore nothing to bear but a time of separation.

Spiritual science must help us learn to feel and experience this in the most living way we can.

—RUDOLF STEINER, JUNE 17, 1915

Know the spiritual world! Then, among the many other blessings that humanity will gain will be this: that the living and the dead will be able to form a unity.

—RUDOLF STEINER, NOVEMBER 17, 1916

Introduction

We must regain the understanding that we are not on earth just to build things in the physical universe during our physical existence. We must understand that during our whole existence we are connected to the whole world. Those who have passed through the gates of death want to work with us on the physical world. This working together only appears to be a physical collaboration, for everything physical is only an outer expression of spirit. Materialism has alienated human beings from the world of the dead. Spiritual science must help us make friends again with that world. The time must come when we no longer alienate ourselves from the dead for it is our alienation that prevents them from spiritualizing the physical world. The dead cannot grasp things in the physical world with their hands or do physical work. To believe that would be superstition. The dead can, however, work in a spiritual way. To do so they need tools placed at their disposal; they need the spirit to live here in the physical world. We are not just human beings, we are also tools—instruments for the spirits who have passed through the gate of death. While incarnated in a physical body we use a pen, or a hammer, or an axe; but once we are no longer physically incarnate, the tools we use are human souls themselves. This has to do with the special way in which the dead perceive....

For instance, suppose you have before you a small vessel containing salt. You can see that. The salt looks like a white substance, a white powder. The fact that you see the salt as a white powder depends upon your eyes. Your spirit cannot see the salt as a white powder; but if you put a little salt on your tongue and taste its special taste, then the spirit can begin to become aware of it. Every spirit can perceive the taste of salt in you. In fact, everything that takes place in human beings through the outer world can be perceived by every spirit, including human souls who have passed through the gate of death. Within us, the sense world extends to our tasting, smelling, seeing, hearing, and so forth; the world of the dead also reaches down into what we hear, see, and taste. The dead can experience with us what we experience in the physical world. This is because these experiences belong not only to our world but also to theirs. Our experiences belong to their world when we thoroughly spiritualize what we experience in the outer world with spiritual ideas. Otherwise, what we experience as the effects of matter remains dark and incomprehensible to the dead. To the dead, a soul devoid of spirit is a dark soul. This is why the dead have become estranged from earthly life. We must overcome this estrangement. The so-called dead and the so-called living must learn again to live together inwardly....

—Rudolf Steiner, *Cosmic and Human Metamorphoses*

Dying touches us all deeply. We all die and so, in our ordinary lives, in the midst of the joys and sorrows we experience, in our work and play, the relations we form, and the children we have, we are continually accompanied—if not consciously then unconsciously—by our own mortality. We are reminded of this daily by loved ones we lose, friends and acquaintances who die, as well as by the myriad anonymous deaths that fill the newspapers, films, and television.

Dying is part of living. Yet, during the last few centuries, we have preferred to deny death by making it an end so final that it is unthinkable—a void, absolute negation. We thought we did so because we loved life. In fact, we did so because in our obsession with material things occupying space, we lost the ability to understand that life extends far beyond the limits of our five senses. We lost the sense that the visible world is merely the tip of an unquantifiable, qualitative, invisible reality. That is to say, we "lost" the spiritual world and, having lost it, can no longer imagine that life can take forms other than the purely physical form we have made supreme: the only reality. This was brought home to me with great intensity when, after my wife died, a friend received a spiritual vision in which my wife, living in luminous form, looked down upon the earth and said, "Love me, and live with me in the great life."

Truly, there is a great life. Life is boundless; it is greater than our wildest dreams. And we are part of it—forever. What a puny notion it is to believe that meaning and love in the universe are restricted to what we can achieve with our brain and brawn during the few brief years allotted each lifetime on earth!

On the contrary, life goes on, life continues, life is endless. We live it now. We live it every moment. This means that all life is always here, now, and that the dead, as well as the unborn—and the hierarchies of angels and Jesus Christ and Mary and all the divine beings—are always with us, seeking our participation and help in the ongoing work of God in the universe.

The implications of this are staggering. It implies that the earth we inhabit is a center of the universe and that what we do makes a profound difference in multitudes of worlds. As the cabalists say, "Every time I move my finger, an angel awakens." More startling still is the message that it sends *us*: "Wake up! Get real! More than your own personal enlightenment or pleasure is at stake. More depends on you than you know."

In ancient times, when humanity was less physicalized than it is today, everything spoke and every human being was a prophet, able to hear and interpret the words of the gods sounding through all phenomena. Not so much distinction was made as now between interior and exterior, subjective and objective. Heaven and earth were one world and everything was alive with meaning and calling for response. Human beings were still heavenly beings and felt themselves woven into and part of a great symphonic stream. The world, the cosmos, was music; and music was the world, the cosmos. Every plant and tree and rock, the sunlight on the water, the shape of the clouds, the dew, the wind, the flame, all feeling and intention, every smile and tear and burst of laughter, the dance of the synapses and the tremors of the inner organs—everything sang. And in this singing the voices were those of the gods and the ancestors and the elemental beings who help sustain the earth.

Gradually, we lost this sense of floating between worlds—between heaven and earth—in harmonies and rhythms. We came down to earth, to solidity, density—to body consciousness where we could unfold a consciousness of our "I" in action.

For a long time we still knew of our heavenly origin. Then we began to forget, and needed to be reminded.

Rudolf Steiner is a twentieth-century representative of a long line of what the Koran calls "warners," who remind us of our divine destiny in the language and manner appropriate to our time.

His message is that we are twofold creatures, children of heaven and earth: visible beings embodied in space and time, and invisible beings of soul and spirit. We live and work and have being in both realms. In both, we are at home. Yet these two—heaven and earth—are in a sense not really two but one: a single reality in two forms. After all, they interpenetrate and reflect each other so perfectly point for point that there is nothing "There" that is not also "Here." Therefore our lives and our work are continuous, and the relationships and connections we form Here continue There, as does our activity and participation in the divine-spiritual-human cosmic process we call the universe.

This radical spiritual and social teaching that Rudolf Steiner brings has a history. Having forgotten, we have had to struggle to remember. The great gift evolution has bequeathed us—our "I"—has also given us our great temptation: our ego. The struggle has always been, and is, the struggle to overcome our egotism. For this, the great religious teachers—Abraham, Moses,

Krishna, Buddha, Mohammed, to mention only a few—worked. For this, Christ, too, came to earth. Here, too, however, we shall overcome.

Orpheus, the legendary prophet, divine poet, musician, and culture-bringer of ancient Greece was perhaps the first to preach this message in the new way, twelve to fifteen hundred years before Christ. He brought the good news of the "Orphic way of life"—a way of conscious effort, sacrifice, and suffering—and made it open to all. He universalized the Mysteries, freeing them from the sacred geography of the Mystery Centers. At the same time, he broke down the elitism of the Temple initiations of the previous epoch. In doing so, he created a free community of seekers, bound not by ties of blood or place, but by karma and by the shared pursuit of a common goal by common means: nonviolence, kinship with all life, continual recollection, purity, and belief in both life after death and reincarnation.

A fragment from an "Orphic Book of the Dead," found at Petelia in Greece and now in the British Museum, vividly illustrates this Orphic point of view:

> To the left of the House of Hades you will find a spring.
> And, beside it, a white cypress.
> Do not approach it.
> But you will find another spring, from the Lake of Memory,
> Cold water flowing from it, guardians before it.
> Say: "*I am a child of Earth and starry Heaven;*
> *But my race is of heaven.* You know this.
> I am parched with thirst. Quickly, give me
> Cool water flowing forth from the Lake of Memory."[1]

Pythagoras and Plato took up this Orphic teaching, each amending it in his own way and fitting it to the times which, as

---

1. Orphic tablet (Petelia tablet], British Museum.

the millennium unfolded, became increasingly materialistic. Plotinus, the Neoplatonic philosopher, expresses it well:

> Before we had our becoming Here, we existed There, human beings other than now, some of us gods; we were pure souls, Intelligence inbound with the entire of reality, members of the Intellectual, not fenced off, not cut away, integral to that ALL. Even now, it is true, we are not put apart; but upon that Primal Human Being there has intruded another, a human being seeking to come into being and finding us there, for we were not outside the universe. The other has wound itself about us, foisting itself upon the Human being that each of us was at first. Then, it was as if one voice sounded, one word was uttered, and from every side an ear attended and received and there was effective hearing, possessed through and through by what was present and active upon it: now we have lost that first simplicity; we are become the dual thing, sometimes indeed no more than that later foisting, with the primal nature dormant and, in a sense, no longer present.[2]

Nevertheless, before Orpheus—and even after him, and after Pythagoras, Plato, and Plotinus, and even after God had dwelled in a human body, in Christ Jesus, and had died and resurrected—many still believed, as they do today, that it is "better," as Homer put it, "to be a beggar on earth than a shade in Hades" or—as a late post-Christian Latin inscription has it *non fui, fui, non sum, non curo,* ("I was not, I was, I am not, I don't care").

But Orpheus and his followers knew otherwise. They understood that there is a perfect correspondence between heaven and earth, macrocosm and microcosm, and that these two are

---

2. Plotinus, *Enneads,* IV, 4, 14.

our one home and that we are immortal. *We are at home in the universe.* The task was to connect heaven and earth—within and through humanity. Socrates taught that this was done by a process of soul purification that he called "dying"—dying to the visible so that the invisible could be all in all.[3] With connections made and the soul purified, Socrates believed, death was overcome; the world was one, single, and invisible.

But Socrates was only a precursor. The incarnation of Christ and his unconditional "overcoming" of death had not yet affirmed the centrality of earthly existence. Earthly, visible life was still seen as secondary to heavenly life; redemption lay in escaping it. The earth was still a prison; the body, a tomb. The supreme sanctity of human, earthly embodiment had not yet been announced. Yet when the announcement came on the Mount of Golgotha, the full import of Christ's deed of "overcoming death" was not recognized immediately. Nor is it fully understood even today.

The early Christians struggled to understand, caught as they were between the two realities of the Orphic announcement of the continuity of life and the radical good news of the resurrection. Nevertheless, they understood that, as Christians, they died "into Christ"—who is eternal life in whom spiritual reality resides.

The primitive church therefore saw the central act of preparing for death as the Eucharist. Receiving and participating in Christ on earth would ensure reception by him in heaven. Just as angels bore witness and rejoiced to witness Christ's cosmic sacrifice, so too angels would descend rejoicing to accompany the soul to God. There might be an interim state of dormancy, but death would not be final. God, the giver of life, was also the recreator, the resurrector. Thus, the dead person, identified

---

3. Rainer Maria Rilke, the supreme Orphic poet of the twentieth century, spoke of human beings as "bees of the invisible." For him, angels were those who had already made the world invisible. He writes in his *Duino Elegies:* "Earth, is not this what you want/To rise in us *invisibly.*"

with Christ, both through the Eucharist and through deathbed readings of the Passion, would rise again. To die was to enter into the light.

A prayer still in use today expresses this feeling beautifully:

> We seem to give them back to you O God who gave them to us. Yet as you did not lose them in giving, so we do not lose them by their return. Not as the world gives, do you give, O Lover of souls. What you give you do not give away, for what is yours is ours also if we are yours. And life is eternal and love immortal, and death is only an horizon, and an horizon is nothing save the limit of our sight. Lift us up, strong Son of God, that we may see farther; cleanse our eyes that we may see more clearly; draw us closer to yourself that we may know ourselves to be nearer to our loved ones who are with you. And while you prepare a place for us, prepare us also for that happy place, that where you are we may also be for evermore.[4]

Through the early Middle Ages, the emphasis changes. More attention begins to be paid to the transitional period. At first, this took the form of increased penance as the means of avoiding the fires of hell. Increasingly, however, and with greater frequency, prayers to accompany the dead on their path and masses for the dead came to play a more important role. There was a growing sense that those on earth could truly aid the dead and help them in their passage. At the same time, through the spreading influence of the Celtic Church in Ireland, the reality of the resurrection, death actually overcome— that is, the true spiritual continuity of life—began to take stronger hold. The whole Mystery of the Passion—still preeminently in the Eucharist—became recognized as true medicine

---

4. *St. Benedict's Prayer Book*, Ampleforth: Ampleforth Abbey Press, Ampleforth Abbey, 1994.

for body and soul. This did not mean, however, that the conviction that the dead needed the living lost any of its power. On
the contrary, the realization of the real power of the living to
aid the dead through prayers and votive masses only increased,
and voluntary confraternities were formed of those who
prayed for the dead.[5]

The first movement of the relation between the living and
the dead culminated around the turn of the first millennium
with two symptomatic gestures: the introduction of the Feast of
All Souls in 997/ 998 by Abbot Odilo of Cluny and, as a corol-
lary to that, the gradual rediscovery or invention of purgatory.[6]
Together, these two focused the attention of the later Middle
Ages on the interdependency of the living and the dead. Theo-
logically, this expressed the idea that the whole Church (and
ultimately the whole of humanity) was a single, reciprocating,
interconnected, interdependent body, the Body of Christ, perpetually dying, perpetually resurrected. Some may be on earth,
some in heaven, some in purgatory, but all, though scattered,
are one, mutually implicated and responsible each for all.

Thus the reality arose that we could suffer, pray, and live for
each other across the great threshold of death. Women, above
all, took up this work—the only priestly work allowed them. Most
of the great mystics of the period—Mechtild of Hackeborn,
Hildegard of Bingen, Elizabeth of Schonau, Christian Mirabi-
lis—became such "apostles to the dead," working closely with
souls in purgatory. At the same time, the primitive notion of the
"Communion of Saints"—risen human beings, companions and
coworkers with the heavenly hierarchies—began to take on a

---

5. For this condensed history, I am indebted to Frederick S. Paxton,
Christianizing Death: The Creation of a Ritual Process in Early Medieval Europe,
Ithaca: Cornell University Press, 1990.

6. See Jacques le Goff, *The Birth of Purgatory*, Chicago: Chicago University
Press, 1984. And Barbara Newman, "On the Threshold of the Dead: Purga-
tory, Hell, and Religious Women," Chapter 4 in *From Virile Woman to Woman
Christ: Studies in Medieval Religion and Literature*, Philadelphia: University of
Pennsylvania Press, 1997.

stronger presence. Not only could we work with the dead, the dead could also work with us.

With the scientific revolution and the rise of materialistic modernism, everything changed. Death became the end. In a world constituted of matter and space—a spatialized world—there was no place for a spiritual world, nor any way to understand the spiritual beings who lived there, including human beings who had died. Death ruled.

Then, in the mid-nineteenth century (1848), things began to change. The story becomes stranger. Spiritualism was born in the village of Hydesville in upstate New York.

It may seem tawdry to mention spiritualism in such august company. It is true that spiritualism led to fantastic excesses and materialistic delusions of all kinds and that the spiritualist movement had more than its fair share of hustlers of every complexion—charlatans, con artists, illusionists, fakes of every kind. Nevertheless, for all its errors—the most grievous of which was "mediumship"—spiritualism accomplished two great feats: it made the idea of a spiritual world thinkable again in a contemporary, nonsectarian way, and it did so thoroughly democratically, that is, it was open to all, thus making it anathema not only to the atheist but also to the esotericists who then, as to a certain extent still today, were mostly elitist.

The first phenomena—various noises, displacements of objects, and so forth—were produced in December, 1847, in the home of the Fox family. As René Guénon points out, there was nothing new in these.[7] They were the familiar trappings of "haunted houses." What was new was the interpretation, the use to which they were put. For, after several months, someone had the idea of "posing questions" to whatever it was that was rapping, questions to which the rapper responded correctly. At first, these questions were simply arithmetical computations.

---

7. René Guénon, *The Spiritist Fallacy*, Harlemville, New York: Sophia Perennis, 1999.

Then, one Isaac Post had the genial intuition of mentioning the letters of the alphabet, inviting the spirit to designate with knocks the letters spelling out what he or she wished to say. The "spirit" declared that he was a certain Charles B. Rosna, a peddler, who had been murdered in the Fox house and buried in the cellar—where, in fact, skeletal remains were later found. Thus the *spiritual telegraph* was invented.

That is one side of the story. The other side is that it was gradually noticed that the phenomena occurred more frequently and successfully in the presence of the Fox *sisters.* "Mediumship" thereby came into being and swept across the country. Among the multitudes that came to witness these events, many, mostly women, believed that they had the same powers and that they, too, were "mediums." This gave feminism an enormous boost; women were able to declare themselves independent of the male ecclesiastical hierarchy. They became, in a sense, a new kind of priestess. "Spiritual circles" quickly began to form around these mediums, and everywhere regular relations began to be established between "this world" and the "next." Naturally, as the spiritualist movement proliferated, the means of communication between the worlds was continuously improved. Table tapping led to alphabetical dials, pencils attached to mobile boards, and so forth. "Scientific" research into apparitions, manifestations, and different orders of psychic and spiritual phenomena proliferated. Famous figures like Benjamin Franklin began to appear. Building on great precursors like Paracelsus, Jacob Boehme, and Emmanuel Swedenborg, spiritualist, visionary philosophies like that of the seer of Poughkeepsie, Andrew Jackson Davis, began to be written. The impact of all this was enormous. By mid-century, sixty percent of Americans claimed "spiritualism" was their religion.[8] Meanwhile, esoterically,

---

8. Anne Brande, *Radical Spirits: Spiritualism and Women's Rights in America,* Boston: Beacon Press, 1989.

many occult groups began to form and come into the open, above all, H. P. Blavatsky's Theosophical Society.

With regard to this, C. G. Harrison tells a bizarre behind-the-scenes story:

> About the year 1840 the nations of modern Europe touched a certain point in their evolutionary cycle called the "*point of physical intellectuality.*" One of those crises had arrived which necessitated immediate action of *some* kind on the part of those who keep watch over the signs of the times.... At the period of which I am speaking, the spiritual evolution was proceeding at its minimum rate, and the intellectual at its maximum rate, and a strong current had set in toward materialism in all departments of human activity. Now the great danger of materialism is the adoption of a utilitarian standard of goodness; and intellectual *evolution*, under these conditions, is spiritual *involution*, or death.
>
> It became, therefore, a serious question with occultists (1) how far they were justified in concealing longer the fact that there is an unseen world around us as real as the world of sense, and (2) how this could be revealed with safety. In other words, how could a safe course be steered between Scylla and Charybdis.
>
> It was admitted on all hands that something must be done, but the party of secrecy were averse to a straightforward policy of tentative elementary instruction. "Let us proceed cautiously," they said in effect, "and endeavor to ascertain indirectly how far the public is disposed to receive such instruction." Accordingly experiments were made, first in America, then in France, and afterward in England, with certain individuals of a peculiar psychical organization, since called mediums. But the whole thing was a failure. The mediums, one and all, declared that they were controlled by spirits who had departed from the earth. "It was just what might have been expected," said those who are always wise after the event, but, in

point of fact, no one had expected it. I can only account for this strange oversight by the fact that "the children of this world are wiser in their generation than the children of light." The occultists were like the man in the fable who was so absorbed in the contemplation of the stars that he walked into the ditch at his feet.

As, under the circumstances, the "Spiritualists" could not be undeceived as to the source of their inspirations, there was no alternative but to withdraw from the experiment. But the mischief was done. The door had been opened to extramundane influences, and could not be reclosed. Spiritualism was a Frankenstein monster, and a Proteus into the bargain. Mediumship (especially in America) became a profession, and mediums, subject to every kind of psychic influence, were largely exploited by "Brothers of the Left" for their own purposes. The party of secrecy were almost wholly employed in endeavoring to counteract these influences, with the assistance of many who called themselves "Liberals" (quite a new name by the way), when an event occurred which united both parties in defense against a common danger. A person who was known to exist, but who had not been discovered, suddenly appeared in Paris, presented herself at an occult lodge, and demanded admission into the brotherhood on terms which could not be entertained for a moment. She then disappeared, and the next thing that was heard was that a certain Madame Blavatsky had been expelled from an American brotherhood for an offense against the Constitution of the United States, and had gone to British India in order to carry out a certain threat which it would seem there was a fair prospect of her putting into execution....[9]

---

9. C. G. Harrison, *The Transcendental Universe*, Hudson, New York: Lindisfarne Press, 1994.

In other words, without entering into details of esoteric history, the suggestion (confirmed by Rudolf Steiner[10]) is that spiritualism was "created" by adepts of the time to combat materialsm.

Whatever interpretation one puts on these facts, however, several things remain clear. Spiritualism, out of which Theosophy arose, and thereby in a certain sense also Anthroposophy, as well as Jungian psychology[11] and most modern Western spiritual movements, was an enormously significant cultural impulse. Regardless of how foolish, materialistic, fantasist, and plain deluded many aspects of spiritualism were, it nevertheless affirmed the presence of an invisible, spiritual world permeating this one: a world waiting only for the physical world to wake up to it.

Spiritualism had its errors—it was both materialistic and atavistic. It was foolish (and epistemological nonsense) to believe that the spiritual world—and the dead—used physical, material means to communicate. As Rudolf Steiner says in the opening quotation, speaking of those who have died and wish to continue working with us on the earth, "This working together only *appears* to be a physical collaboration, for everything physical is only an outer expression of spirit." That is, the spiritual world lives with us in soul and spirit; "matter" is our fantasy alone. "Mediumship," the other great fallacy, is likewise quite easily disposed of. We need only realize that we are surrounded by the spiritual worlds and need only awaken our own organs of perception to perceive these consciously. This is another aspect of the great democratization effected by spiritualism. We can *all* communicate with the dead and the spiritual worlds. They are always around and with us and it does not take priests, mediums, or otherwise specially chosen people to enter into the

---

10. Rudolf Steiner, *The Occult Movement in the Nineteenth Century, and its Relation to Modern Culture*, London: Rudolf Steiner Press, 1973. And for another perspective: Rudolf Steiner, *The History of Spiritism, Hypnotism, and Somnambulism*, New York: Anthroposophic Press, 1943.

11. See Richard Noll, *The Aryan Christ*.

working relationship that is a true collaboration between heaven and earth.

What is most interesting in the present context is that the means chosen by spiritualism to reopen humanity to this spiritual world was to demonstrate the reality of the continued existence—the continuing life, work, and love—of those who had died. In other words, the living, active presence of the dead in earthly life was presented as the door to the exploration of a whole spiritual world.

It is still so today. The phenomenon of death, as that of life itself, still defeats materialistic explanations of the world and demonstrates, if not their fundamental error, then at least their narrow limits. Anyone who has accompanied another across the threshold knows that once the fact of death's imminence is certain, medical science must bow out: it can do nothing, it knows nothing. It can only deny. At the same time, many of those who have witnessed someone "dying" know that a person does not die in any absolute sense but is always in transition—leaving the visible world, he or she becomes only more invisibly and immediately present. It is one of the best kept secrets of the late twentieth century that multitudes of ordinary people know from their own experience that no one dies in the sense of disappearing forever. The bestselling books on the subject of communication with the dead are only the most sensationalist heralds of an enormous and growing social reality—the fact that, although we pay lip service to materialism and hedonistically consume its fruits (all too easily becoming addicted to them and to the comforts they provide), we know in our heart of hearts that our lives encompass so much more than mere "things," and that we are spiritual beings living in a spiritual world.

This collection of Rudolf Steiner's lectures and meditations on staying connected with those who have died can help deepen one's understanding of these things. More than that, it provides concrete and practical instructions for all who wish to consciously engage in the great work that the living and the so-called dead can do together.

Specific indications are given about how we can learn to work together with those we love who have passed through the gates of death into the invisible world. The cumulative effect is staggering. Gradually, we come to realize that the so-called dead and indeed the whole spiritual world are involved in and care deeply about every aspect of earthly life. Thereby, we come to understand the supreme importance of earthly life as the only sphere in the universe where death can be experienced. And not only death: earth is above all the place of connection, of relationship and love. *Love, connection, relationship occur only on the earth.* We had better take care of them. Those fruits we take to heaven.

Above all, we learn that we do not live—or love or experience—for ourselves alone. All our experience feeds the universe. We are the books the dead read. Our thoughts and feelings are the works of art that brighten and instruct their lives. When we meditate (or pray) and do our spiritual practice, when we organize our lives to serve and make manifest the good, the true, and the beautiful, then we are doing so not only for ourselves but for all beings in all worlds. Truly, we are called to serve: to offer up our experience for the sake of the world's evolution. Not only do we take it all with us, we must also give it all away. When we do so, we live together with world evolution. We cannot do it alone, but only in and through and with those we love—in and through and with love. For the work of the earth is love: that the substance of the earth become love. And work with the dead, as Rudolf Steiner shows, is an important part of this task.

Finally, on a personal note, I must say that living and working with the concepts and exercises contained in these talks and meditations has changed my life. This is a most practical book. Do what it recommends and you will experience the presence of the dead in your lives. You will know that the community of human beings on both sides of the threshold is not theory, but reality.

Christopher Bamford

PART ONE

"Entry"

1

To communicate with the dead, we need a common language—a living language, not a dead language of old thoughts, unconscious habits, and mechanical emotions. Thoughts sent to the dead must be in a language they can understand; what we think must have meaning for them. Thus it must have meaning for us, too. To communicate with the dead therefore requires freshness, spontaneity, creative intention, and truly felt feelings. The first approach to this must include the understanding that the language must be "spiritual," not "material." The dead cannot understand dead, materialistic thoughts, but only living, spiritual thoughts. Spiritual thoughts are those that we make our own. First, we think them afresh and try to raise them to their highest meaning for us. Then, emptying ourselves, we offer that experience to the spiritual world. Once thoughts can become a living reality for us in this way, they are able to cross the abyss between the living and the dead. The dead can share in such thoughts and learn from them; they can even act within them and take them further. In fact, without such thoughts we are not present for our loved ones who have died. They look in vain for us. They depend upon us but cannot find us. More than that, they are constrained, even fettered, by our absence. We do not provide a medium within which they can live and continue to participate in the earthly stream that is their karma. When our souls are

*filled with materialistic thinking, we are like a void to
them: nothing. Nowadays, many souls are cut off in this
way! Therefore, spiritual reading—what is called* lectio
divina [1]*—the meditative reading of spiritual literature
to the dead—can be a great comfort to them. At the same
time, through this process and through the process of living thinking and living feeling, the dead can also communicate with us. After all, they continue to care and
still have a great deal to offer. To establish relationships
with the dead, however, requires effort. This effort is part
of the greater work of overcoming materialism and spiritualizing human life on earth. Since this work is an
aspect of cosmic evolution as a whole, it involves the
entire spiritual world and all the beings in it.*

Overcoming the Abyss

STUTTGART, FEBRUARY 20, 1913

... Here on earth, by means of our souls and bodies, we have
the most varied kinds of relationships with the physical world,
as well as with the spiritual world that underlies it. Likewise,
between death and a new birth we exist in relationship with the
facts, happenings, and beings of a supersensory world. Human
beings have an occupation or activity in the physical world

---

1. See Michael Casey, *Sacred Reading, The Ancient Art of* Lectio Divina,
Liguori, Missouri: Triumph Books, 1995, and Guigo II, *The Ladder of Monks
and Twelve Meditations*, Garden City, NY: Image Books, Doubleday & Company, Inc., 1978, pp. 81-82.

between birth and death; likewise, they have activities—occupations as it were—between death and a new birth. What we can learn about human life and human activity between death and a new birth will lead humanity more and more toward what we may call the overcoming of "the abyss" that, especially in our materialistic times, separates those who live on earth from those whom we call the "dead." In this process, communication and a mutual entering-into-relationship will increasingly come to be established between the living and the "dead."

Today, I want to highlight the details of such relationships between the living and the "dead," and speak about how souls live and work in the period between death and a new birth. Naturally, those who die before others with whom they had relationships on earth often gaze back from the spiritual world at those they loved who remain here. This being the case, we may ask whether such souls living between death and a new birth can perceive human beings who live here on earth between birth and death.

Anyone who develops the faculties that enable a person to become a seer and to penetrate the life between death and a new birth can have very special, even deeply moving, experiences. For instance, such seers may find souls among the dead who sometimes say something like the following (of course, they say it in a language comprehensible only by one who can look from our world into the world of the "dead").

A soul who was last incarnated in a male body, for example, was able to express itself to a seer after death in this way: "All my thoughts and memories go back to that person who was my faithful wife. When I was below in earthly life, she was the sunshine of my life. When my business for the day was finished and I came home in the evening, my soul was refreshed by what she was able to be for me and by what then entered my soul from hers. Truly, she was spiritual food for me. The longing for her has stayed with me. Now my spiritual eye is directed toward the earth, but I cannot find her; she is not there. From all that I have learned, I know that this soul, my wife, must be on earth in a physical body as she was before, but for me it is as though she is extinguished and not there."

Seers can often have this kind of heart-wrenching experience with souls who feel fettered when they think of those they left behind. Such souls feel that they cannot get through, cannot look down on those earthly souls. They are fettered not by their own essential being, but by the other souls left behind.

Investigation into why a soul in the spiritual world cannot perceive souls who remain on earth reveals that, because of the circumstances of our time, those souls who have remained on earth have been unable to take in or allow any thoughts to live in them that might otherwise become visible and perceptible to a soul who has passed through the gate of death.

In other words, souls who have gone through the gate of death and long for the sight of those left behind sense their existence on the physical plane, but they cannot announce themselves to them. Just as mutes cannot announce themselves through language, earthly souls also remain mute for the disembodied souls who long for them. In other words, souls left behind remain inaudible in their spiritual nature to the one who has already passed through the gate of death.

There is a great difference among souls here on earth, depending on their makeup. Imagine a soul living here in the physical body who, between awaking and going to sleep, is concerned only with thoughts taken from the material world. Such a soul—filled entirely with thoughts, concepts, ideas, and sensations taken solely from the material world—cannot be perceived at all from the other world. No trace of it can be seen. But a soul filled with spiritual ideas such as those provided by spiritual science—a soul glowing and illuminated by spiritual ideas—is perceptible from the other world. Consequently, no matter how good they may be as human beings, the souls left behind who are immersed in materialism are not real to the world beyond and cannot be perceived. This makes a shocking, terrible impression upon the seer, despite the detachment such souls have attained.

It is especially true these days, when it seems as if every contact were cut off between souls who were often so closely linked
here on earth, that one can have countless experiences of this
kind in relation to the world beyond. Nevertheless, one can
always find souls who live in that world. They have gone
through the gate of death and now look down on those who
have spiritual thoughts, even if only occasionally. If human
beings on earth allow spiritual thoughts to permeate their
souls, those thoughts can be perceived by souls in the beyond,
and those earthly souls remain real for them. What we are
touching upon here is the fact that the spiritual thoughts nurtured by souls here on earth can not only be perceived but be
understood by the souls beyond. And, even more significantly,
this fact can have a practical consequence. Building on this
insight, we can do something that could become very significant for the relationship between souls here and souls beyond.
I refer to what we may call "reading to the dead." Reading to
the dead is often extraordinarily important.

Again, a seer can have the experience that human beings
who have entirely disregarded spiritual wisdom have a strong
longing for it, and wish to hear about it after they have passed
through the gate of death. If souls who have remained behind
make a clear mental image of the dead person, and at the same
time bring to mind a spiritual train of thought or read from a
spiritual book (in thought, not aloud), then the dead person
whose spiritual image stands before them will become aware of
it. We have experienced in our [spiritual] movement the most
excellent results when those still living have read to their
departed relatives. One can often see how the dead long to
hear what gets through to them from here.

To enter into a relationship with a soul, it is especially important to remember one thing during the time immediately following death. One cannot establish a relationship with a
suprasensory being without *doing* something. There is often
much deception and illusion about this. It is not as easy as it
seems. It is a grave error to think that a human being merely

needs to die in order to contact the whole spiritual world. I met a person once who was not really very intelligent but, nevertheless, spoke incessantly about Kant, Schopenhauer, and so on. He even gave lectures on Kant and Schopenhauer. When I lectured about the nature of immortality, he answered me rather smugly, saying, "Here on earth we cannot know anything about immortality, since we do not experience it until we die." It might be said that, given his present capacities, after death this person will not differ very much from what he is now in his soul. Indeed, it is a deep misconception to believe that souls become wise as soon as they pass through the gate of death. A soul cannot be easily instructed by souls in the beyond immediately on passing through the gate of death if there is no basis for a connection with them.

Furthermore, as I have said, it is not so easy to establish connections with human beings after death if we have not already been connected before death. On the other hand, connections that have been established here are effective for a long time. But a departed human being does have connections with people on earth, and in the afterlife those people can bring that soul the food it is starving for. They can bring spiritual wisdom by reading to the dead, thereby bringing about immensely valuable effects.

The dead would not be helped if we read them external, materialistic science—chemistry or physics, for instance. That is a language they do not understand because these sciences are useful only for life on earth. But what is said about the spiritual worlds in the language of spiritual science remains understandable to the dead. However, one thing must be taken into consideration during the time immediately following death. During the period immediately following death, souls retain an understanding for things communicated to them in the languages they spoke here on earth. The dead become independent of language only after a certain time. Then one may read to them in any language and they will understand the thought content. A departed person who has spoken only one language will surely be more connected immediately following death with the language last spoken. We should really consider that during the time immediately following death we have to send our thoughts to the dead—we must send our thoughts to them—in the language they were accustomed to.

Here we come to a point that can teach us how the abyss may be bridged by the fact that spiritual science flows into our spiritual life in this world and in the other world—the world we live in between death and a new birth. While materialism permits us to bring to life only relationships between souls confined to their earthly existence, spiritual science opens the way for free communication and exchange between souls on the earth and souls that dwell beyond the earth in the other world. The dead will live with us. And, when that happens, what we may call the passage through the gate of death will often after a time be experienced as merely a change in the form of existence. The whole transformation in the life of spirit and of soul that will take place when such things become common knowledge will be of enormous significance.

We have just dealt with one example—reading to the dead—of the effect of the living on the "dead." We may likewise begin to understand the way in which the "dead," in their turn, affect the living. Several times I have ventured to mention—please excuse the personal reference—that in the past I taught many children. I had to teach several children in a family in which only the mother was alive, and I felt it to be my task—this must be the task of any educator—to discover the potentialities and talents of the children in order to guide and instruct them as their educator. Something about these children remained incomprehensible to me; no matter what was tried they showed a certain behavior that was a consequence neither of their inherent qualities nor of their surroundings. One could not quite manage them. In such cases, one must call on everything for help. My spiritual research produced the following. The father had died, as I said, and he did not agree with how the children were being treated by the relatives nor with what happened within the intimate family circle and, because of special circumstances, his influence had an effect on the children. I did not know what to do until the moment when I considered that there was something special at work that derived neither from potentialities nor from surroundings, but came out of the suprasensory world from the departed father, who directed his forces into the souls of his children. I had to consider what the father really wanted. I succeeded in my task as soon as I investigated the will of the father who had passed through the gate of death, and considered him as a real person like the other persons in physical existence who had their joint effects on the children.

In this case it was clearly shown to me that spiritual knowledge can indicate to us the effect that forces from the suprasensory, spiritual world have on this physical world. But to perceive such a thing one needs the right moment. One must try, for instance, to develop a kind of force that makes it possible to perceive, as it were, the raying in of the suprasensory force—in this case that of the father—into the souls of the children. This is often difficult. It might be easy, for instance, to try to recognize how the dead father wants to implant this or that thought into the children's souls. But that often proves incorrect and, above all, the experience cannot always be repeated. It helps to obtain a picture that gives the father's form, the way he looked at the last, and meditate on it—or, if you have access to it, a distinct picture of his handwriting may be held in memory and kept before the mind's eye. By such means, we can prepare ourselves for the kind of teaching I am talking of here. By concentrating on handwriting or a picture, we take into our own work the dead person's views, intentions, and aims. The time will come when we are going to have to take into account what the dead want for those left behind. Today we can only take into account the will of those who are on the physical plane; but in the future, there will be a mutual, one might say, a free exchange between the living and the dead. We shall learn to investigate what the dead want for the physical plane.

Just imagine the great upheaval in the external factors of physical life when the dead play a part and have an effect on the physical plane through the living. Spiritual science, if it is rightly understood—and it must always be rightly understood—will then not be a mere theory. Spiritual science will become more and more an elixir of life, pervading all existence, transforming it the more it spreads. And it will certainly accomplish this, for its effects will not be those of an abstract ideal that is preached or "sold" by societies. On the contrary, spiritual science will slowly but surely take hold of souls on earth and transform them.

Our understanding will be enriched in many other respects as well. We will live together with the dead in quite another way, because we will understand what the dead are doing. Many things about the relationships between the world here on earth (the physical plane) and the world we experience between death and a new birth remain quite incomprehensible today. Much that happens here in the physical world remains incomprehensible. Since everything that happens here corresponds to what happens there, the relation of the physical world and humanity to the suprasensory world remains incomprehensible. But if spiritual science is rightly understood, comprehension will increasingly take the place of noncomprehension.

For instance, relationships will be established that show what strangely devious ways are taken by the beings who, as it were, carry out the further development of world wisdom. These beings take strangely devious ways, but nevertheless, if we follow them, they show themselves to be full of wisdom in every respect.

Let us consider various conditions. First, let us consider souls whom the eye of the seer may perceive in their work between death and a new birth. There we see many souls—again this is something that deeply affects the seer—who are condemned for a certain time between death and a new birth to be the slaves of the spirits who send sickness and death into physical life. We see souls who, between death and a new birth, are under the dominion of beings we call the "ahrimanic" spirits, or the spirits of hindrance, those who bring obstacles or hindrances into life. It is a hard fate indeed that the seer observes in some souls who have to submit to the yoke of slavery in this way. If one traces such souls back to the life they led before they passed through the gate of death, one finds that souls who must serve the spirits of resistance for a certain time after death prepared themselves for this by self-indulgence during life on earth, while the slaves of the spirits of sickness and death prepared this fate for themselves by having been unscrupulous before death. So we see a certain relation of human souls to the evil spirits of sickness and death, and to the evil spirits of resistance.

Let us now look more closely at the souls here on earth who are subjected to what such souls must do—that is, visit sickness and death upon us and work hindrances into our lives. Let us look at the souls who perish here on earth in the flower of their youth without reaching the death of old age. Let us look upon the souls here on earth who are subjected to sickness, who are pursued by misfortune, as obstacle upon obstacle arises before them. What does the seer observe when considering souls who die early or are pursued by misfortune and then pass into the spiritual world? What does the seer notice about such souls? One may have strange experiences concerning human destinies on earth. We shall point to one example, to one very moving destiny on earth, which in a certain way is paradigmatic.

A child, a little girl, is born. The mother dies at her birth— the child is motherless. The father, on the day the child is born, learns that his whole fortune, which was tied up in a ship on the high seas, is lost—the ship has been wrecked. Because of this, he becomes melancholic. Then he, too, dies, leaving the child completely orphaned.

The little girl is adopted by a wealthy woman, who is very fond of the child and wills a large fortune to her. The woman then dies while the child is still comparatively young. But when the will is probated, a technical error is found. The child does not get a penny of what was willed to her. For the second time she is cast out into the world penniless, and must hire out as a servant, do menial work.

She meets a man who falls in love with her, but they cannot be united because of the prejudices governing the community: they belong to different denominations. But the man loves her so much that he promises to adopt her faith as soon as his father, already very old, dies. The man goes abroad. There he learns that his father has fallen ill. His father dies. The man adopts the girl's faith. He speeds back to her. But as he is returning, she falls ill and dies. When he arrives, she is dead. He feels the deepest pain and will not be satisfied until the grave is opened so that he can see her once more. And from the position of the corpse, it can be seen that the girl was buried alive.

This is a legend—Robert Hamerling, the Austrian poet, retold it.[2] It is a legend, not reality, but it might occur in innumerable instances. We see a human soul who does not merely perish in the flower of her youth, but in a certain way is pursued by misfortune from the beginning of her life. Such conditions are worked out through the cooperation of those souls who, on account of unscrupulousness, become the servants of the evil spirits of sickness, death, and misfortune. In other words, unscrupulous souls are active in the preparation of such hard fates. To the seer this is especially evident in such happenings as, for instance, the catastrophe of the *Titanic*. There we may investigate the effect of the souls who for lack of conscience have become the servants of the spirits of sickness and misfortune. Karma must be carried out, and these things are necessary; but it is an evil fate that engulfs the souls who, after death, are bowed down under such a yoke of slavery.

But let us ask further: What about the souls who suffer such a fate here on earth, who perish in the flower of their youth, who are destroyed early by epidemics? What about these souls, when they pass through the gate of death into the spiritual world before their time? We learn the fate of these souls when

---

2. Robert Hamerling, pseudonym of Rupert Hammerling, 1830-1889. Austrian poet best known for his epics *Ahasverus in Rom* (1865) and *Homunculus* (1889).

we penetrate with the eye of the seer into the work of the spirits who give a forward impulse to the evolution of the earth—or, indeed, to all evolution. These spirits are beings of the higher hierarchies. They have certain forces, certain powers to advance evolutionary development; but they are limited in a certain way with regard to these forces and powers.

Thus we notice the following. Completely materialistic souls who lose all sense of the suprasensory world are in fact already threatened today by a kind of blight, a kind of cutting off from progressive development. Already in our time, in a certain way, the danger exists that a large portion of humanity may not be able to keep up with evolution because they are, so to speak, bound to the earth by the heaviness of their own souls. Because their souls are completely materialistic, they may not be taken along for the next incarnation. This danger is to be deflected, according to the decision of the higher hierarchies. The truth is that the decisive hour for the souls who, having cut themselves off completely, are not to be carried along with evolution does not come until the sixth period—actually, not until the Venus stage of evolution.[3] Souls must not fall prey to the downward pull of gravity to the extent that they are compelled to remain behind. The higher hierarchies have actually decided that this must not happen. But these beings of the higher hierarchies are, in a certain way, limited in their forces and capabilities. Nothing is unlimited, even among the beings of the higher hierarchies. If it were only a question of the forces of these higher hierarchies, then completely materialistic souls would, through themselves, already in a certain way have to be cut off from progressive evolution. The beings of the higher hierarchies really cannot save these souls by themselves, so an expedient is used.

Those who die an early death have, as souls, a possibility before them. Let us say they have died through some catastrophe; for

---

3. For a description of the various stages of evolution, see for instance *An Outline of Esoteric Science*, Hudson, N Y: Anthroposophic Press, 1998.

instance, they are run over by an express train. The bodily
sheath is taken from such a soul; the soul is now free from its
body, denuded of its body, but it still contains the forces that
would have been active in the body here on earth. By going into
the spiritual world, such souls carry up with them very special
forces—forces that would still have been effective here on earth,
but that have been prematurely diverted. Those who die early
carry with them forces that are especially helpful. The beings of
the higher hierarchies then use these forces to save the souls
whom they cannot save by their own power, which is only sufficient for the regular course of human evolution

Souls that are materialistically inclined are thus led away to
better times and saved. Salvation is achieved because the
beings of the higher hierarchies experience increased
strength through the unused forces that come from the earth
and still have available energy. These forces accrue to the
beings of the higher hierarchies. Thus the souls who perish
early help their fellows who otherwise would be submerged in
the morass of materialism. This is what those souls who depart
early must do. What a strange interdependence exists in the
complicated ways of cosmic wisdom. Cosmic wisdom permits
the sentencing of human souls for lack of conscience to cooperate in bringing sickness and early death into the world. But
then the souls who suffer sickness and early death are used by
the good beings of the higher hierarchies to help other souls.
Thus, things that seem evil outwardly in maya are often transformed into good, but in complicated ways. The ways wisdom
takes in the world are very complicated. Only gradually do we
learn to find our way in these paths of wisdom.

One might say that up above, the spirits of the higher hierarchies sit in council. Because human beings must be free, they
are given the possibility of plunging into materialism, into evil.
The hierarchies give them so much freedom that some human
souls, so to speak, escape from them—souls who could not, by
their own strength, carry on up to a certain point of time. Such
souls need other souls who develop forces on earth that retain

their inner potential because of being prematurely separated from the body when the latter souls have to return to the spiritual world because of accident and early death. This early death is brought about by the agency of human souls who, in pursuit of their freedom, have fallen into unscrupulousness. A wonderful cyclic path is opened up here, a cyclic path of cosmic wisdom, we may say. We should not believe at all that the so-called simple things are the universal ones. The world has become complicated. Nietzsche's saying, which was revealed to him as though by inspiration, is truly significant: "The world is deep, and deeper than the day had thought." Those who believe that everything can be grasped by the day wisdom of the intellect are completely wrong. For the higher spiritual light does not shine into the wisdom of the day, but shines into the darkness. We must seek this light in order to find our way in the darkness where, nevertheless, cosmic wisdom is at work.

If we accept such concepts, we may contemplate the world with different eyes from before. And it will become increasingly necessary to learn to contemplate the world with new eyes—for humanity has lost much since ancient times.

To understand what we have lost, consider this: during the third post-Atlantean period—the Egypto-Chaldean—there were intermediate states between sleeping and waking. In those states, souls looked up into the world of the stars and saw not just physical stars, as we do today, but the spiritual beings of the higher hierarchies. They observed the guiding and directing forces of the destiny and movement of the stars. And what existed from immemorial times in the form of old stellar maps with all kinds of drawings of group souls that looked like animals without being animals, was not born out of fantasy, but was spiritually perceived. Souls perceived this in the realm of the spirit, and they were able to carry this spiritual element through the gate of death. The soul has now lost this vision of the suprasensory world. When souls are born today, they confront the physical world with the bodily sense organs and see nothing but the external physical world. They no longer see

what surrounds the external physical world as the world of
spirit and soul, the world of the higher hierarchies, and so
forth. But what is the nature of the souls who appear in today's
bodies? All the souls of those here now were incarnated in
former times. The great majority were incarnated in
Egypto-Chaldaic bodies, and through them looked out into a
world they saw with spiritual as well as with physical perception. They took this spiritual experience into themselves; it
exists in them today. Not in all souls. Yet, the souls who today
no longer see anything but physical facts once lived in contemplation of the spiritual world, lived a life completely perceptive of the spiritual world.

How do these souls live now? They live exactly as though
they had totally forgotten the spiritual world. They have forgotten the spiritual perceptions they once absorbed. But what
we have forgotten is forgotten merely for our present consciousness; it still exists in the deepest recesses of our souls.
Thus this peculiar situation exists: souls living today have
around them consciously nothing but a physical-sensory image
of the world; but in their inner being perceptions they once
received as true spiritual vision still live unconsciously in the
depths of their souls. They know nothing of these perceptions,
which manifest only as peculiar conceptions that burrow in the
depths of the soul, but do not rise into consciousness; these
conceptions have a paralyzing, deadening effect. And thus
something actually arises in the human beings of today that
exists in them as a deadening element.

If one contemplates human beings today as a seer—contemplates them anatomically—one finds, especially in the nervous
system, certain currents, certain forces that are forces of death,
stemming from conceptions that were alive in former incarnations. The spiritual ideas that human beings have now forgotten
have a consuming quality. Indeed, if there were not something
present that counteracts it, this consuming quality would show
itself more and more as humanity moves further into the
future. What could avert this? Nothing but the bringing up into

consciousness of what was forgotten. One must remind souls of what they have forgotten. That is what spiritual science does. Fundamentally, it does nothing but remind the souls of ideas they have absorbed. Spiritual science lifts these conceptions into consciousness. In this way, it provides the possibility of enlivening what would otherwise be like a dead impulse in life.

Please note two things you have heard in the course of these reflections. On the one hand, the seer perceives human souls who have passed through the gate of death and long for the souls left behind, who cannot be perceived because, although they may perhaps belong to quite good people, they contain only materialistic images of the world. Though the seer may have achieved calmness of soul, it is deeply moving to perceive these starving souls. On the other hand, the seer looks into a future in which humanity will contain more and more dead matter, which will kill it if people do not raise into consciousness and revivify the ideas they once received. If humanity does not do this, the seer would have to look into a future in which people, through all kinds of hereditary traits, would show signs of old age much earlier than is the case today. Just as today one may see examples of infantile old age, even senility, so then would people show, soon after birth, wrinkles and other indications of old age, if through lack of spiritual knowledge forces do not appear that are memories of conceptions once received in a natural way. The seer is conscious of this and searches for a language that will provide the dying human race with a life-giving elixir and will give the dead possibilities of coming into contact with the relatives they have left behind on earth. Such a language would be understood and spoken both by souls living on earth between birth and death and by those living beyond, between death and a new birth—a language common to the living and the "dead."

2

LIFE ELUDES NATURAL-SCIENTIFIC OBSERVATION because life is not a material phenomenon, but a gift, a grace, from the spiritual world. Death, however, is experienced only on earth; this is why, of all the beings of the divine-spiritual worlds, only Christ knows death. In the spiritual world, the only experience similar to death is loneliness—the loneliness of knowing only oneself.
Those who live on earth only for themselves may encounter such loneliness in the life after death. Therefore, we must live on earth in a way that prepares us for continuing life in the spirit. From this point of view, the purpose of earthly life is to establish connections and relationships with others. This is because, in the first period after death, those who have died connect only with those they have known on earth or those who died with them. Later, other relational faculties developed on earth come into play, without which the soul after death experiences loneliness. The first of these is a moral *disposition that acknowledges the unity and value of all human beings. Second is the* religious *sensibility developed through the devotion and reverence that grow in us through the practice of a particular religious life. And third, there is an expanded understanding of the unity of all religious striving, and that Christianity contains the seed of universal religion. The presence and knowledge of the Christ—whether recognized by that name or not—is thus tremendously important.*

The Life of the Dead

DÜSSELDORF, APRIL 27, 1913

The relationship between life and death is mostly misunderstood. One often finds in theosophical writings the remark that the human soul and spirit could disappear completely. It is said, for example, that if a soul burdens itself with enough evil, it could disappear in the course of evolution. Furthermore, it is often emphasized that those black magicians who have worked such evil will meet that fate.

Those who have shared our goals for some time will know that I have always opposed such statements. *Above all, we must maintain the knowledge that what we call death on the physical plane is meaningless in the suprasensory world.* This is true even for the region of the suprasensory immediately bordering our world. Today, I will deal with a certain aspect of this matter.

The science that deals with the physical world has arrived at a number of laws and relationships within the physical realm. When these laws are applied to the outer phenomena of nature, they can tell us only about the structure of outer, sensory reality. For example, a natural-scientific investigation of a flower will reveal certain facts about the physical and chemical laws that act within the plant, *but life itself always eludes such scientific observation.* It is true, of course, that in recent times a few especially imaginative scientists have constructed a body of hypotheses to explain how plant life arises from mere dead substances. Such attempts are quickly being recognized as false, because any understanding of the reality of life remains a mere ideal for science. Science continually accumulates knowledge of chemical laws and so on, but nothing about life itself. The investigation of life is only an ideal for the natural-scientific method, because life is something that flows from the suprasensory realm into the physical world, within which the laws of life cannot be understood.

The truth of life in the physical world is true of death in the suprasensory world, except that in the suprasensory world it is a matter of the will. There, an act or impulse of will can never lead to what we know as death on earth. At most, a longing for death may arise in the suprasensory world, but not death itself; death does not exist in the realms beyond the physical. This fact is particularly moving for the human soul who realizes that no being of the hierarchies can ever know death. Death can be experienced only on earth.

According to a biblical saying, the angels hide their faces so they will not see the mysteries of birth; it is also true that they hide their faces so as not to see the mysteries of death. The being whom we know as the one who gave the greatest impulse to earth evolution, the Christ, is the only being in divine realms who encountered knowledge of death. No other divine spiritual beings know death. They know it only as a transformation from one form into another.[1]

The Christ had to descend to the earth to experience death. Christ alone among all the suprahuman, suprasensory beings knows death through experience. As I have said, it is deeply moving to view the experience of death in relation to Christ.

Now, it is literally true that human beings, after passing through the gate of death, live in the suprasensory world where there is no dissolution. They can enter those realms but cannot die, because they are received into a world where there can be no destruction.

In the suprasensory world, however, there is something similar to death, yet quite different from death as we know it. In human language, one would have to call it *loneliness*. Death can never mean the annihilation of something in the suprasensory world, but loneliness does arise. Loneliness in the suprasensory world is comparable to death here. It is not destruction,

---

1. See also "Reality and Illusion: The Inner Aspects of Evolution," lecture 5, in *The Spiritual Hierarchies and the Physical World: Reality and Illusion.*

but it is far more intense than the loneliness we know on earth. It takes the form of looking back upon one's own being. One knows fully what this means only when it happens—when there is nothing to know except oneself.

Consider, for example, those who developed little sympathy for their fellow human beings while on earth—people who lived essentially for themselves. Those souls encounter difficulties after death, especially in getting to know other human souls. They can live together with others in the suprasensory world without being the least aware of their existence. They are filled only with their own soul content. After death, such a soul is aware only of what lives within itself.

After passing through the gate of death, those who, because of an exaggerated sense of egoism, have avoided any form of human love on earth may be able to live only in the memory of their last earthly existence. They cannot gain any new experiences, because they do not know and cannot contact any other being. They must depend completely on themselves, because as human beings on earth we prepare a particular world for ourselves after death.

Here on earth we do not actually know ourselves. Science, because it knows only the corpse, can teach us only about what we are no longer. The brain thinks, but it cannot think *itself.* We see a portion of ourselves, and a larger portion when we look in the mirror, but this is only our outer aspect. We do not live in ourselves on earth. We live together with the surrounding world that impinges upon our senses. But through ourselves, through all that we experience here, we are preparing to expand into the macrocosmos and *become* a macrocosmos, to become all that we see around us on earth.

Here on earth we see the Moon. After death, we expand so that we become the Moon, just as on the earth we are our brain. We expand into Saturn so that we become Saturn, just as we are now our spleen. After death, the human being becomes a macrocosmic being. When the soul has departed from the body it expands into the entirety of the planetary system, so all souls simultaneously dwell within the same spatial area. They interpenetrate one another but without being aware of it. Only spiritual connections determine whether we know about one another or not. We prepare ourselves during our life on earth to expand into the whole of the universe that we behold here in its physical reflection. But what in fact is our world after death?

Now we are surrounded by mountains, rivers, trees, animals, and minerals; then we will live in the universe. The universe becomes our organism; it constitutes our organs. We are our world. We view ourselves from the surroundings. This process begins in the etheric body immediately following death, when we see the tableau of our life.

Were it not for the fact that, while we are on earth, we make connections with other human beings and (more and more frequently through spiritual science) with beings of the higher hierarchies, we would have nothing to do after death apart from continuously observing ourselves. This is not intended to be trivial; it is a truly shattering fact. To observe only oneself throughout several centuries is not an especially enviable prospect. We become a world for ourselves, but it is the connections we have made on earth that open wider vistas for the self after death. *The purpose of earthly life is to develop connections and relationships that can be continued after death.* Everything that makes us into sociable beings after death must be prepared on earth. Fear of loneliness is the torment in the spiritual world. We can experience it. This fear falls upon us repeatedly, because we move through a number of stages between death and rebirth. Even if we experience a measure of sociability at one stage, we may fall into loneliness during the next.

The first period after death is such that we can establish a good connection only with souls who have remained on the earth, or with those who died about the same time as we did. In this situation, the closest connections continue to have an effect beyond death. The so-called living who have remained on earth can do much. One who has a connection with a departed soul can remind that soul of what it knew of the spiritual world while on the earth. This is possible above all by reading to the dead.

We can perform the greatest service for a dead person by forming a picture of that individual in our soul and softly reading a work of spiritual science, thus instructing that soul, so to speak. We can also convey thoughts to the departed—thoughts we have made our own—always with a vivid image of the one who has passed on. We should not be miserly in this respect. This enables us to bridge the abyss that separates us from the dead. It is not just in extreme cases that we can help the dead in this way. It is true in every case. This provides a comforting feeling that can alleviate the sorrow experienced when someone we have loved passes on.

As we go more deeply into the suprasensory world, particular relationships become less established. We still find individual relationships in the astral world, but the higher we ascend, the more we find a cessation of what weaves between separate beings. Now there are beings everywhere. The relationships among these are of a soul nature and we need them to avoid loneliness. It is the mission of the earth to establish relationships between one human being and another. Otherwise, we would remain alone in the spiritual world.

During the first phases after death, our world consists of the relationships, the friendships we formed with our fellow human beings on earth. These friendships continue. For example, one who investigates with suprasensory perception finds the departed soul in the vicinity of a person on earth whom it can follow. Many people in our time live with those who have died recently or, perhaps, at some earlier period. One also sees how many come together with a number of their ancestors, to whom they were related by blood.

The seer often encounters the fact that a departed soul links itself to ancestors who died centuries ago, but this lasts only for a certain period. The soul would again feel extremely lonely if there were not other connections that, though far removed, prepare the person to be sociable in the spiritual world. Within our movement we have discovered a basic principle that stems from a cosmic task entrusted to us. This principle involves the formation of relationships among people in the most varied ways. Consequently, anthroposophy is cultivated not just by giving lectures. Within the Anthroposophical Society, we try to bring people together so that personal relationships may form. These connections are valid for the suprasensory world, as well, to the degree that a person who belongs to a particular stream in our society creates connections for the realm beyond the physical.

There comes a time, however, when more general connections are necessary. A phase comes when a feeling of loneliness arises in souls who have gone through the gate of death without any *moral* soul disposition and without moral concepts—souls who have rejected a moral disposition of soul during their earthly life. It is a simple fact that those endowed with a moral soul disposition are of greater value here on earth than those lacking in morality. A moral human being is of greater worth for humanity as a whole, just as a sound healthy stomach is more valuable to the whole person than one that is sick.

It is not easy to put your finger on where the value of the moral human being lies for all of humanity, or to pinpoint the harm created by one who is immoral. But you can understand what I mean when I say that a person devoid of a moral soul disposition is a sick member of humanity. Through that immoral soul disposition, such a person becomes increasingly alienated from others. To be moral also means to acknowledge that one has a relationship to *all* human beings. This is why love of all humanity is self-evident to all moral people. Immoral people feel lonely in a certain phase after death because of their lack of morality. The torments of loneliness at this stage can be dispelled only by the moral disposition of the soul.

Consequently, when we investigate the lives of human beings spread out after death in the macrocosmos, we see that the immoral individuals are in fact lonely, whereas moral individuals find a connection with others of similar moral ideas. Here on earth, human beings are grouped by nationality, for example, or in some other way. Between death and rebirth people also group themselves, but according to the moral concepts and soul dispositions they have in common.

This phase is followed by one of development in which even those endowed with a moral soul disposition feel lonely if they lack religious concepts. A *religious* turn of mind is the preparation for sociability at a particular stage of life between death and rebirth. Here we also discover that people are condemned to loneliness if they are unable to have religious feelings and connections. We find people of the same religions grouped together.

This period is followed by one in which it is no longer enough to have lived within a religious community. A phase approaches when one can again feel loneliness. This period is particularly important in the life between death and rebirth. We feel alone if we cannot now bring understanding to every human soul in its essential character, even though we experienced togetherness with those of like religion. We can prepare for this communion only by understanding *all* religious confessions.

This was unnecessary before the Mystery of Golgotha, because experience in the spiritual world was different then. Now it has become essential. A correct understanding of Christianity is a preparatory step. We cannot encounter the essential being of Christianity in other religious creeds. It is not correct to place Christianity next to other religious creeds. Although certain Christian confessions are perhaps narrow-minded, nevertheless Christianity, when properly understood, bears within it the impulse to understand all religious creeds and tendencies.

How has the West understood Christianity? Consider Hinduism. For the most part, only those who are Hindu can be true adherents. If, for instance, that kind of racial religion were prevalent in Europe today, we would still have a Wotan cult, which would be the Western equivalent of a racial religion. But the West has accepted a religion that did not arise from its own folk substance, but one that came from the East. Something was accepted that could work only through its spiritual meaning. The Christ impulse cannot be subsumed into a racial or folk religion. In fact, the truth is that those among whom Christ appeared did not acknowledge him. That is the remarkable fact about Christianity. It contains the seed that enables it to become the universal religion.

One cannot, therefore, take an intolerant attitude toward other religions. The mission of Christianity is not to bring dogma to people. Of course, Buddhists smile at a religion that lacks even the idea of reincarnation. Such a religion must seem false to them. But Christianity, if correctly understood, presupposes that all are Christian in their innermost being. If you say to a Hindu, "You are a Hindu and I am a Christian," it will be obvious that you have not understood Christianity. Christianity has been truly understood only when you can say that inwardly the Hindus are as much Christian as you are, but have as yet only had the opportunity to become acquainted with a preparatory religion. We must try to show them where our religions correspond. The best thing would be for Christians to teach Hinduism to the Hindus and then attempt to take Hinduism a stage further so that Hindus can gain a point of contact with the general stream of evolution. We understand Christianity only when we see all individuals as Christians in the depths of their hearts. Only then is Christianity the religion that transcends race, color, and social position. That is Christianity.

We are entering a new age. Christianity can no longer work as it has during past centuries. It is the task of anthroposophy to bring the new understanding of Christianity that is needed. From this perspective, the anthroposophic worldview is an instrument of Christianity. Among the religions of the earth, Christianity appeared last. New religions can no longer be established. That belongs to the past. Religions followed one another and brought forth Christianity as the last flower. Today the task is to form and apply the impulses of Christianity. This is why, in our spiritual scientific movement, we try to consider all the religions of the world more consciously than before, and in loving participation. In this way, we are also preparing ourselves for the period between death and rebirth, when we will experience loneliness if we cannot perceive and have access to other souls in that realm.

If we misunderstand Hinduism while on earth, then we might only sense the presence of a Hindu in the world beyond, while being unable to gain any contact with that soul.

You see, this is the phase during life between death and rebirth when we have also expanded our astral body to the extent that we enter the Sun sphere and live there. In fact, we expand into the entire macrocosmos, and when we need the capacity for love of our neighbor we reach the Sun being. The encounter with the Sun occurs in this way: first, we lose the possibility of understanding all human beings unless we have gained a connection to the words, *For where two or three are gathered together in my name, there am I in the midst of them* (Matt. 18:20). Christ did not mean that wherever two Hindus or one Hindu and one Christian are gathered together, there he is in the midst of them, but that wherever two human beings who have a genuine understanding for his impulse are gathered, he is there in the midst of them.

Until a certain moment, the Christ being was in the sphere of the Sun. His throne was there. Then he united with the earth. Since then, we must experience the Christ impulse here on earth and carry it up into the spiritual world. If we arrive in the sphere of the Sun without the Christ impulse, we are faced with an unintelligible entry in the akasha chronicle.[2] Since the Christ united with the earth, we must come to understand the Christ on earth. We have to take that understanding with us,

---

2. The Sanskrit term *akasha* (literally "primordial spatial substance") *chronicle*, or *akasha record*, refers to what a clairvoyant sees as a suprasensory record of history going back to primordial times; see *Cosmic Memory: Prehistory of Earth and Man*, chapter 2.

otherwise we cannot find Christ after death. If we have gained an understanding for the Christ on earth, then as we approach the sphere of the Sun we understand the entry in the akasha chronicle, because it was Christ who left the akasha chronicle behind in the Sun. The important fact is that our *understanding of Christ must be aroused on the earth.* It can then be preserved in higher worlds as well. Things become clear only when they are viewed within a certain framework.

Some theosophical groups cannot understand that the Christ impulse exists as a fulcrum at the center of earthly evolution; it is the point from which the "ascending curve" begins. To maintain that Christ can appear repeatedly on earth is like saying that the beam of a balance must be supported at two points. But one cannot weigh with such scales. A conviction of this sort makes no more sense in relation to the physical world than the statement of certain esotericists that Christ goes through repeated earthly lives. One can understand the Christ impulse only with the understanding that Christ is the only god who has experienced death. For that he had to descend to the earth. One who has come to understand the Christ here will not find the throne in the Sun to be empty.

This understanding also enables us to recognize the nature of a particular encounter at this stage. We meet Lucifer, not as the tempter but as a lawful power who must travel by our side if we are to progress on our journey. Qualities that are beneficial in the proper sphere become destructive in the wrong sphere. The activity of Lucifer in the physical world is evil, but after death—from the Sun sphere on—we need Lucifer as a companion. We must meet Lucifer, and we must continue our journey between Lucifer and Christ. Christ preserves our soul nature with the whole wealth accumulated by our soul through previous incarnations. The task of the luciferic power is to help us learn to apply the forces of the other hierarchical beings in the right way for our next incarnation.

Irrespective of when this stage occurs, we are faced with the need to determine where on the globe and in which nation we are to reincarnate. This must be determined midway between death and rebirth. In fact, the first thing that must be determined is the location and country where the soul is to reincarnate. We prepare for this stage on earth inasmuch as we acquire a connection with the suprasensory world, but we need the support of Lucifer. Now, as we return, the beings of the higher hierarchies give us the forces that guide us to a certain place at a certain time.

Consider this excellent example. The appearance of Luther at a specific moment had to be prepared for from the ninth century on. Even then, forces had to be directed within the appropriate people. Lucifer must cooperate to this end so that the time and place of our reembodiment can be determined. What one has gained through effort is preserved when one harbors Christ in the soul. But human beings are not mature enough to know the best place to work out their karma; Lucifer's assistance is needed for this.

After another period of time elapses, a serious matter must be decided, which involves a deeply stirring activity. It cannot be described in our everyday language except as follows. The matter must now be resolved concerning the characteristics of the parents of this soul who will incarnate at a certain time and place, so as to give birth to that particular being. All this has to be determined far in advance. This means, however, that the higher hierarchies (again, supported again by Lucifer) must work in a preparatory way through the whole genealogical stream long before the incarnation of a particular individual. In the case of Luther, for example, his ancestors had to be determined as early as the tenth and eleventh centuries so that he might have the right parents.

Science believes that we assume the characteristics of our ancestors. But, from the suprasensory world, we in fact influence the characteristics of our ancestors. In a certain sense, we ourselves are responsible for the way our great-great-great-grandparents were. Obviously, we cannot influence all their characteristics, yet, among others, those we ourselves later require must be present. We first instill in our ancestors what we later inherit from them.

First, the time and place of birth are determined; then, the ancestry is chosen. Fundamentally, a child's love for the parents is the emergence of a union with a stream into which the incarnating being has worked for centuries from the suprasensory world. At the moment of conception, the individual receives the forces that cooperate in forming the body—specifically, the head and general physical form. From then on, we must picture these forces to be active primarily in the deeper structure of the head, less in the hands and feet, and even less in the torso—that is, going from the head toward the torso. We lay the foundation for this, and then continue to shape it after birth.

First, everything is woven into the astral body. The shape of the head is prefigured astrally. This proceeds to the degree that, in fact, it is only at the final stage that the shape of the cranium is incorporated into the astral prototype, which then unites with the bodily formation. The shape of the head is individual, and the shape of the brain is sculpted during the last stage.

Thus what we receive through the hereditary stream is able to unite with what we bring with us from the suprasensory world. Imagine what comes from the suprasensory world as the chalice. It is filled with water provided by the hereditary substance. The pure stream of heredity provides only the characteristics of our bodily constitution that is more independent of the circulatory and nervous systems. Whether our bones are big and strong or weak and fine depends more on heredity than on the forces we receive from the preparatory spiritual powers.

The individual is to be born at a particular time and place in order to work out its karma, and thus may be the child of parents with strong bones, blond hair, and so on. This is made possible by the hereditary stream. If theories of physical heredity were correct, we would appear with deformed nervous systems and a mere indication of hands and feet. Only suprasensory insight can lead to matters that are truly meaningful.

Let me relate a real example. I met a hydrocephalic boy who was different in many respects from the rest of his family. Why was he hydrocephalic? Because the council of higher powers together with Lucifer had decreed this particular individual should be born in a particular place, and his parents were the best ones available for him. But he had been unable to work into the ancestral line properly, so that he could create what would become the appropriate substance for his head to harden correctly. Only during his lifetime would he be able to adapt his brain to the head's general structure. This individual did not find the right conditions that would allow him to influence his ancestry so that his head could harden appropriately.

These are considerably important matters; they demonstrate the technique that must be adopted to enter the world. When such matters are correctly understood by science, the activities of the higher worlds will also be felt. If we continue our journey with Lucifer *and* Christ, we can acquire the right relationship to the progressive stream in evolution.

In conclusion, during our life after death we must first overcome the dangers of loneliness through our relationships to other human beings, and then through moral and religious connections. After that, we fashion the new person that is to incarnate in the future, a task that involves facing ourselves instead of facing the world.

If we go through stages on earth condemned to loneliness when we could be sociable, a longing arises in us after death. We long for unconsciousness, but in the higher worlds, where matter no longer exists, everything is a matter of consciousness. Therefore, we do not lose consciousness but merely become lonely. This is true of souls who lack a connection to other souls. Death does not exist in the world beyond.

Here we live in a rhythm between waking and sleeping; likewise, life in the other world alternates between withdrawal into ourselves and social interaction with other souls. As I have explained, our life in the higher worlds depends on how we have prepared ourselves here on earth.

. . . .

Rudolf Steiner answered a question about whether one also could read to children who have died at birth or in early childhood.

Rudolf Steiner. One is a child only here on earth. Suprasensory vision frequently reveals that a person who dies at an early age is less childlike in the spiritual world than many who cross the portal of death at eighty.... I have spoken before about the painting by Raphael, the *School of Athens,* and how it should be understood in an esoteric sense. Recently I came to know an individual, a child, who died an early death. My connection with this soul made it possible for me to become aware of Raphael's original intention in this painting. The soul explained to me that, on the left, near the group in the foreground, a part had been painted over. This is the spot where something is being written down. Today, we find a mathematical formula there. Originally, however, there was a gospel passage. So you see that a "child" can be a highly evolved individual, able to guide one to things that can otherwise be discovered only with great difficulty. Consequently, I would say that, yes, one also can practice reading to children who die young.

3

BECAUSE THE BEINGS of the spiritual world cannot read, the best way to communicate spiritual truths is orally rather than through the written word. They understand and learn from thoughts that have come to life in human hearts. The modern habit of abstraction and literalism has set up a wall between those living on earth and those who live in the spiritual world, including those who have died. In earlier times, it was much easier for the love of those on earth to enter loved ones in heaven. Today, we must try to reestablish those relationships and build a bridge between the living and those who have died. To do this, it is important to understand the power of love and hate; love aids the dead, and hatred hinders and obstructs them. It places an obstacle in their path of development. The souls of the dead need nourishment, just as we need food on earth. Thoughts filled with heart and love become food for those who have died. At night, they draw near to our sleep and partake in our life of thinking and feeling. Often, they find nothing and must turn away hungry. Insofar as we do not live spiritually, we starve those who have died and, indeed, the whole spiritual world. For the most part, of course, this nourishment comes from those souls to whom the dead were related when alive. In ancient times, the community of blood relations provided that nourishment for their ancestors. Now, the communities we create must be based on love. Souls are complex. What we see in life is only the merest surface. Many souls hunger for spiritual ideas once they are on the other side, even those who seemed averse to anything spiritual while on earth. We are "books" for them. They hunger for the spiritual knowledge we can gain only on the earth. We must work to make the wall between these worlds thinner.

Recovering the Connection

BERGEN, OCTOBER 10, 1913

... Today I want to speak aphoristically about matters related to the spiritual world. This is better and more easily expressed orally than in writing, partly because prejudices in the world make it difficult in many ways to commit to writing everything that one gladly conveys to *hearts* devoted to anthroposophy. But it is also difficult, because spiritual truths lend themselves better to the spoken word than to writing or to print.

This applies especially to the more intimate spiritual truths. When these things are written down and printed, it always goes rather against the grain, though it must be done these days. It is always difficult to allow the more intimate truths of the higher worlds to be written down and printed. The precise reason for this is that writing and printing cannot be read by the spiritual beings about whom one is speaking. Books cannot be read in the spiritual world.

It is true that for a short period after death books can still be read through remembrance, but the beings of the higher hierarchies cannot read our books. And if you ask whether these beings therefore want to learn to read, I must say that in my experience they show no desire at present to do so. They find that reading what is produced on earth would be neither necessary nor useful for them.

Spiritual beings begin to read only when earthly human beings read books—when the contents of a book *come to life in human thoughts.* Then spiritual beings read in those thoughts; but what is written or printed is like darkness for the beings of the spiritual worlds. So when something is committed to writing or to print, one has the feeling that we are communicating behind the backs of the spiritual beings. Although people of today's culture may not wholly share it, every true esotericist will experience this feeling of distaste for writing and print.

As we penetrate the spiritual worlds with clairvoyant vision, we come to see that it is particularly important for knowledge of these worlds to spread more and more widely in the immediate future. There is an increasingly necessary change in human soul life, and it will depend a great deal on the spread of spiritual science.

If we look back with spiritual eyes over a period of a few centuries, what we find may greatly astonish those who have no knowledge of these things; communication between the living and the dead has become increasingly difficult. Even a relatively short time ago, it was far more active and alive.

When Christians of the Middle Ages—and even Christians of more recent centuries—turned their thoughts in prayer to the dead who had been related or known to them, their prayers and feelings bore them up toward the souls of the dead with much greater power than today. It was far easier in the past for souls of the dead to feel warmed by the breath of love flowing from those who looked up or sent their thoughts upward to them in prayer—that is, if we allow conventional culture to be our only guide.

Again, the dead are cut off more drastically from the living in the present age than they were a comparatively short time ago, which makes it more difficult for them to perceive what stirs in the souls of those left behind. This is part of humanity's evolution, but that evolution must also lead to rediscovering the connection, the real communion between the living and the dead.

In earlier times, the human soul could still maintain a real connection with the dead, though it was no longer fully conscious; human beings have not been clairvoyant for a long time now. During even more ancient times, the living were able to look up to the dead with clairvoyant vision and follow the events of their lives. It was once natural for a soul to have a living relationship with the dead; likewise, it is now possible for a soul to reestablish this communication and relationship by acquiring thoughts and ideas about the spiritual worlds. And it will be one of the practical tasks of anthroposophic living to ensure that such a bridge is built between the living and the dead.

To help us truly understand one another, I want begin by speaking about certain aspects of the mutual relationship between the living and the dead. I will start with a very simple phenomenon that will be explained according to the discoveries of spiritual research. Souls who occasionally practice a little self-contemplation will be able to observe the following (and I believe that many have done so).

Let us suppose that someone has hated another person in life, or perhaps it was, or is, really a question of aversion or dislike. When the one who was the object of the hatred or aversion dies, the other will not feel that this same hatred or aversion can be maintained. If that hatred persists beyond the grave, sensitive souls will feel a kind of shame that it exists. This feeling—and it is present in many souls—can be observed by clairvoyance. During self-examination one may well ask, Why does this feeling of shame over some hatred or aversion arise in the soul? After all, the existence of that hatred was never acknowledged to another person.

By following the one who has passed through the gate of death in the spiritual worlds, the clairvoyant investigator finds that the soul generally looks back to the earth and very clearly perceives a definite feeling of hatred in the soul of the one who is living. The one who has died (if I may speak figuratively) "sees" the hatred. The clairvoyant investigator can confirm the truth of this with absolute certainty, and is also able to perceive the meaning of that hatred for the one who has died. It represents an impediment to the soul who died—an obstacle to that soul's intentions for spiritual development. Such an obstacle is comparable to the earthly hindrances that block our way to an outer goal. In the spiritual world, that hatred becomes an obstacle to the good endeavors of those who have died. Consequently, we can understand why hatred dies in the souls of those who practice a little self-contemplation, even when hatred in life was justified. Hatred dies because a feeling of shame arises in the soul when the person who was hated dies. Of course, a person who is not clairvoyant does not know why, but a feeling of being observed is implanted in the very soul. One feels that the dead individual sees one's hatred and that it acts as a hindrance to that soul's good aspirations.

Many feelings that are deeply rooted in the human soul are explained as we rise into the worlds of spirit and recognize the spiritual facts behind those feelings. When we do certain things on earth, we prefer not to be physically observed, and we would refrain from doing them if we knew we were witnessed; likewise, hatred does not persist after a person's death because we have the feeling that we are being observed by the soul who has passed over. At the same time, the love or warmheartedness we extend to the dead eases their path by removing hindrances.

What I am saying—that hatred creates hindrances in the spiritual world and love takes them away—does not have an impact on, or pierce, karma. Nevertheless, many things happen here on earth that we must not attribute directly to karma. If one stubs a toe on a stone, it cannot necessarily be attributed to karma—at least, not to moral karma. Similarly, it is not a violation of karma when the dead feel put at ease by the love flowing toward them from earth or when they encounter hindrances to their good endeavors.

There is something else that will make an even stronger appeal for communication between the dead and the living. The souls of those who have died need nourishment in a certain sense—not, of course, the kind needed by human beings on earth, but spirit and soul nourishment. On the earth, we must have cornfields where grain for our physical sustenance ripens; likewise, the souls of the dead must have "cornfields" from which to gather the sustenance they need between death and a new birth. The clairvoyant eye sees that cornfields for the souls of the dead are in fact the souls of sleeping human beings. One who experiences this for the first time in the spirit world is not only surprised but deeply shattered to see how the souls living between death and a new birth hurry, so to speak, toward the souls of sleeping human beings, seeking their thoughts and ideas. *Such thoughts are food for the souls of the dead—nourishment they need.*

When we go to sleep at night, the ideas and thoughts that have passed through our consciousness in our waking hours come to life as living beings. The souls of the dead approach and share those ideas, feeling nourished as they perceive them. Clairvoyant vision can see the dead as, night after night, they make their way toward sleeping human beings left behind on earth (especially blood relations, but also friends), seeking refreshment and nourishment from the thoughts and ideas carried into sleep. And it is a shattering experience to see that they often find nothing, because in the sleep state there is a great difference between one kind of thought and another.

If we are caught up all day in thoughts related to material life, with the mind directed only toward what is happening in the physical world and what may be accomplished there, and if we have no thought for the spiritual worlds before going to sleep but, in fact, often take ourselves into those worlds by means quite other than such thoughts, then we have no nourishment to offer the dead. I know of towns in Europe where students induce sleepiness by drinking a lot of beer. Consequently, they carry with them thoughts that cannot live in the spiritual world. When the souls of the dead approach such souls, they find barren fields. They fare no better than our own physical body would during a famine, because our fields do not yield crops. Today especially (because materialism is so widespread), one can observe great famine among souls in the spiritual worlds. Many people consider it childish to involve themselves with thoughts of the spiritual world, but this is exactly how they deprive souls after death of needed nourishment.

Before one can understand this correctly, it must be said that nourishment after death can be drawn only from the ideas and thoughts of those with whom the dead had some connection during life. Nourishment cannot be drawn from those with whom there was no connection at all. Today, when we cultivate anthroposophy so there may again be in souls a spirituality that can nourish the dead, we are not working only for the living, or merely to provide them with some kind of theoretical satisfaction; we try to fill our hearts and souls with thoughts of the spiritual world because we know that the dead who were connected with us on earth must draw their nourishment from these thoughts. We feel ourselves to be not only workers for living human beings, but workers too in the sense that anthroposophical activity, the spread of anthroposophical life, is also of service to the spiritual worlds. In speaking to the living for their life by day, we promote ideas that bring satisfaction in the life by night as fruitful nourishment for the souls whose karma it was to die before us. So not only do we feel the urge to spread anthroposophy by the ordinary means of communication, but deep down within us there is the longing to cultivate anthroposophy in communities, in groups, because this is of real value.

As I have said, the dead can draw nourishment only from souls they were associated with in life. We therefore try to bring souls together so that the harvest fields for the dead may become more and more extensive. Many human beings who after death find no harvest fields in their families, because they are materialists, find them in the souls of anthroposophists with whom they had some connection. That is the deeper reason for working together in communities, and why we are anxious that the dead should have been able before death to know anthroposophists who are still occupied on earth with spiritual things. For when these people are asleep, the dead can draw nourishment from them.

In ancient times, when a certain spirituality pervaded the souls of human beings, religious communities and blood relatives were where help was sought after death. But the power of blood relationship has diminished and must be replaced by cultivation of the spiritual life, as we endeavor to do. Anthroposophy can therefore promise that a new bridge will be built between the living and the dead, and that by it we can mean something real to the dead. And when with clairvoyant vision today we sometimes find human beings in the life between death and a new birth suffering because those they have known, including their nearest and dearest, harbor only materialistic thoughts, we recognize how necessary it is for cultural life on earth to be permeated with spiritual thoughts.

Suppose, for example, we find in the spiritual world a man we knew who died fairly recently and left behind certain members of his family, also known to us. The wife and children are all of them good people in the ordinary sense, with a genuine love for one another. But clairvoyant vision now reveals that the man, whose wife was the very sun of his existence when he came home after heavy and arduous work, cannot see into her soul because she has no spiritual thoughts in either her head or in her heart. And so he asks, Where is my wife? What has become of her? He can look back to the time when he was united with her on earth, but now, when he is seeking her most urgently of all, he cannot find her. This may well happen. There are many people today who believe that as far as consciousness is concerned, the dead have passed into a kind of void, who can think of the dead only with materialistic thoughts, not with any fruitful thoughts. In the life between death and rebirth, a soul may be looking toward someone still on earth who had loved him, but the love is not combined with belief in the soul's continued existence after death. In such a case, at the very moment after death when this desire to see one who was loved on earth arises, all vision may be extinguished. The living human being cannot be found, nor can any link be established, although it is known that contact could indeed be made if spiritual thoughts were harbored in that person's soul.

This is a frequent and sorrowful experience for the dead. Thus it may happen, and this may be seen by clairvoyant vision, that many human beings encounter obstacles after death in the way of their highest aims because of the thoughts of antipathy that follow them, and they find no consolation in the living thoughts of those they were dear to on earth, now hidden from sight due to their materialism.

The laws of the spiritual world, perceived in this way by clairvoyant vision, hold good unconditionally, as shown by an example it has often been possible to observe. It is instructive to see how thoughts of hatred, or at least antipathy, take effect even if they are not conceived in full consciousness. There are schoolteachers, of the type usually called "strict," who are unable to gain the affection of their pupils. In such cases, of course, the thoughts of antipathy and hatred are formed half-innocently. But when such a teacher dies it can be seen how these thoughts, too—for they persist—are obstacles in the way of good endeavors in the spiritual world. After the teacher's death it is not often that children or young people realize that hatred ought to cease, and they preserve the feeling of how the teacher tormented them. From such insights a great deal can be learned about the mutual relationships between the living and the dead.

I have been trying to lead up to an anthroposophical endeavor that can have a fundamentally good result: *reading to the dead.* It has been proved in our own movement that very great service can be rendered to the souls of those who have died by reading to them about spiritual things. This can be done by directing your thoughts to the dead, which is easier to do if you picture them as you knew them in life, standing or sitting

before you. In this way you can read to more than one soul at a
time. You do not read aloud, but follow the ideas with alert
attention, always keeping in mind the thought that the dead are
standing before you.

That is what is meant by reading to the dead. It is not always
essential to have a book, but you must not think abstractly and
you must think each thought to the end. In this way you are able
to read to the dead.

Although it is more difficult, this can be carried so far that
one can even read to a soul with whom the connection has been
no closer than thoughts held in common—in the realm of some
particular world conception or indeed in any domain of life—if
there has been some degree of personal relationship. Through
the warmth of the thoughts directed to them, the dead gradually become attentive. Thus it may be of real use to read to distant associates after their death.

The reading can take place at any time. I have been asked
what the best time is for such reading, but it is quite independent of time. All that matters is to think the thoughts through to
the end—to skim through them is not enough. The subject matter must be worked through word by word, as if one were recit-
ing inwardly. Then the dead read with us. And it is not correct to
think that such reading can be useful only to those who have
come into contact with anthroposophy during their lifetime.
This is by no means necessarily so.

Very recently, perhaps less than a year ago, one of our friends,
and his wife too, felt a kind of uneasiness every night. As the
friend's father had died a short time previously, it struck him at
once that his father was wanting something and was turning to
him. When this friend came to me for advice, it was found that
the father, who during his lifetime would not listen to a word
about anthroposophy, was feeling an urgent need after his
death to know something of it. Then, when the son and his wife
read to the father my lecture course on the Gospel of St. John,
that soul felt deeply satisfied, as though lifted above many dis-
harmonies that had been experienced shortly after death.

This case is noteworthy because the soul concerned was that of a preacher who had regularly presented the views of his religion to other people, but who could find satisfaction after death only by being able to share in the reading of an anthroposophical elucidation of the Gospel of St. John. It is not essential that the ones we wish to help after death should have been anthroposophists in life, although in the nature of things very special service will be rendered to anthroposophists by reading to them.

Such a fact gives us a view of the human soul quite different from the one usually held. There are factors in the souls of human beings of far greater complexity than is generally believed. What takes its course consciously is actually only a small part of human soul life. In the unconscious depths of one's soul a great deal is going on of which one has at most a dim inkling; it hardly enters at all into clear waking consciousness. Moreover, the very opposite of what people believe or think in their upper consciousness may often be astir in their subconscious life. A very frequent case is that one member of a family comes to anthroposophy and the brother or the husband or the wife become more and more hostile to it, often scornful and rabidly opposed; great antipathy to anthroposophy then develops in the family. Life becomes very difficult for many people because of the scorn and even anger of friends or relatives.

Investigation of the hostile souls often reveals that in their subconscious depths an intense longing for anthroposophy is developing. Such souls may be longing for anthroposophy even more intensely than those who attend anthroposophical meetings avidly. But death lifts away the veils from the subconscious and balances out such things in a remarkable way. It often happens in life that people deaden themselves to what lies in the subconscious. There are people who may have an intense longing for anthroposophy, but they deaden it by raging against anthroposophy and delude themselves by repudiating it. But after death the longing asserts itself all the more forcibly. The most ardent longing for anthroposophy often shows itself after death in the very people who have raged against it in life. Do not, therefore, refrain from reading to those who were hostile to anthroposophy while they were alive, for by this reading you may often be rendering them the greatest service imaginable.

A question often raised is, How can one be sure that the soul of the dead person is able to listen? Admittedly, without clairvoyance it is difficult to be sure of this, although if you steep yourself in thoughts of one who has died you will in time be surprised by a feeling that the dead person is actually listening. This feeling will be absent only when the reader is inattentive and fails to notice the peculiar warmth that often arises during the reading. Such a feeling can indeed be acquired, but even if this proves impossible it must nevertheless be said that in our attitude to the spiritual world the following principle always applies: when we read to the dead, we help them under all circumstances if they hear us. But even if they do not hear us, we are fulfilling our duty and may eventually succeed in enabling them to hear. In any case, we gain something by absorbing thoughts and ideas that will quite certainly be nourishment for the dead in the way indicated. Under no circumstances is anything lost. Actual experience has shown that awareness of what is being read is in fact extraordinarily widespread among the dead, and that we render a tremendous service to them by reading the spiritual wisdom that can be imparted to us today.

Thus, we may hope that the wall dividing the living from the dead will become thinner and thinner as anthroposophy spreads through the world. And it will be a beautiful and splendid result of anthroposophy if in a future time people come to know—as actual fact, not just theory—that in reality, when we pass through so-called death and are together with the dead, it is only a matter of a transformation of experience. We can actually enable the dead to share in what we ourselves experienced during physical life. A false idea of the life between death and rebirth is indicated by asking, Why is it necessary to read to the dead? Do they not know through their own vision what those on earth can read to them? Do they themselves not know it far better? These questions will of course be asked only by one who is not in a position to know what can be experienced in the spiritual world. After all, we can live in the physical world without acquiring knowledge of it. If we are not in a position to form judgments about certain things, we have no real knowledge of the physical world. The animals live together with us in the physical world, but do not know it as we know it. Because a soul is living in the spiritual world after death does not mean it has knowledge of that world, although it is able to behold it. The knowledge acquired through anthroposophy can be acquired only on earth; it cannot be acquired in the spiritual world. If, therefore, beings in the spiritual world are to possess knowledge, it must be learned through those who themselves acquire it on earth. It is an important secret of the spiritual worlds that the soul can be in them and behold them, but that knowledge of them must be acquired on earth.

At this point, I must mention a common misconception about the spiritual worlds. When human beings are living in the spiritual world between death and a new birth, they direct their longing to our physical world somewhat as physical human beings direct their longing to the spiritual world. Human beings between death and a new birth expect people on earth to show and radiate up to them knowledge that can be acquired only on earth. The earth has not been established without purpose in spiritual world-existence; the earth has been summoned to life so that what is possible nowhere else may come into being. *Knowledge of the spiritual worlds—which means more than vision, more than merely looking on—can arise only on earth.*

I said before that the beings of the spiritual worlds cannot read our books, and I must now add that what lives in us as anthroposophy is for the spiritual beings, and also for our own souls after death, what books here on earth are for physical human beings—a source of knowledge of the world. *We ourselves are living books for the dead.* Try to feel the importance of these words: we must provide reading for the dead!

In a certain sense our books are more faithful and long-suffering, for they do not allow their letters to vanish into the paper while we are reading them, whereas, by filling our minds with material thoughts—which are invisible in the spiritual worlds—we human beings often deprive the dead of the opportunity of reading. I am obliged to say this because a question often raised is whether the dead are not capable of knowing for themselves what we are able to give them. They cannot be, because anthroposophy can be grounded only on the earth and must be carried up from there into the spiritual worlds.

When we penetrate into the spiritual worlds and come to know something about the life there, we encounter conditions altogether different from those prevailing in physical life on earth. That is why it is so very difficult to describe these conditions in terms of human words and human thoughts. Any attempt to speak concretely about them often seems paradoxical.

To take one example only, I can tell you of a human soul who, after death, was able because of its special knowledge to help me make certain discoveries in the spiritual world about the great painter Leonardo da Vinci, particularly about his famous picture *The Last Supper.* When one investigates a spiritual fact in association with such a soul, that soul is able to indicate many things that ordinary clairvoyance might not otherwise have found in the akasha chronicle. The soul in the spiritual world is able to point things out, but only when there is some reciprocal understanding of what it is trying to convey. Something very noteworthy then comes to light.

Suppose that in company with such a soul one is investigating how Leonardo da Vinci created his famous picture, which today is hardly more than a few patches of color. In the akasha chronicle, one can watch Leonardo as he painted, one can see what the picture was once like—although this is not easy to do. When the investigation is carried on in company with a discarnate soul who has some connection with Leonardo da Vinci and his painting, one perceives that this soul is showing one certain things—for example, the faces of Christ and of Judas as they actually were in the picture. But one perceives, too, that the soul could not reveal this unless at that moment there is understanding in the soul of the living investigator. This is a *sine qua non*. And only at the moment when the soul of the living investigator is receptive to what is being disclosed does the discarnate soul itself learn to understand what is otherwise merely vision. Figuratively speaking, in experiencing something together—something that can be experienced only in the way described—the discarnate soul says to the living investigator, You have brought me to the picture and I feel the urge to look at it with you. (The investigator's desire to investigate the picture is what brings the discarnate soul to say this.) Numerous experiences then arise. But a moment comes when the discarnate soul is either suddenly absent or says that it must depart. In the case I have just described, the discarnate soul said, Up to now the soul of Leonardo da Vinci regarded with approval what was being done, but does not now desire the investigation to continue.

My object in telling you this is to describe an important feature of the spiritual life. Just as in physical life we know that we are looking at this or that object—we see a rose, or whatever it may be—so in the spiritual life we know that this or that being is seeing us, watching us. In the spiritual worlds we have the constant feeling that beings are looking at us. Whereas in the physical world we are conscious that we are observing the world, in the spiritual world the experience is that we ourselves are being observed, now from this side, now from that. We feel that eyes are upon us all the time, but eyes that also impel us to make decisions. With the knowledge that we are being watched by eyes favoring what we ought to do or ought not to do, we either do it or refrain. Just as here we reach out to pick a flower that delights us because we have seen it, in the spiritual world we do something because a being there views it favorably, or we refrain from the action because we cannot endure the look directed at it. This experience must become ingrained in us. In the spiritual world, we feel that we ourselves are being seen, just as here in the physical world we feel that we ourselves are seeing. In a certain sense, what is active here is passive there, and what is active there is passive here.

It is obvious from this that quite different concepts must be acquired to correctly understand descriptions of conditions in the spiritual world. You will therefore realize how difficult it is to describe the spiritual world in ordinary human language. You will realize too how essential it is that the necessary preparatory understanding be created first....

4

OUR DREAMS AND OUR CONTACT with the dead have in common the absence of a subjective sense of our self, or I, and the absence of our sense of touch. Like the world of dreams, the world in which we encounter the dead is not a world of "things," but primarily a world of images. There, we are not outside but inside what we perceive; we "fuse" with beings of the spiritual world. Occasionally, those who have died appear as they did in life. More often, however, they take on the form of another person. If we allow our feelings to penetrate this image, we can begin to sense the underlying meaning. This is a kind of "reading" in which we go beyond underlying meaning to the cognitive essence. It is a different kind of reading. In the world of waking consciousness, we perceive things (objects), but in the other world we have to become accustomed to the feeling of being perceived—the feeling of presences perceiving us. We must become aware of their spiritual gaze resting upon us, and not just resting but acting and giving us strength. To experience this we must develop a specific kind of selflessness and the capacity to love objectively, not subjectively out of personal needs. If we can do this we will experience the gaze of a loved one who has died as a warm mildness, but if we cannot we shall experience a piercing, burning sensation. What we feel tells us who is with us. This is true of all spiritual beings. Esoteric training reveals this world of beings as,

for instance, the world of living and weaving thoughts,
the world of the angels and the next world, and the world
of the archangels. There, too, we can encounter the astral
bodies of those we have loved as great cosmic paintings. If
we remain selfish and unloving, however, we release
luciferic and ahrimanic beings.

The Presence of the Dead

PARIS, MAY 25, 1914

... What happens to our soul when it becomes clairvoyant can be compared with our dreams, which are like a surrogate clairvoyance. When we dream, we live in a world of images, which contains nothing of what we call the "sensation of touching an object outside us." In our dreams, there is usually nothing we can compare with normal I consciousness. If any aspect of our I does appear in our dreams, it seems to be separate from us, almost like another being outside us. We face our I like a separate entity. Thus, we can speak of a doubling of the I. However, in dreams we perceive only the part of ourselves that has separated, not the subjective I. All statements apparently contradicting what I have just said can be traced to the fact that most people know of their dreams only from memory, and cannot remember that in the actual dream the subjective I was extinguished.

The images of clairvoyant research resemble dreams because in both of them the subjective I and the sense of touch are absent. A clairvoyant recalling his or her experiences must feel that the clairvoyant reality is permeable and, unlike physical objects, offers no resistance to touch. In the physical world we have I awareness because we know: I am here, the object is out-side me. However, in clairvoyant perception, *we are inside the object, not separated from what we perceive.* Consequently, individual objects are not fixed and distinct like physical ones, but are in continuous movement and transformation. Objects in the physical world are fixed because we can touch them and because they offer us boundaries, which objects of clairvoyant perception do not have. The same thing that causes our I to fuse with the objects of clairvoyant perception also forces us to be very careful when we encounter in the physical world what we call another I, another human being.

Let us first look at what happens when through our clairvoyant faculties we encounter a person who has died. Such an encounter can come about when the figure of the deceased approaches us in clairvoyant perception like a very vivid dream image, looking every bit as we remember the person looked in life. However, this is not the usual type of such encounters, but a rare exception.

Another possibility is that we clairvoyantly perceive a dead person who has taken on the form of either a living or another dead individual, and thus does not appear in his or her own form. The appearance of the deceased, then, is of very little relevance in identifying the individuality. Perhaps we were particularly fond of another dead person or have a particularly close friendship with a living one; the deceased approaching us can then take on the form of either of those other individuals. In other words, we lack all the usual means of identifying the I and appearance of a person in the physical world. It will help us find our way to remember that the appearance or form is not at all important; a being is meeting us in one form or another, and we need to note what this being does. If we take our time and carefully observe the image before us, we will realize that, based on everything we know about, the individual in question could not act the way this image is acting in the clairvoyant sphere; the actions are totally out of character. We will often encounter a contradiction between how the person we knew, whose image appears before us, acted and how the image acts.

If we allow our feelings to accompany these actions, ignoring the individual's appearance, we will get a sense in the depths of our soul telling us what being we are actually dealing with. Let me repeat that we are guided by a feeling that rises up from the depths of our soul, for that is very important. The individual's appearance in the clairvoyant sphere seems to resemble a physical figure but can be as different from the being really present as the symbols for the word *house* are from the actual house. Since we can read, we do not concentrate on the symbols that make up the word *house* and do not describe the shape of the letters, but instead get right to the concept *house*. In the same way, we learn in true clairvoyance to move from the figure we perceive to the actual being. That is why we speak of reading the occult script, in the true sense of the word. That is, we move inwardly and actively from the vision to the reality it expresses, just as written words express a reality.

How can we develop this ability to go beyond the appearance, the immediate vision? We do so, above all, by looking at new ideas and concepts we will need if we want to understand the clairvoyant sphere—new, that is, in contrast to the ideas we use in the physical world.

In the physical world we look at an object or a being and say, quite rightly, I perceive that being, that object. We perceive the plant, mineral, and animal kingdoms, the realm of physical human beings, as well as clouds, mountains, rivers, stars, Sun, and Moon. The feeling expressed in the words *I perceive* undergoes a transformation when we enter the clairvoyant sphere.

Let me try to explain this with an analogy, though it may sound simplistic. If you were a plant, how would you relate to people perceiving you? If this plant had consciousness and could speak, it would have to say, People look at me, I am perceived by them. Of course, we say, I perceive the plant, but at its level of consciousness, the plant would have to say that it was perceived by human beings. It is this feeling of being perceived, being looked at, that we must acquire in relation to the beings of the clairvoyant sphere. For example, concerning the beings of the first hierarchy, the angels, we must be aware that, strictly speaking, it is not correct to say, I perceive an angel; instead we have to say, I feel an angel perceiving me.

Based on our Copernican worldview, we know full well that the Sun does not move. Nevertheless, we say that it rises and moves across the sky, thus contradicting our better knowledge. Similarly, in everyday language we can say that we see an angel. But that is not the truth. We would actually have to say that we feel ourselves seen or perceived by an angel. If we said we experience the being of an angel or of a dead person and can feel it, we would speak the truth from the clairvoyant point of view.

Perhaps an example from clairvoyant observation will help you understand this. More than ten years ago, at the beginning of our work with spiritual science, a dear friend of ours worked with us for a short time.[1] This individual possessed not only enthusiasm for what we could give her in the early stages of spiritual science, but also a profound artistic sensitivity and understanding. One could not help but love her, a love that may well be described as objective because of her qualities. Having worked with us for a relatively short time and having learned a great deal about the results of spiritual science, she left the physical world. There is no need to go into the next four or five years after her death, so let me get directly to what happened after that. In 1909, we presented our mystery plays in Munich[2]—preceded, to our great delight, by *Children of Lucifer* by our highly respected friend Edouard Schuré.[3] Whatever you may think about the way the plays were produced then and later, we had to

---

1. Maria Strauch Spettini (1847–1904).

2. Rudolf Steiner, *Four Mystery Plays*, London: Rudolf Steiner Press, 1982. These plays were premiered in Munich between 1910 and 1912, under Steiner's direction.

3. Edouard Schuré, born in Strasbourg in 1841, was an early esoteric student of Steiner.

present them the way we did. The circumstances under which we had to work on the performances were such that we needed an impulse from the spiritual world, an impulse that also included the artistic aspect we wanted to incorporate. Now, I can assure you that even at that time, in 1909, and even more so in later years, I always felt a specific spiritual impulse as I was working on the arrangements for the performances.

You see, when we have work to do in the physical world, we need not only intellect and skills but also the strength of our muscles. Our muscles help us objectively; they are given to us, unlike the intellectual capacities we ourselves dwell in. Now, in dealing with matters of the spirit we need forces from the spiritual world to combine with our own, just as we need the strength of our muscles for physical action. In the case I mentioned, the impulse from the individual who had left the physical world in 1904 entered more and more into our artistic work on the Munich plays. To describe what happened, I would have to say the impulses from this individual came down from the spirit plane and flowed into my intentions, into my work. She was the patron of our work.

We develop the right feelings toward the dead if we become aware that their spiritual gaze—if I may use that expression—and their powers focus on us; they look at us, act in us, and add to our strength.

To experience such a spiritual fact in the right way, we need to develop a very specific type of selflessness and a capacity for love. That is why I stressed that one should love people objectively, as it were, because of their qualities; one must love them because they were as they were. A subjective love, a love arising out of personal needs, can easily be egotistical and can potentially keep us from finding the right relationship to such a dead individual. The difference between the right love, the selfless love we have for such a person, and selfish love becomes perfectly obvious in clairvoyant experience.

Let us assume a person like the one mentioned would want to help us after her death, but we cannot develop true selfless love for her. Her spiritual gaze, her spiritual will streaming toward us would then be like a burning sensation, causing a piercing, burning feeling in our soul. If we can feel and maintain a selfless love, this stream, her spiritual gaze as it were, flows into our soul like a feeling of warm mildness and pours itself into our thoughts, imagination, feeling, and willing. It is out of this feeling that we recognize who the dead person is and not on the basis of his or her appearance, because the dead may manifest in the guise of a person we feel close to at the moment. The form in which the beings of the higher world appear to us—and after death we are all beings of a higher, spiritual world—depends on our subjective nature, on what we habitually see, think, and feel. The reality is what we feel for the being manifest before us, and how we receive what comes to us from this being. Regardless of what Joan of Arc said about the appearance of the higher beings in her visions, the spiritual researcher able to investigate these things knows that it was always the genius of the French nation that stood behind them.

I described how we can feel the gaze of spiritual beings resting upon us and their will flowing into our souls. To learn this is analogous to learning to read on the physical plane. Those who merely want to describe their visions would be like people describing the shape of the letters on a page rather than their meaning. This shows you how easy it is to have preconceived notions about the experiences in the spiritual realm. Naturally, it seems most obvious to attach great importance to the description of what the vision looked like. However, what really matters is what lies behind the veil of perception and is expressed in the images of the vision.

Thus, in the course of occult development, the soul immerses itself in specific moods and inner states different from those of our everyday life. We have entered the world of the hierarchy of angels and the hierarchy—we could also say hierarchies—of the dead as soon as our occult exercises have brought us to the stage where the sense of touch characteristic of the physical world no longer exists, and where a person's appearance is no longer characteristic of the I concerned. Then our thinking changes, and we no longer have thoughts in the sense we have them here in the physical world. In that world, every thought takes on the form of an elemental being. In the physical world, our thoughts can agree or contradict each other. In this other world we enter, thoughts encounter other thoughts as real beings, either loving or hating each other. We begin to feel our way into a world of many thought beings. And in those living thought beings, we really feel what we usually call "life." Here life and thinking are united, whereas they are completely separate in the physical world.

When we speak on the physical plane and tell our thoughts to someone, we have the feeling that our thoughts come from our soul, that we have to remember them at this particular moment. Speaking as a true occultist and not someone who just tells his or her experiences from memory, we will feel that our thoughts arise as living beings. We must be glad if we are blessed at the right moment with the approach of a thought as a real being.

When you express your thoughts in the physical world, for example, as a lecturer, you will find it easier to give a talk for the thirtieth time than you found it the first time. If, however, you speak as an occultist, thoughts always have to approach you and then depart again. Just as someone paying you the thirtieth visit had to come to you thirty times, the *living* thought we express for the thirtieth time has to come to us thirty times as it did the first time; our memory is of absolutely no use here.

If you express an idea on the physical level and someone is sitting in a corner thinking, "I don't like that nonsense, I hate it," you will not be particularly bothered by it. You have prepared your ideas and present them regardless of the positive or negative thoughts of someone in the audience. But if as an esotericist you let thoughts approach you, they could be delayed and kept away by someone who hates them or who hates the speaker. And the forces blocking that thought must be overcome, because we are dealing with living beings and not merely with abstract ideas.

These two examples show that as soon as we enter the sphere of clairvoyance, we are immersed in living and weaving thoughts. It is as if the thoughts are no longer subjective and as if you yourself are no longer within yourself, as if you are living outside in the wide world.

When you are in this world of living and weaving thoughts, you are in the hierarchy of angels. And just as our physical world is everywhere filled with air, the world of the hierarchy of angels is filled with the mild warmth I spoke about earlier, which the beings of this hierarchy pour out. When our inner development has brought us to the stage where we can live in this spiritual atmosphere of streaming mildness, we feel the spiritual eyes of the hierarchy of angels resting on our souls.

Now, in our earthly life, we have certain ideals and think about them abstractly. As we think of them, we feel obligated to pursue these ideals. In the clairvoyant sphere, however, there are no abstract ideals. There ideals are living beings of the hierarchy of angels and flow through spiritual space, looking at us with warmth.

In the physical world, we may have ideals and know them well, and yet we may not do anything to apply them. Our emotions, and perhaps passions, can tempt us to shirk them. However, if we knowingly ignore an ideal in the clairvoyant sphere, we feel the spiritual gaze of a being of the hierarchy of angels directed at us with reproach, and this reproach burns. In the spiritual world, ignoring an ideal is thus a reality, and a being of the hierarchy of angels reproaches us. Their gaze makes us feel the reproach; it is the reproach we feel.

You see, learning to develop a real feeling for ideals is one way of entering the world of the hierarchy of angels. Limiting our consciousness to the physical plane may lead us to think that nothing will happen if we are too lazy to act on our ideals. However, we can learn to feel that if we do not act on an ideal, then, regardless of other consequences, the world becomes different from what it would have been had we followed our ideal. We are on the way to the hierarchy of angels when we begin to see that not acting on our ideals is something real, and when we can transform this insight into a genuine feeling. Transforming and vitalizing our feelings allows our souls to grow into the higher worlds.

Through continued esoteric training, we can rise to an even higher level, that of the hierarchy of archangels. If we ignore the angels, we feel reproach. With the archangels we feel reproach as well as a real effect on our being. The strength and power of the archangels works through our I when we live in their world.

For example, a few months ago we lost a very dear friend when he left the physical plane.[4] A profound poet, he had quickly found his way into the anthroposophical worldview in the last five years, and the feelings it evoked in him are beautifully reflected in his recent poetry. From the time he joined us, and even before that, he had been struggling with an infirm and deteriorating body. The more his body deteriorated, the more his soul was filled with poetry that reflected our worldview. Only a short time has elapsed since his death, so one cannot yet say that this individual possesses a clearly existing consciousness. Nevertheless, the first stages of his development in the existence after death can be seen. The astral body, now separated from the physical and living in the spiritual world, reveals the most wonderful tableaux of cosmic development as we understand it in spiritual science. Having left the deteriorated physical body, the astral body has become so illuminated, comparatively speaking, that it can present the clairvoyant observer with a complete picture of cosmic evolution.

Let me use an analogy to explain what I mean. We can love nature and admire it, and still appreciate a beautiful painting that recreates what we have seen in nature. Similarly, we can be uplifted when what we have seen in the clairvoyant sphere lights up again, as a cosmic painting so to speak, in the astral body of a

---

4. Rudolf Steiner is referring here to the poet and translator (of Ibsen, Strindberg, and Hamsun), Christian Morgenstern (1871-1914).

person who has died. The astral body of our departed friend reveals after death what it absorbed, at first unconsciously but later also consciously, in the course of his anthroposophical development when the beings of the hierarchy of archangels worked actively on the poetical transformation of his anthroposophical thoughts and ideas.

Our progress in our esoteric development can be called mystical, because it is initially the inner progress of the soul. We transform our ordinary personality and gradually reach a new state. This step-by-step growth of the soul is mystical progress because at first it is experienced inwardly. As soon as we can perceive the mildness looking down from the spiritual world, we are objectively in the world of the angels, which reveals itself to us. And as soon as we can recognize that real forces of strength and power enter us, we are in the realm of the archangels. With each stage of inner mystical progress we have to enter another world.

However, if we fail to develop selflessness and reach the stage of living in the world of the angels while remaining selfish and unloving, then we carry the self intended for the physical world into their realm. Instead of feeling the mild gaze and will of the angels upon us, we feel that other spiritual powers are able to ascend through us. Instead of gazing at us from outside, they have been released by us, shall we say, from their underworld while we were raised to a higher world. Instead of being overshadowed, or rather illuminated, by the world of the angels, we experience the luciferic beings that emerge from us.

Then, if we reach the stage of mystical development that allows us to enter the world of the archangels, but without having first developed the wish to receive by grace the influences of the spiritual world, we carry our self up into their realm. As a result, instead of being strengthened and imbued with the power of the archangels, the beings of the ahrimanic world emerge from us and surround us.

At first glance, the idea that the world of Lucifer appears in the realm of the angels and the world of Ahriman in that of the archangels seems terrible. However, there is really nothing awful about this. Lucifer and Ahriman are in any case higher beings than we are. Lucifer can be described as an archangel left behind at an earlier stage of evolution, Ahriman as a spirit of personality also left behind at an earlier stage.[5] The terrible thing is not that we encounter Lucifer and Ahriman, but that we encounter them without recognizing them for who they are. Encountering Lucifer in the world of the angels really means encountering the spirit of beauty, the spirit of freedom. But the all-important thing is that we recognize Lucifer and his hosts as soon as we enter the world of the angels. The same is true of Ahriman in the realm of the archangels. Unleashing Lucifer and Ahriman in the higher worlds is terrible only if we do not recognize them as we release them, because then they control us without our knowledge. It is important that we face them consciously.

When we have advanced in our mystical development to the level of living in the world of the angels and want to continue there with really fruitful occultism, we have to look for Lucifer as soon as we expect the spiritual gaze of the angels to rest on us. Lucifer must be present—and if we cannot find him, he is within us. But it is very important that Lucifer is outside us in this realm, so that we can face him.

These facts about Lucifer and Ahriman, angels and archangels explain the nature of revelation in the higher worlds. From our viewpoint in the physical world, we are easily led to believe that Lucifer and Ahriman are evil powers. But when we enter the higher world, this no longer has any meaning. In the clairvoyant sphere, Lucifer and Ahriman have to be present just as much as the angels and archangels. However, we do not perceive them the same way. We identify the angels and archangels not by their appearance, but by the mildness that flows into us from the angels and the strength and power that flow into our feeling and willing from the archangels, if we allow it. Lucifer

---

5. For more about Lucifer and Ahriman, see Rudolf Steiner, *Evil: Selected Lectures*, London: Rudolf Steiner Press, 1997. Also *Lucifer and Ahriman*, North Vancouver, Canada: Steiner Book Center, 1976.

and Ahriman appear to us as figures, merely transposed into the spiritual world; we cannot touch them, but we can approach them as spiritual projections of the physical world. Clearly, it is important that we learn in our mystical clairvoyant development to see forms in the higher world and to be aware that we are seen, that a higher will focuses on us.

You see, higher development does not consist merely in acquiring clairvoyant faculties, but in developing a certain state of soul, a certain attitude or relationship to the beings of the higher world. This new attitude and state of soul must be developed hand in hand with the training of our clairvoyant faculties. In other words, we must learn not only to see in the spiritual world but also to read in it. Reading is not meant here in the narrow sense of a simple learning process, but as something we acquire through transforming our feelings and sensations. It is important to keep in mind that a split of our personality occurs when clairvoyance begins and we attain a revelation of the higher worlds. Our earthly personality is left behind, and a new one is acquired upon ascending into a higher world. And just as the beings of the higher hierarchies look at us in the higher world, so we perceive our own ordinary personality from a higher perspective. Our higher self discards the lower one and observes it. So, to make valid statements about the higher worlds we had better wait until we are able to say, That is you; the person you see in your clairvoyant vision is yourself. "That is you" on the higher level corresponds to "this is I" on the physical one.

Now remember when you were eight or thirteen or fifteen years old and try to reconstruct from your memory a small part of your life at that time. Try to recall as vividly as possible your thinking in those years. Then concentrate on your current feelings about the girl or boy you were at eight, thirteen, or fifteen. As soon as we move from the physical level to the higher world, the present moment we live in now becomes a memory of the kind we have just recalled. We look back at our current existence on the physical level and at what we may still become during the remainder of our physical life in the same way you look back to your experiences at eight, thirteen, or fifteen from your vantage point in the present moment.

Everything we consider part of ourselves on the physical level, such as our feelings, thoughts, ideas, and actions, becomes a memory as soon as we enter the higher world. We look down at the physical world and become a memory to ourselves when we live in the higher world. We have to keep our experiences in the higher worlds separate from those in the physical realm, just as we distinguish between our present situation and an earlier one. Imagine a forty-year-old person who vividly remembers the feelings and abilities he or she had as an eight-year-old boy or girl. For instance, the person might be reading a book now, at the age of forty, and all of a sudden begin to relate to the book as an eight-year-old would. That would be a confusion of the two attitudes, the two states of soul, and is analogous to what happens when we confuse our state of soul on the physical level with what is required in the higher worlds.

Of course, this has nothing to do with the fact that every unbiased person can understand what I say about the higher worlds; in other words, you do not have to believe these descriptions, because you can understand them if you approach them without preconceived ideas. People may object that we cannot describe the higher worlds with concepts, thoughts, and ideas from the physical world because the former are completely different from the latter. This objection makes as much sense as saying that we cannot give people an idea of what we mean by writing h-o-u-s-e; that, for them to understand that concept, we have to bring them a house.

We talk about physical facts and objects by means totally independent of the object or fact, so we can also describe phenomena of the spiritual world with what we understand on the physical plane. However, we cannot understand the higher worlds with our everyday concepts and ideas, but need to acquire others and expand our thinking. People who honestly tell us about the higher world must also extend our concepts beyond our everyday life; they must give us concepts that are new and different and yet comprehensible on the physical plane.

People find it difficult to understand genuine spiritual science and serious esotericism because they are so reluctant to expand their concepts. They want to understand the higher world and its revelations with the ideas they already have and don't want to create new ones. When people in our materialistic age hear lectures on the spiritual world, they believe all too easily that the esoteric world can be understood simply by looking at it. They think the shapes there may be slightly more delicate and more nebulous than in the physical world, but similar nevertheless. It may seem inconvenient to some that the serious occultist is expected to do more than merely follow instructions on how to see angels. A change in thinking is necessary, and the concept *angel* must include that we are perceived by them, that their spiritual gaze is focused on us.

Mystical development, or ascending to the higher worlds, cannot be separated from enriching and giving greater scope to our ideas, feelings, and soul impulses. To understand the higher worlds, we must not let our life of ideas remain as impoverished as it is on the physical plane....

5

BY FREEING OUR THINKING, FEELING, AND WILLING from the physical body, we can begin to encounter the beings of the spiritual worlds. To sensitize ourselves to the presence of the dead we must develop new faculties and a new sense of being. Meditation and concentration—the practice of attention—are ways that we can begin to experience ourselves as soul-spiritual beings independent of our bodies. We begin to experience our thinking, feeling, and willing as not dependent on our bodies, but existing independently of us as a cosmic medium. Clairvoyance begins with perception in this medium; one begins to sense otherwise hidden realities. Steiner speaks of trying to understand the consciousness of a particular historical era. No matter how hard he tried to think his way into that period, his thoughts were not strong enough. As he continued his effort, however, he began to feel "a foreign will and feeling" enter his own. Thoughts appeared in his mind as "gifts of this external feeling and willing and solved the original problem of investigating a certain historical epoch." The lesson here is that, whereas in the physical world we meet people and exchange ideas with them, the opposite happens in spiritual experience; we discover "something foreign" within us and we discover that this foreign thing is a being of the spiritual world. In this case, a person Steiner had known well had died in midlife. She had taken her unused energy into the spiritual worlds and so offered it to Steiner to aid his spiritual research. Steiner's understanding of this dawned only gradually, because the way we come to know a being in the spiritual world is the reverse of how we do this in the physical world. In the spiritual world, first we learn to recognize the being's presence and to live with it, and then, gradually, we come to know the being as such. This being is, in a sense, the individuality who structures its various incarnations. It was through knowledge of a past incarnation that this friend was able to help Steiner unravel his historical problem. Beyond that, when one encounters in this way those who have died, it naturally opens one to the whole world of spirit, which is a world of beings. The dead, too, are spiritual beings like all spiritual beings. They seek to assist in the evolution of humanity by helping human beings on earth think thoughts (and feel feelings and will acts) that they would not otherwise think, feel, or do. But this is possible only when we have freed ourselves from the body. Then we can work together with those who have died and receive their blessings. These relationships are reciprocal.

The Blessings of the Dead

PARIS, MAY 26, 1914

... In everyday life and in conventional science, we learn about the external world through ideas we develop in our soul, but as researchers of the spirit, we first have to work with our thinking deep within us to develop abilities that are quite different from those we normally have. Spiritual science is basically in accord with the natural sciences, as we can see in its attempt to enter the spiritual world through spiritual chemistry. We cannot tell from the looks of it that water can be split into hydrogen and oxygen. Though water is liquid and does not burn, hydrogen is a combustible gas—clearly something quite different from water. We can use this as a metaphor for the spiritual process I am about to explain.

Just as water is a combination of hydrogen and oxygen, human beings are a combination of soul-spiritual and material-physical elements. Thus, there is a kind of "spiritual chemistry" in which the soul-spiritual is separated from the material-physical, just as in ordinary chemistry water is separated into hydrogen and oxygen. Just looking at people will tell you little about the nature of the soul-spiritual element.

The methods we use to separate the soul-spiritual from the material-physical in us—and this experiment in spiritual chemistry can be carried out only within us—are *concentration and meditation*.

Meditation and concentration are not some kind of miraculous mental performance, but the highest level of mental processes whose lower, elementary levels we find also in our everyday life.

Meditation is a devotion of the soul, raised to limitlessness, such as we may experience in the most joyful religious feelings.

Concentration is attentiveness, raised to limitlessness; we use it at a more basic level in ordinary life.

By *attentiveness* in everyday life we mean not allowing our ideas and feelings to range freely over anything that catches our attention, but pulling ourselves together so that our soul focuses our interest on something specific, isolating it in our field of perception. There are no limits to how far this attentiveness can be increased, particularly by voluntarily focusing our soul on certain thoughts supplied by spiritual science. Ignoring everything else, all worries and upsets, sense impressions, will impulses, feeling, and thinking, we can center our inner forces completely on these thoughts for a certain amount of time. The content of what we are concentrating on is not as important as the inner activity and exercise of developing our attentiveness, our powers of concentration.

Focusing, concentrating the forces of the soul in this way is crucial. And regular training, often involving months, years, or even decades, depending on individual predisposition, is necessary for the soul to become strong enough to develop inner forces. Qualities otherwise merely slumbering in the soul are now called up by this boundless enhancement of attentiveness, by concentration. In the process we must develop the capacity in our soul to feel that through this inner activity the soul is increasingly able to tear itself away from the physical body. Indeed, this tearing away, this separation of the soul and spirit from the physical-material element, will happen more and more often as we continue the activities I have described. You will find detailed descriptions of the individual exercises in my book *How to Know Higher Worlds.*[1]

If you practice attentiveness—concentration and meditation—you will learn to understand the meaning of the statements, *I experience myself as a soul-spiritual being. I am active in myself without using my senses or my limbs. I have experiences independent of my body.* Progress will be evident when you can perceive

---

1. Rudolf Steiner, *How to Know Higher Worlds*, Hudson, NY: Anthroposophic Press, 1994.

your own body with all its physical attributes as separate and independent of our soul and spirit, just as you see a table or a chair in physical life.

This is how one begins to separate the soul's ability to think and form ideas from its physical tools, namely, the nervous system and the brain. We learn to live in thinking and the forming of ideas, fully aware that we are outside the nervous system and the brain, the physical instruments we normally use for these processes.

To put it more concretely, let me add that our first experience in this self-development is the realization that in thinking we live as though outside our head. We live in our weaving thoughts just as we do when we use our brain, but we know with certainty that these thoughts are outside our head. The experience of immersing ourselves again in the brain and the nervous system after having been outside the head for some time remains indelibly with us. We feel the resistance of the substance of brain and nervous system in such a way that the soul-spiritual that emerged from those physical organs needs to use force to reenter them. This is an unforgettable moment.

The method I have described also allows us to release the feeling and will activities of the soul, which is necessary for true spiritual research. To achieve this, we must raise devotion to the infinite. This enhanced devotion, which is also called meditation, is similar to what happens when we sleep. The sense organs are laid aside in sleep; there is no activity of the senses, and the limbs are at rest. While we sleep, we are given over to the general course of the world without contributing anything through our I, thinking, feeling, and willing to the course of events. We are unconscious in sleep; our consciousness dissolves into general darkness and obscurity. In meditation, we must voluntarily create the state that sleep causes as a natural necessity. The only difference is that sleep leads to a loss of consciousness, but intensified devotion leads to an enhanced awareness. As spiritual researchers, we must be able to silence our senses at will. We must divert them from all impressions of the external world and suppress the activity of our organs and limbs as we do in sleep. In terms of our body, we have to behave just as in sleep. However, in sleep we sink into unconsciousness, but in enhanced devotion controlled by our will we awaken into the divine-spiritual stream of cosmic forces. To this level of consciousness we then reach, our everyday consciousness is what sleep is to our ordinary state of consciousness.

If we persevere and patiently train our soul, we will be able to separate out, through a kind of spiritual chemistry, another soul capacity, namely, our thinking, so that it continues only in the soul-spiritual sphere. Similarly, through devotion we can gradually separate out that power of the soul we use in language, in speaking. As I am speaking to you now, I am using a soul-spiritual force that flows into my nerves and speech organs and uses them. Through the exercises described above, we can unfold this same power when the entire speech and nervous systems are completely inactive. In this way, we discover in the depths of our soul a faculty we know nothing of in our everyday life, because it is employed in speech and the use of our speech organs. When we are not using this faculty, it lies dormant deep within our soul, but in spiritual research, it is drawn up and separated by spiritual chemistry, so to speak, from our physical speaking. If we learn to live in this weaving, hidden activity of language creation, we can recognize what we may call, perhaps inaccurately, the perception of the inner word, the spiritual word. As soon as we can control this hidden power, we can also detach our thinking and feeling from our personality, leave ourselves behind, and enter the spiritual world. Then we can perceive feeling and willing outside ourselves just as we did within us. We begin to know beings of will and feeling in the spiritual world, and we can perceive our own willing and feeling only when they are immersed in these beings.

... Clairvoyant perception begins with the emancipation of the power of thinking from the physical body and continues with the freeing of our willing and feeling. Clearly, then, we can know and truly experience encounters with other spiritual beings only by leaving our body and by immersing our own feeling and willing soul in the spiritual world.

In view of the widespread opposition to spiritual science in our time, it is risky to give concrete examples, yet it is a risk I am willing to take. I am sure you will not mind that it is an example from my personal experience. After all, our own experiences are the examples we know best since they are the only ones where we are actually present for every detail.

Some time ago I had to solve a problem in my work. I knew very well that the capacities I can develop with my constitution in this life would not suffice to perform the task, which was to understand the mentality of a certain historical period. I knew exactly what questions I had to answer, but I also realized that no matter how much I exerted my thinking, my thoughts were not strong enough to gain insight into this problem. It was like wanting to lift a weight but lacking the strength to do so. I tried to define the issue as clearly as possible and to develop the active will to find a solution one way or another. As far as I could, I tried to feel vividly the particular qualities of that period. I tried to get a vivid sense of its greatness, its color, and to project myself completely into that period. After I had repeated this inner soul activity often enough, I could feel a foreign willing and feeling enter my own. I was as sure of its presence as I am that the external object I see is not created by my looking at it, but exists independently of me and makes an impression on me.

From a materialistic point of view, people can easily object that this was nothing but an illusion, a deception, and that I did not know I was drawing out of my own soul what I thought were external influences. To avoid falling prey to illusion, hallucination, and fantasies in this field, we need true self-knowledge. Then we will begin to know what we can and cannot do. Self-knowledge, particularly for the researcher of the spirit, means knowing the limits of our abilities. We can train ourselves in self-knowledge in the way described in my above-mentioned book, and then we will be able to distinguish between our own feeling and willing and the external feeling and willing entering them from the spiritual world. We will reach the stage where not being able to tell the difference between our own feeling and willing and that from outside will seem as absurd as not being able to distinguish between hunger and bread. Everyone knows where hunger stops and bread begins, just as everyone knows that hunger itself does not make bread appear—desirable as this would be from a social standpoint. True self-knowledge enables us to differentiate between the hunger of our own feeling and willing and what comes to meet them from the spiritual world (as hunger is met with bread). Once the outside feeling and willing have penetrated our own, the two will continue to exist in us side by side.

In my case, the close relationship between my feeling and willing and what I recognized as external feeling and willing fertilized my thinking. As a result, thoughts appeared in my mind as gifts of the external feeling and willing, and solved the original problem of investigating a certain historical epoch.

What happens there in our spiritual experience runs counter to a similar process in the physical world. When we meet people in the physical world and get together with them, we first see them, then speak to them and exchange ideas. The opposite happens in the spiritual experience I have described; there we observe thoughts in ourselves and have the feeling that a foreign feeling and willing are present. Then we perceive a separate spiritual individuality as a real, separate being, but one that lives only in the spiritual world. Then, we gradually get to know this individuality in a process reverse to meeting someone in physical life. In the spiritual sphere, we approach the individual through the foreign feeling and willing we find within us, then get closer to the personality by being together with it.

In my case I found out that the foreign feeling and willing that fertilized my own thinking came from an individual I had known well, who had been torn from our circle of friends by her death a little more than a year ago. She had died at a relatively early age, in her best midlife years, and had taken unused life energy into the spiritual worlds. The feeling and willing that entered my own originated in the intensity of this unused life energy. Generally, people live to a ripe old age and use up their vitality during their lifetime. However, if they die relatively young, this strength remains as unused potential and is available to them in the spiritual world. The life forces that were not used in our friend's short life enabled me, because of our friendship, to solve a problem that required her strength.

What I earlier called "the capacity of the inner word" leads to such revelations of the spiritual world as this one of a dead person. At the same time, this capacity allows us to look beyond our life enclosed between birth and death, or between conception and death, and gain insight into human life extending into infinite periods of time through repeated earthly lives. Then we can understand the life of those we were very close to, as I was to our dead friend.

As we get to know ourselves or another person through the soul faculties I have described, we discover not only the physical life between birth and death, but the spiritual human being who structures the body, lives in repeated earthly incarnations, and lives in the spiritual world between each death and new birth. Now you will easily understand that I could gain deeper insight into the soul-spiritual being of our dead friend because she stood before my soul as a spiritual being.

The process of getting to know another being in the spiritual world is the reverse of that in the physical realm. At first, we learn how to be together spiritually with the other being, then we come to know the being itself as a spiritual being. And then entering the spiritual world becomes a reality.

To return to our example, it became clear that the friend we knew in her short life here had taken in, during an earlier incarnation in the first Christian centuries, much of that Christian culture. However, she had not been able to digest it all because of the restrictions of the time, and had entered this life with the undigested material. It burst the confines of this incarnation, but remained present as life energy. And now through my connection with her, I was blessed with insight into the period my work was concerned with, the age in which our friend had lived in a past incarnation.

It doesn't matter that many people in our age make fun of what I have just described and belittle an attitude that guides us into the spiritual world. If you have developed yourself along these paths, you know that when you accomplished something you could not possibly have done by yourself, it was because specific spiritual beings helped you. In addition, your view of the world will expand because you will know that you cannot expect hunger to produce bread, and because you know that the power of spiritual beings has entered your own abilities. As our view into the sphere of the dead widens, our insight into the spiritual world also deepens through the methods I have described and finally encompasses concrete events and beings that are just as real as the physical world around us.

People do not mind our talking about the spiritual world in general terms; they admit there is a spiritual realm behind the sensory one. But they are less tolerant if we talk about concrete beings in the spiritual world whom we perceive just as we do beings of the mineral, plant, animal, and human kingdoms. However, if we do not shy away from developing our slumbering soul forces, we find that it is just as wrong to talk about the spirit in general terms, or in vague pantheistic terms, as to speak about nature in general terms. For example, if, while walking across a meadow and looking at flowers, perhaps some daylilies here, violets there, and so on, we point to them but instead of saying their names just say, "This is nature, that is nature, there is nature, everything is nature and more nature," then that is no different from talking about spirit, spirit, and more spirit in a vaguely pantheistic way. We can understand the spiritual world only if we really know the individual beings living there and what happens between them.

People often object to the possibility of knowing the spiritual world by claiming that harboring such fantasies about the realm of the spirit simply runs counter to intelligent behavior in the physical world. Although this conclusion seems justified based on the capacities of human intelligence, it can be sustained only as long as one is ignorant of the extensive power of the intellect, that is, the power of human thinking, as we can know it through spiritual research.

To return to our example, imagine that someone who has the task of developing certain ideas here on earth learns how to encounter a spiritual being, in this case the soul of a dead person, which adds its thinking—now modified by the spiritual world almost into willing that thinks and thinking that feels—to the living person's thinking and feeling. The intelligent ideas that the soul in the spiritual world wants to produce emerge in the human being on earth. The dead possess feeling and willing, just as they did on earth, as well as other soul capacities not developed on earth. Therefore, the dead have the desire to connect their thinking and feeling with human thoughts. That is why they unite with the person on earth. As the thinking, feeling, and willing of the dead penetrate the living person, ideas are stimulated. Thus, the dead can experience these ideas, something they could not do on their own. That is why they communicate with human beings on earth. However, this communication and stimulation of ideas is possible only if the thinking of human beings on earth has been freed from the nervous system and the brain, that is, only if we have developed thinking independent of the brain.

As we liberate our thinking from the body, we feel as though our thinking has been snatched away from us, as though it has expanded and spread out in space and time. Thinking, which we normally say takes place inside us, unites with the surrounding spiritual world, streams into it, and achieves a certain autonomy from us similar to the relative independence of the eyes, which are set in their sockets rather like autonomous organs. Thus, although our liberated thinking is connected with our higher self, it is independent enough to act as our spiritual organ of perception for the thoughts and feelings of other spiritual beings. Its function is thus similar to that of our eyes.

Gradually, the thinking processes, normally limited by our intelligence, become independent from our being as spiritual organs of perception.

To put it differently, what we experience subjectively, what is comprised by our intelligence, namely our outer thinking, is nothing but shadowy entities, thought entities, mere ideas reflecting external things. When thinking becomes clairvoyant and separates from the brain and nervous system, it begins to develop inner activity, a life of its own, and to stream out, as our own experience, into the spiritual world. In a sense, we send the tendrils of our clairvoyant thinking out into the spiritual realm and, as they become immersed in this world, they perceive the willing that feels and feeling that wills of the other beings in that realm.

After what we have said about self-knowledge being a necessity on the path of spiritual development—and from this it follows that modesty is a must—allow me to comment on clairvoyant thinking; please do not think me presumptuous for saying this. When we enliven our thinking through clairvoyant development, it becomes independent and also a very precise and useful tool. True clairvoyance increases the precision, accuracy, and logical power of our thinking. As a result, we can use it with more exactness and closer adaptation to its subject; our intelligence becomes more practical and more thoroughly structured. Therefore, the clairvoyant can easily understand the scope of ordinary scientific research, whereas conventional science requires bringing out ... [text missing] of the mind. It is easy to see why modern natural science cannot comprehend the findings of clairvoyant research, while those who have developed true clairvoyance can comprehend the full significance of the achievements of the natural sciences. There can be no question, therefore, of spiritual science opposing conventional science; the other way around is more likely. Only clairvoyant development can organize the power of the mind, making it inwardly independent, alive, comprehensible. That is why the materialistic way of thinking cannot penetrate to the logic that gives us the certainty that clairvoyant knowledge really does lead to perception of the spiritual world.

The example of my clairvoyant experiences with a dead person shows that intelligence and thinking are specific qualities of souls living in a physical body, of human beings on earth. The deceased wanted to connect herself with a human being so that what lived in her in a completely different, supersensible way could take the form of intelligent thoughts. The dead individual and the living person were thinking their thoughts together in the head of the latter, as it were.

As specifically human qualities, intellect and thinking can be developed only in human beings on earth, and they allow even people who are not clairvoyant to understand the results of clairvoyant research. You see, our independent thinking becomes the spiritual eye, as it were, for the perception of the spiritual world. Supersensible research, which uses this spiritual eye for clairvoyant thinking, has found that this eye is active, that the spiritual feelers are put out in all directions, but our physical eyes only passively allow impressions to come to them. When we as spiritual researchers have taken the revelations of the supersensible world into our thinking, they continue to live in our thoughts. We can then tell other people about what we have taken pains to bring into our living thought processes, and they can understand us if they do not allow materialistic prejudices to get in the way.

There is a sort of inner language in the human soul that normally remains silent. But when concepts acquired by allowing one's willing and feeling to be stimulated by the spiritual world and its beings enter the soul, this language responds immediately with an echoing sound. Careful and thorough study of spiritual science will gradually silence the objection that the spiritual researcher's reports of the realm of the spirit can only be believed, because they cannot really be understood. People will see that human intelligence is indeed able to understand information from the spiritual world, but only if it is the result of true spiritual experiences and true spiritual research. They will realize that it is wrong to say human intelligence does not suffice to comprehend revelations from the spiritual world and that therefore they have to be accepted on authority. They will come to know that the only obstacle to such understanding is having preconceived notions and prejudices.

Eventually, people will treat information from the spiritual world as they treat the insights of, say, astronomy, biology, physics, and chemistry. That is, even if they are not astronomers, biologists, physicists, or chemists, they accept the scientists' findings about the physical world based on a natural feeling for truth, which we may call a silent language of the soul.

The harmony between intelligence and clairvoyance will become much more obvious, and then people will admit that clairvoyant research approaches the world of spiritual beings and processes with the same attitude that also motivates the natural sciences. In view of the considerable opposition to spiritual science, it will comfort us to know that our modern culture will eventually come to the point Giordano Bruno did. Looking up to the blue vault of the sky, which people then considered to exist exactly as they perceived it, Bruno declared that they saw the blue dome of the sky only because that was as far as their vision reached. They themselves in a way imposed that limit; in reality space extends into infinity. The limits people saw so clearly, based on the illusion of their senses, were created by the limitation of their vision.

You see, now and in the future, the spiritual researcher will have to stand before the world and say that there is also a firmament of time, the time between birth and death. We perceive this firmament of time through the illusion of the senses. In fact, we create it ourselves because our spiritual vision is limited, just as in earlier times people "created" the blue firmament of space. Space extends endlessly beyond the blue dome of the sky, and time also continues infinitely beyond the boundaries of birth and death. Our own infinite spiritual life is embedded in this infinite time together with the rest of spiritual life in the world.

The time will come when people will realize that clairvoyant research strengthens and deepens our intelligence, producing a more subtle and refined logic. Such improved understanding will silence many, seemingly justified, current opinions on spiritual science claiming that the philosophical writings of several authors prove that our cognitive and intellectual capacities are limited. After all, aren't the reasons these philosophers present to prove the limits of human cognition convincing? Are they not logical? How can researchers of spiritual science hope to refute these convincing, logical arguments for the limits of our capacity to know?

The time will come when people will see the lack of substance and precision in such logic, when they will understand that something can be irrefutably correct as a philosophical argument, and yet be completely refuted by life. After all, before the discovery of the microscope or the telescope people could have "irrefutably" proven that human eyes can never see a cell. Still, human ingenuity invented the microscope and the telescope, which increased the power of our eyes. Similarly, life has outdistanced the irrefutable proof of the philosophers. Life does not need to refute the arguments of this or that philosopher. Their proofs may be indisputable, but the reality of life must progress beyond them by strengthening our cognitive capacity and spiritual understanding through spiritual instruments.

In the present state of our culture with its prevailing belief in the incontrovertibility of the philosophers' proofs, these things are not generally or readily accepted. However, as our culture continues to develop, it will reach a higher logic than the one supporting these proofs of purely external philosophy. This higher logic will be one of life, of life of the spirit, of insights based on spiritual science. A time will come when people, while still respecting the accomplishments and discoveries of the natural sciences as much as we do now, will nevertheless realize that for our inner life these marvelous achievements have brought more questions than answers. If you study biology, astronomy, and so on, you will see that they have reached their limits. Do these sciences provide answers? No, they are really only raising questions. The answers will come from what stands behind the subject matter of the natural sciences. The answers will come from the sources of clairvoyant research.

To summarize, let me repeat that the world extends beyond the realm of the senses, and behind the sensory world we find spirit. In spiritual science, the spirit reveals itself to clairvoyant perception, and it is only then that we can see the divine nature of the magnificent sensory world around us. The world is vast, and the spirit is the necessary counterbalance to the physical world. A proper perspective on our future cultural development reveals that in trying to understand the world in its entirety, people will not strive for a one-sided exploration of the natural world, as many now assume. Instead, they will seek to unite science, intellect, and clairvoyant research. Only in this union will human beings truly come to understand themselves and their own spirit. Only then will they realize solutions to the world's future riddles, never to be solved completely, and feel satisfaction in that knowledge.

Those who have taken the true impulse of spiritual science to heart can sense even now in our culture the yearning and the latent urge in many souls to go beyond the immediate and sensory in science. Through use and inner assimilation of the capacities the sciences have created in recent centuries, these souls long to be strengthened so that they can live in the spiritual worlds whence alone can come true satisfaction for the human soul.

6

---

*IT IS IMPORTANT to direct our thoughts to the realm
between death and a new birth because this will help
us to live our earthly lives more fully. Therefore, we
must always hold the mystery of death before us as a
key to many of life's mysteries. A human being dies and
passes through the gate of death. That human being
enjoyed relationships while on earth, and those who
remain on earth retain memories of the departed loved
one. Such memories differ from all others, because the
being who is remembered is still present, but in the spiritual world. Nevertheless, the fact remains that a
human soul becomes a memory. In other words, we
carry an image of a being in the spiritual world. And
that being in the spiritual world may perceive these
images as well as the thoughts and feelings that surround them. We should note that for those who have
died and dwell in the spiritual world, the earthly world
is an "other" world. The spiritual world itself has
become their world, and to engage in relationships
there requires great inner activity on their part. But
their "other" world (which is "this" world to us) rises
spontaneously into their awareness. Our memories rise
to them. How do they experience these? To answer such
a question, we must first ask it with all the intensity,
seriousness, and attention we can muster, and then*

wait; the answer will come by grace. In this case, the answer is that the dead experience our thoughts and feelings as "art," or "creation"; they experience our memories and loving thoughts analogously to the way we experience art in this world. Not only do we then become "living books" for the dead, we also become their "art." This is the deeper meaning of remembering the dead. Something in our memories transcends the ordinary level of existence. For the dead, this functions just as beauty does in our world. Thus, the two worlds—the earthly and the supra-earthly—are intimately interconnected. Our "inner" world is their "outer" world. How much richer our lives would be if we were conscious of this.

Works of Art, Acts of Grace

BERLIN, DECEMBER, 7, 1915

Spiritual science seeks to show the connection that exists in every domain between the spiritual worlds and the world that, while in our earthly bodies, we perceive through our senses and grasp with our reason. In recent lectures, I have been especially concerned with considering the connection that exists between the life we lead as souls between death and rebirth, and the life we pass through here, while incarnated in a physical body. It is important to remember that we must always bear firmly in mind the reality that, as long as we live in physical bodies, we must direct our thoughts to the sphere we will experience after death and before rebirth. We direct our thoughts there not to satisfy mere curiosity, but because we have been able to convince ourselves through spiritual science that when we direct our thoughts to the other world, we can make a contribution to *this world* by ennobling and invigorating the concepts we need for our doing, thinking, and feeling.

We must therefore hold firmly to the thought that many of life's secrets can be solved only if we have the courage to approach what may be called *the riddle of death.*

Today, in order to consider the connection between the spiritual and the sense worlds from a particular point of view, I want to begin with an observation that is trivial and yet contains profound feeling. We shall start with a fact we have often spoken of: a human being passes through the gate of death. I repeat, we start with something that is an everyday occurrence but one connected with very deep experiences—experiences that grip us in the depths of our soul. As you know, when we stand face to face with human beings here in the physical world, we form thoughts that can unite us with them. We surround the person with feelings of sympathy, antipathy, and so on. We feel either friendship or enmity. In brief, we form a certain relation to another person here in the physical world. This relation may arise through ties of blood, or it may be brought about by the preferences that arise in daily life. All this may be summed up in the expression "the relation of human beings to one another."

When someone we have been united with through various ties leaves the physical world and passes through the gate of death, at first that person's memory remains, that is, a collection of feelings and thoughts we have experienced as a result of our relation with that person. But since the person has passed from us through the gates of death, the thoughts and feelings that united us now live on in a very different manner. While the person lived with us here on the physical plane, we knew that at any time, in addition to the relation our souls had formed, the outer physical reality itself might also appear. We knew that we could bring our inner experience to bear upon this outer reality. And if at any time the person had somehow changed, we had to expect that the feelings we formerly had toward them would also change in one way or another. We do not often think of the radical difference it makes when suddenly (or even not suddenly), the moment comes after which we can carry in our soul only the memory of our friend—when we know, My eyes will never see him again, my hands will never again hold his hand.

The image we have formed of the person remains essentially unchanged, but a radical change appears in our relationship. As I have said (and although it may sound trivial it cuts deeply into the inner life in each individual case), *a human soul whose physical incarnation once impressed us becomes a memory.*

Let us now compare a memory like this with others that we construct from our experience. We live a great part of our physical life in memory. We know what we ourselves have experienced. We know, for example, the events that have befallen us. We retain these in thoughts. And we know that through these thoughts we can revert to the times when the events in question took place. When we examine the content of our memories, we find that in the greater part of our thoughts we bear something in us that no longer exists—past events, events that we can no longer meet in the external world as reality, for they belong to the past. Our memory of one who has gone through the gate of death, however—if we have absorbed some of the thoughts of spiritual science—is quite different to our psychic gaze. In the case of the dead, we hold thoughts in us, but these thoughts are fixed on *a reality*—a reality that is certainly not accessible to us in the external physical world, but that exists in the spiritual world. Although it cannot enter the sphere of our vision, *the object of such thoughts is present.* That is quite a different kind of memory from the mere memory of what occurred here in the physical world.

If we observe this fact in relation to the entire cosmos, we realize that when we remember someone who has died, *we carry in our soul thoughts of a being who is in the spiritual world.* Now we

know—and this must be clear from the last three lectures[1]—
that the longing of souls incarnated on earth ascends to the spiritual world and that the consciousness of those who have passed
through the gate of death (and now live in the intermediate
world between death and rebirth) extends down to what happens here in the physical world. We can say, *The souls, who live discarnate lives in the spiritual world, receive into their consciousness from
the physical world whatever their spiritual gaze and their spiritual
vision directed down to earth enables them to perceive.* I pointed out in
one of the last lectures how souls still incarnated here in physical bodies can be perceived by the souls of the so-called dead,
and contrasted this with the perception such souls have of other
discarnate souls living in the intermediate stage between death
and rebirth. I explained how, in order to perceive in the spiritual world, souls living there must continually be active. For
instance, they may be aware that another soul is near them, but
to perceive that soul, they must become inwardly active. They
must, as it were, construct an image. The image will not appear
by itself, as it does here in the physical world. In the spiritual
world you first have the thought, "someone is there." Then you
must, as it were, inwardly experience the "being there" of whoever it is. Then the image of the other soul will arise. The per-
ceptual process is reversed.

There is an important difference between how souls in the
spiritual world construct images of other souls in the spiritual
world and how they construct images of souls still incarnate on
earth. Discarnate souls must produce the image of other souls in
the spiritual world entirely out of themselves. They must be
thoroughly active in doing so. But when it is a question of a soul

---

1. This lecture is the fourth of a series given in Berlin, *The Forming of Destiny and Life After Death.* The titles of the previous three lectures were "Spiritual Life in the Physical World and Life Between Death and a New Birth";
"The Experience of the Effects of the Last Earthly Existence and Its Transformation into Forces for the Next Incarnation"; and "The Substrata of Soul
Life and Spirit Life after Premature Death."

still living on the earth, a discarnate soul may remain more passive. In this case, the image rather comes to it. The effort
needed to approach the image of a soul living on the earth is
much less than that required to produce the image for one
already discarnate. Less inner activity is required. For those
souls living between death and rebirth, this difference in inner
activity represents the distinction between discarnate and incarnate souls. If you grasp this, you will realize that after the soul
has passed through the gate of death and lives the life of the
spiritual world, it not only beholds the beings of the higher hierarchies and the other human souls living with it in the spiritual
world, but also beholds the world of souls to which it was related
before going through the gate of death.

This is an important distinction. Human beings on earth are
actually surrounded by earth existence and can only grasp the
other world in spirit, but on entering the spiritual world this is
reversed. A soul in the spiritual world can see our world
unaided, without any effort, although from there it is the "other
world." But to make its own world—the world where it exists
after death—perceptible, the soul must always exert itself. It
must always construct this world for itself. Thus, when a soul is
in the spiritual world, it must continually work on that world,
while what is then "the other world" always arises as if by itself.

For discarnate souls, it is in this other world (which for us is *this*
world, but from there is the *other* world) that earthly souls and
what lives in them—above all in those human souls with whom
relations were established during life on earth—rise up into
awareness. Such human souls appear to the discarnate. At the
same time, within "the ocean of spiritual perception" (if I may
put it this way) created in our earthly souls by the spiritual world,
memories of those who have passed through the gate of death
occasionally appear. Imagine this very vividly. Let us suppose
hypothetically that we lived in a time when no one could remember any dead person. The dead would still perceive those human
souls—in which no memory of the dead existed. And then suppose that into "the ocean of spiritual perception" that discarnate

souls can offer, memories of the dead now enter. *They live there.* That is something added by *human free will and love* to what the dead can always see from the other side. It is something *added.*

Here again we come to a point where an important question arises for the spiritual researcher, a question that the spiritual investigator must research. *What does it mean for souls who have passed through the gate of death to see, streaming by them, embedded in the souls ebbing and flowing in our world, memories of the dead?* When those souls perceive these memories, what do they mean to them? When such a question arises in spiritual investigation, it must first of all be thoroughly experienced. One must really live into it. If one begins to seek speculatively for a possible solution, a possible answer to such a question, one will certainly arrive at a false conclusion. For the efforts of the ordinary brain-fettered understanding provides, as a rule, no solution. A solution can be arrived at only through inner activity. The answers to questions relating to the enigmas of the spiritual world descend from the spiritual world as by an act of grace. One must wait. There is really nothing else to be done but to live with the question, and meditate upon it again and again. One must allow the question to live in the soul with all the feelings it arouses, and then calmly wait. One must wait until one is worthy—that is the right word— *worthy* to receive an answer from the spiritual world. And, as a rule, this comes from a place quite different from what one would expect. The answer comes from the spiritual world at the right moment—that is, at the moment when one has sufficiently prepared one's soul to receive the answer. Whether it is the right answer can as little be decided theoretically as any statement concerning physical reality. Only experience can furnish the criterion. To those who always deny spiritual reality by saying that it cannot be proved, and that everything must be proved, I would like to ask a question: Would it have been possible to prove the existence of a whale in the physical world if no whale had ever been discovered? Nothing can be proved, unless it can be shown to be a reality in the same way. Even in the spiritual world one must *experience* reality.

What enters one's consciousness as the solution may, of course, appear in many different forms, according to the preparation of one's soul. The truth may present itself in many ways, but nevertheless it must be experienced as the truth.

For example, if one lets the above question live rightly in the soul, there can appear—apparently from quite a different place—an image, an inner image, which, I may say, gives one an inner impression of offering something toward the solution to the riddle in question. The image may arise of a person who lets themselves be photographed, or allows a portrait to be painted. The principle point in the picture will be something physical, an image of a physical thing, and around it, finally, also all that has to do with the realm of art, the artistic presentation. Now, if you consider how physical life runs its course, you can recognize that it does so in such a way that we are confronted with external beings, the outer occurrences of nature. These run their course and expire. Likewise all our human concerns run their course, all that we do and plan to meet our needs—all that we create as history. But, beyond all this transience, we also seek something that really has nothing to do with the immediate needs of life. The human soul is aware that if nature and history merely ran their course in relation to the satisfaction of human needs, life would become barren and desolate. Therefore we create something above and beyond the course of nature and necessity in physical existence. We feel the need not merely to see a certain landscape, but also to copy it. We organize our lives so that anyone connected with us can get "copies" of it. From this starting point, we can think of the whole realm of art as something we create on earth that is of a higher reality than the ordinary reality of nature and history. Just think what the world would lack if there were no art, if art did not produce something from its own resources to add to what is self-existing. Art creates something that, one may say, need not exist. If art did not exist, all the necessities of nature might still go on. One may suppose that even if no single copy of nature had been made, no artistic representation, life would still pursue its course from the beginning to the end of the earth. You can imagine what humanity would then lack. Theoretically speaking, our earth could be punished by its inability to evolve art, for in art we have something that extends beyond life. Think of all that art has created in the world, and also consider human progress. In a sense, these are two parallel processes: the necessities of nature and history, and, inserted into them, the stream of art.

Now, just as art, in a sense, enchants a spiritual world into the world of physical reality, so the memories that fill our souls here likewise conjure another world into the world of those who have gone through the gate of death. As far as the dead are concerned, the world here might run its course without any memories living in the souls here, memories born of love and all our human relationships. But then the world of the dead would be the same for them as our world would be for us if we could find nothing in it that transcended ordinary reality. That is an extraordinarily significant thing. *Our thoughts of love, our memories, and all that passes through our soul in connection with those no longer with us in the physical world create for the dead in their world something analogous to artistic creations in ours.* Here in the physical world we must bring forth artistic creations out of our own soul, we must contribute something out of our own being. But for those in the spiritual world, the opposite must occur. Their "art" must be brought to them from *their other world,* from the souls who are still incarnated here—souls whom they can contemplate more passively than they contemplate those already with them in the spiritual world. What the course of nature and history would be to us were it to run on simply of itself without art, without everything we can create above and beyond our immediate reality—such would our world be for the dead if the souls still on earth retained no memories of them.

We do not really know that this is so in our ordinary physical lives. These things are not known by our ordinary consciousness, but our deeper subconsciousness is aware of them. And our life is always directed in accordance with this subconscious knowledge. Why, for instance, have human communities always placed a high value on the celebration of All Souls' Day, Days of the Dead, and so on? And those who cannot share in the usual memorials for the dead nevertheless have their own days set apart for this.

Why is this? Because in the depths of our subconsciousness lives what may be called a dim knowledge of what takes place in the world through our keeping alive the memory of the dead. The receptive soul of the seer who celebrates All Souls' Day, or a Sunday devoted to the dead, or some similar day when many people come together full of the memories of their dead, *sees the dead participate in the ceremony.* With certain natural differences, the experience for the dead is similar to what happens on earth when people visit a cathedral and see forms they could never have seen if something had not been created out of the artist's imagination, if something had not been added to physical existence. For the dead, the experience is similar to what happens when those on earth listen to a symphony or music of that sort. *Something is reproduced in all our memories, that, in a sense, transcends the ordinary level of existence.* And just as art inserts itself into the physical course of human history, so do these memories insert themselves into the images of *their* world that the souls between death and rebirth receive. In customs such as All Souls' Day that have arisen in human communities, the secret knowledge contained in the depths of the soul finds expression. Many worthy customs are connected with this deeper subconscious knowledge.

We stand before such interconnections of life with still greater admiration if we can permeate them with what spiritual science offers us. Each time a dead soul encounters a remembrance of itself in the soul of a living human being with whom it was in some way connected here on earth, it is as if something streams over to that soul that beautifies its life, enhancing its value. Just as beauty comes to us here from art, so beauty streams to the dead from what rays forth out of the hearts and souls of those who keep them in memory.

That is one connection between the world here and the spiritual world there, and it is closely connected with another thought that should arise from what can be cultivated in spiritual science—the thought of *the value and importance of earthly life.* Spiritual science does not lead us to despise the earth and all that it can bring forth. Rather, it leads us to consider life as a part of the whole life of the cosmos, a necessary part, organized to conform with what is at work in the spiritual world—a part without which the spiritual world would not appear in its perfection. Whenever we turn our attention to the fact that out of our physical world beauty must spring forth for the dead, we must also be struck by the thought that the spiritual world would lack this beauty if there were no physical world with human souls in it who, while still in the body, are able to evolve thoughts full of feeling and emotion for those no longer in their world. It meant a great deal when whole peoples in ancient times repeatedly and reverently devoted themselves in their festivals to thoughts of their great ancestors, uniting themselves in feeling for the sake of the memory of their great ancestors. It was of great significance when they inaugurated such memorial days. It always meant the flashing up of something beautiful for the spiritual worlds—that is, for the souls living there between death and rebirth.

And although here on earth it is somewhat foolish, to put it mildly, to take special pleasure in one's own portrait, nevertheless it is important for the dead to find their images in the souls who still remain here. For we must bear in mind that humanity on earth appears very different to us when we consider it from the standpoint of the spiritual, *from the standpoint of the dead.* We have often emphasized this. Here on earth we are enclosed within our skin. What we designate as "I," and what is most precious to us, is shut in by our skin. This holds good even for the most selfless people—perhaps it even holds good for them to a higher degree than for those who consider themselves less selfless. We value first and above all what is shut up inside this skin; then comes the rest of the world. We look at what lies outside our skin, at this "rest of the world," as the outer world. But the most significant thing is that once we are outside our bodies, for instance when we die or in higher states of meditation, we are one with the outer world and live in it. I have often described this opening, this expansion of oneself over the outer world. And when we are outside our bodies and have gone into the outer world, that outer world is just what we have experienced here between birth and death. In a sense, we may say that the outer world becomes the inner world. What is now our inner world becomes our outer world. Hence that significant experience on entering the land of the spirit, "Thou art That," described in my book *Theosophy*.[2]

As our outer world there, we look out upon what was here our inner world encompassed by our I. But the soul there, which cannot be egotistic as it was here, looks back on the thoughts that come to meet it as thoughts of itself. That is what comes to meet it as an outer world. As such, it really ought to be incorporated within the compass of what we may designate as the "beautiful"—as that which exalts one. Then into what has become the outer world—that is, the memory of all we have undergone between birth and death—comes something that does not live in it, does not belong to our life but lives in other souls and relates itself to us. That really means the insertion into that world of something transcending ourselves, transcending what has then become our outer world—just as here on earth some work of art rises above ordinary reality as it exists in itself. And while it is improper for people here to be in love with themselves—and thus also with their own portraits!—there it is quite natural for a soul to stand in that relation to what arises as an image, another presentation of itself, in the souls left behind. It is natural for a soul in the other world to stand before an image of itself in the same way as on Earth we stand before a landscape and compare it with the scene itself. Thus when the question comes before the soul—*What does it mean for the souls who have*

---

2. *Theosophy: An Introduction to the Spiritual Processes in Human Life and in the Cosmos*, Hudson, NY; Anthroposophic Press, 1994.

passed through the gates of death to see, streaming by them, embedded in the souls ebbing and flowing in our world, memories of the dead?—one is shown a soul presented with his or her image, and from this one finds a way of answering the question.

Speculation as a rule does not help at all; one must learn to wait, to wait patiently. In reality, one should work only on *questions* as these relate to the spiritual world. The answers can be given to the human soul only by a revealing act of grace....

PART TWO

" Practice "

7

BEHIND THE WORLD of sense perceptions lies the elemental, or imaginal, world. This world can be known only through "imaginations," or images. Ordinary consciousness is largely unaware of that world. Nevertheless, unconsciously, imaginations—impressions we receive from the elemental world—are perpetually flowing into us. In a sense, they are more important than our sense perceptions, because they become part of our whole etheric organism. We receive imaginations from all earthly realms—mineral, plant, and animal—but above all from the interhuman realm. Our life with others is a shifting sea of exchanged images. Often we experience these as antipathy or sympathy, a sympathy that can become undying love. We receive such images all the time and carry them with us. They give warmth to our lives, and as we become more interested in our fellow human beings we gain more warmth, and the images that flow between us become more intense. Thereby we become related to the elemental world, to a multitude of elemental beings, and above all to our own etheric counterpart. When we pass through the gate of death, we bear our elemental, imaginal being with us; in a sense, we become that being. For this reason, the first impression we receive from a soul who has died arises through images. After that, our etheric being is absorbed by its etheric counterpart and becomes the "instrument" of the evolving individuality whom we have known and loved and with whom we must continue to work. Many of the ways the dead are present to those on earth are connected to this elemental or etheric being. The interplay of imaginations continues. If we have known the person and can continue our interest and love, the interplay can continue. "Interest and love" mean that we continue to carry something of the departed one within us. If we have not known them, then with difficulty a substitute or aid may be found: a handwriting sample, for instance, or empathy with the grief of those left behind. However difficult this might be, unconsciously, imaginations from the dead work continuously, in many ways, into the lives of the living—for instance, in bringing people together. But there is a still more intimate way of living together with the dead. Besides the elemental world, we live in the soul, or astral, world as well. Ordinarily, we are in this world only while we are asleep, when the I and astral body are outside the physical realm, and we encounter astral beings—soul beings in the soul world. These include the soul beings of the dead. Our interchange with them takes place not through imaginations but through "inspirations." We can train ourselves to take such inspirations into our consciousness; we take into our own being some part of the being who wishes to inspire us. To accomplish this, we must be able to transform ourselves into the other—and to do this, we must purify ourselves of all

egotism. The dead, who want to work into the earth, can-
not work through our egotism—that is, through sympa-
thy and antipathy, love and hate, driven by our egotism.
They see us as we are on earth. They see our love and hate
as luciferic and ahrimanic. Because of this, a great love
arises in the dead for the living. For us to reciprocate, we
must become free of our personal feelings of sympathy and
antipathy. Otherwise, the dead cannot enter our souls.
There is, of course, yet another way we are connected with
the dead: through "intuitions," I to I.

How the Dead Influence
the Living

BERN, NOVEMBER 9, 1916

A goal of spiritual-scientific practice is to form ideas of how
we, as human beings, live with the spiritual worlds. We know that
we are connected with the physical world through the experiences and perceptions of our physical bodies, and we strive to
understand how we are connected with the spiritual worlds.

I may as well start our reflections today with what we already
know from all that has come before our souls during these last
years. First, we have the world of our sense perceptions, the world
to which we direct our impulses of will, our actions. The physical
body mediates this. Immediately behind this world of sense perception lies the next world, the elemental world. What we call it
does not matter, and we could also give it other names, but we will
gain a clear idea of the supersensible worlds only if we enter to

some extent into some of their characteristics and try to recognize what they are for us as human beings. The whole of our earthly life between birth and death—and also our next life, which takes place between death and a new birth—depends on our coexistence with the various worlds spread out around us.

What we are calling the *elemental* world is the world that can be seen only by what we know as *imaginations.* Thus, we may also call the *elemental* world the *imaginal* world. In ordinary human life, under ordinary circumstances, we cannot lift our *imaginal* perceptions, our perceptions of the elemental world, into consciousness. This does not mean that the imaginations are not there, or that at any given moment of our sleeping or waking life we are not in relation with the elemental world and receiving imaginations from it. On the contrary, imaginations perpetually ebb and flow within us. Though we are unaware of it, we constantly receive impressions from the elemental world. Just as we have sensations of color, light, and sound when we open our eyes and ears to the outer world, we also receive continuous impressions from the elemental world that produce imaginations in our etheric body.

Imaginations differ from ordinary thoughts. In ordinary, everyday human thoughts, only the head participates as the instrument of their processing and experience. In imaginations, however, we participate with almost the whole of our organism—our etheric organism. Imaginations take place all the time in our etheric organism, but they rise into consciousness only for trained "occult" cognition. We may therefore refer to them as "unconscious imaginations."

However, even though they do not enter our consciousness directly in everyday life, they are not therefore meaningless for us. On the contrary, they are far more important for our life as a whole than our sense perceptions, for we are united far more intensely and intimately with our imaginations than with our sense perceptions.

As physical human beings, we receive few imaginations from the mineral kingdom. We receive more through all that we develop by living with the plant and animal worlds. But the greater part, by far, of what lives as imaginations in our etheric body is due to our relations with our fellow human beings, and all that these relations entail for our life as a whole. In fact, our whole relation with our fellow human beings, our whole attitude toward them, is based fundamentally on imaginations. Imaginations always result from the way we meet another human being. Although, as I said, they do not appear as imaginations to ordinary consciousness, they nevertheless make themselves felt in the sympathies and antipathies that play such an overwhelming part in our life.

As human beings, we develop sympathies and antipathies, to a greater or lesser degree, with all that approaches us in this world. We have vague undefined feelings, slight inclinations or disinclinations. Sometimes our sympathies grow into friendship and love—love that can be so heightened that we think we can no longer live without this or that human being. All this is due to imaginations that are perpetually called forth in our etheric body by our life with our fellow human beings. In fact, we always carry with us in life something that cannot quite be called memory, for it is far more real than memory. We bear within us as it were heightened memories or imaginations that we have received from all the impressions of the human beings we have ever encountered, and we continue to receive these all the time. We bear them within us. In fact, they make up a goodly portion of what we call our inner life—not the predominant life that lives in clear, well-defined memories, but the inner life that makes itself felt in our prevailing mood and feeling, and above all in our outlook on the world itself, our own life in the world.

We would pass the world around us coldly by and would live indifferently with our contemporary world if we did not unfold this imaginal life by living together with other beings, and above all with other human beings.

We must look upon what makes itself felt here—our soul's interest in the surrounding world—as belonging particularly to the elemental world, and especially to our own etheric body.

This "interest" is inherent in the forces of our etheric body, and it makes itself felt as interest. Sometimes we feel ourselves immediately "caught" and interested. Such interest, often woven from the very first moment between one human being and another, is due to definite relationships that arise between the one etheric human being and the other, bringing about the play of imaginations between them. We live with these imaginations and with our own resulting sympathies, whose effect and intensity we are often largely unaware of, or aware of only in the vaguest way. Indeed, when our everyday life is not wide-awake, but runs along more or less dully, we often fail to observe them at all.

Thereby we belong to the elemental world, for our etheric bodies derive from the elemental world. The etheric body is our instrument of communication with the elemental world. Through it we weave relationships not only with other etheric bodies that belong to physical beings, but also with spiritual beings that have an elemental character. Such "beings of an elemental character" are precisely those able to call forth conscious or unconscious imaginations in us. Human beings are perpetually related to a multitude of elemental beings, and this differentiates one human being from another. Each has several relationships—one human being to a given set of elemental beings, another to another set of elemental beings. Moreover, the relations of one human being to certain elemental beings may sometimes coincide with the relations of another to the same beings. However, it must be observed in this connection that while we are always, in a manner of speaking, related to a large number of elemental beings, we have relations of special intensity only with one elemental being, who is in essence the counterpart of our own etheric body. Our own etheric body is intimately related to one particular etheric being. Just as what we call our etheric body develops its own relations, from birth until death, to the physical world inasmuch as it is inserted in a physical body, so does this etheric entity, the counterpart or counterpole as it were of our own etheric body, enable us to have relations to the whole of the elemental world—the whole surrounding cosmic elemental world.

Hence we may be said to look out upon an elemental world to which we ourselves belong by virtue of our etheric body, and with which we stand in manifold relations—specific relationships to particular elemental beings. In the elemental world we meet beings who are truly no less real than human beings or animals in the physical world—beings who never come to incarnation, however, but only to "etherization," so to speak, for their densest corporeality is ethereal. Just as we go about among physical people in this world, so do we constantly go about among such elemental beings, some of whom are more remote and, in their turn, related to other people. Some of these elemental beings, however, are more closely related to us, and one among them relates to each of us most closely of all, and acts as our organ of communication with the entire cosmic elemental world.

Now, in the time immediately following our passage through the gate of death, when for a few days we still bear our etheric body, we ourselves become precisely such a being as these elemental beings are. In a manner of speaking, *we ourselves become an elemental being.* I have often described this process of the passage through the gate of death, but the more exactly we study it, the clearer the imaginations it provides. For the impressions we receive immediately after the passage of a human being through the gate of death always consist in, and make themselves felt as, *imaginations.*

Observing the process more exactly, we find that there is a certain mutual interplay immediately after death between our own etheric body and its etheric counterpart. The fact that our etheric body is taken from us a few days after death is due mainly to its being attracted—drawn in, as it were—by this etheric counterpart. Henceforth, it becomes one with its etheric counterpart. A few days after death we lay aside our etheric body. We hand it over, as it were, to our own etheric counterpart. Our etheric body is taken from us by our own cosmic prototype or image, and as a result, special relations now emerge between what is thus taken from us and the other elemental beings with whom we have been related in any way during our life. We might describe it thus: a kind of mutual relation now arises between what our own etheric body has become, united as it is now with its counterpart or counterimage, and the other elemental beings who accompanied us from birth until death. We might compare this to the relation of a sun to its associated planetary system. Our etheric body with its cosmic counterpart is like a kind of sun, surrounded—as a kind of planetary system—by other elemental beings. This mutual interplay gives rise to the forces that instill into the elemental world, rightly and in gradual evolution, all that our etheric body is able to take into that world. What we commonly refer to in abstract terms when we speak of the dissolution of the "etheric body" is essentially a play of forces, engendered by this sun and planetary system that we have left behind. Gradually, everything that we acquired and assimilated into our etheric body in the course of our life becomes a part of the spiritual world, weaving into the forces of the spiritual world.

We must be very clear on this. Every thought, every idea, every feeling we develop, however hidden it remains, is of significance for the spiritual world. For when the coherence is broken by our passage through the gate of death, all our thoughts and feelings pass with our etheric body into the spiritual world and become part and parcel of it. We do not live for nothing. What we receive into the thoughts that we make our own, into the feelings that we experience, become the fruits of our life embodied in the cosmos. This is a truth we must receive into our whole mood and outlook—otherwise we do not conduct ourselves rightly in the spiritual scientific movement. *You are not a spiritual-scientist merely by knowing about certain things. You are such only if you feel yourself, by virtue of this knowledge, to exist within the spiritual world—if you know yourself quite definitely to be a part of the spiritual world.* Then you will say to yourself: The thought I am now harboring is of significance for the whole universe, for at my death it will be handed over to the universe in such and such a form.

After a human being has died, we may have to deal, in one form or another, with what is thus handed over to the universe. Many of the ways that the dead are present to those they have left behind manifest because the etheric human being—who has, of course, been laid aside by the real individuality—sends back imaginations to the living. And if those still living are sensitive enough, or if they are in some abnormal state or have prepared themselves by proper spiritual training, the influences of what is thus given over to the spiritual world by the dead—influences, that is to say, of an imaginal kind—can emerge in them in a conscious form.

At the same time, after death there is still a connection between the true human individuality and the etheric entity that has separated from it. There is a mutual interplay between them. We can observe it most clearly when, through spiritual training, we come into actual communication with this or that dead individual. A certain kind of exchange can then take place. To begin with, the dead human being conveys to the etheric body what he or she wishes to transmit to those still in the physical world. For only by the dead person's transmitting it to the etheric body— making, as it were, inscriptions in the etheric body—can we perceive it here in the physical world in terms of what we call imaginations. The moment we have imaginations of a person, the dead person's etheric body is acting as a "switch" or "commutator," if you will pardon my use of the trivial and all-too-realistic term! Do not imagine that our relations to the dead need be any the less deeply felt because such an instrument is needed. People who meet us in the outer world also convey their form to us by the pictures they evoke in us through our own eyes. It is the same with this transmission through the etheric body. We perceive what the dead wish to convey to us by "getting" it, so to speak, through their etheric body. This body is *outside* the dead person, but so intimately related that it can be inscribed with what lives within that person, thus enabling us to read it in imaginations.

There is, however, this condition: a spiritually trained person who wishes to connect through the etheric body in this way with a dead human being must have had some relationship with the dead person, either in the last life between birth and death, or in a former incarnation. Moreover, these relationships must have affected the soul of the one who is still alive deeply enough for the imaginations to make an impression. And this can happen only if in one's heart and mind there is a definite and living interest in the dead person. Interests of heart and feeling must always mediate between the living and the dead if any exchange at all, conscious or unconscious, is to take place. (We shall speak of the latter presently.) Some interest of heart and feeling must be there, so that we really carry something of the dead within us. In a way, the dead person must have constituted a portion of our own soul's experience. However, one who is spiritually trained can make a certain substitute. One can, for instance, give oneself up to the impression of the handwriting, or of something else where the individuality of the dead is living. This may at first seem external, but spiritual training turns it into something far more inward. However, one can do this—contact someone through their handwriting—only if one has acquired a certain practice in making contact with an individuality through the fact that he or she lives in the writing. Or again, one may establish the possibility of contact by entering with sympathy into the feelings of the physical survivors, partaking in their grief and in all the emotional interest they have in the dead person. By entering with sympathy into these real and living feelings that flow from the dead into the dear ones they have left on earth—or that remain in their inner life—a person of spiritual training can prepare his or her soul to "read" the imaginations.

It is also true that although perceiving the imaginations from the etheric body depends on spiritual training or other special conditions, at the same time what passes unperceived by most people is nonetheless there. Therefore, we may truly say that those living in the physical world are not woven around only by the elemental forces in the form of imaginations proceeding from other human beings living with them in the physical body. For, whether we know it or not, our etheric bodies are constantly played through by all the imaginations we absorb from those who stood in any kind of relation to us and who have passed through the gate of death before us. In physical life, in the physical body, we are related to the air around us; so too are we related to the whole of the elemental world, including all that is there of the dead.

We shall never learn to know human life unless we gain knowledge of these relationships, although they are so intimate and fine that most people do not notice them. After all, who can deny that we do not remain always the same between birth and death? Let us look back upon our lives. However consistent we may think the course of our lives has been, we will soon notice that we have, in fact, often gone to and fro in life, or that this or that has occurred. Even if something does not immediately change the direction of our lives (which it can of course do), it nonetheless has the effect of enriching our lives in one way or another—in a happy direction or a painful one. Life always brings us different conditions—just as when you move to another area your general feeling of health may be changed by the different composition of the air.

These soul moods we enter in the course of our lives are due to the influences of the elemental world. They are due in no small measure to the influences that come from the dead who were formerly related to us. Many people in earthly life meet a friend or someone they become connected with in one way or another—to whom, perhaps, they find themselves obliged to do this or that by way of kindness or of criticism or rebuke. The fact that they were brought together required the influence of certain forces. A person who recognizes the occult connections in the world knows that when two human beings are brought together to this end or that, sometimes one and sometimes several of those who have gone through the gate of death before them are instrumental in this. Our lives do not become any less free thereby. We do not lose our freedom because we starve if we do not eat. No one who is not deliberately foolish will ask how we can be free, given that we are obliged to eat. It would be just as invalid to say that we lose our freedom because our souls constantly receive influences from the elemental world.

Just as we are connected with the air around us, with warmth and cold, and with all the things that become our food, so we are also connected with what comes to us from those who have died before us. We are similarly connected with the rest of the elemental world, but above all with what comes to us from the dead. Therefore, we can truly say that *our work for our fellow human beings does not cease with our passage through the gate of death.* Human beings remain connected to the etheric body after death, and through it send imaginations into those with whom they were connected in life. Indeed, the world we are referring to here is far more real than that we commonly call real—even if it remains unperceived in our everyday life, for very good reasons. So much, then, about the *elemental world* for today.

Another realm that is always present in our environment, to which we ourselves belong no less than to the elemental world, is what we may call the *soul world.* (The name does not matter.) We are always connected in our waking life with the elemental world, and we are still connected indirectly with it and with our etheric body in sleep, when our "I" and our astral body are outside the physical and the etheric bodies. But we are connected most directly with the higher soul world to which I now refer. However, as with the elemental world, the soul world cannot rise into our consciousness in ordinary life. We are connected with it in sleep when our astral body is freely around us, and we are connected with it in waking life as well—although then the connection, mediated as it is by forces the physical body has drawn into itself, is no longer so direct.

In this world of soul—*we* shall call it the *soul world* for the present, although medieval philosophers referred to it as the heavenly or celestial world—we find beings who are just as real as we are during our life between birth and death. In fact, these beings are even more real. However, they do not need to come to embodiment in a physical body, or even in an etheric body. They live—in their lowest "corporeality"—in what we call the *astral*

body. We are connected constantly and intimately with a large
number of these purely astral beings both during our life and
after our death. As is the case with elemental beings, we differ
from one another as human beings inasmuch as we are related
to different astral beings. Here again, two people may have relationships in common with one or more astral beings, and at the
same time have several relations to other astral beings.

When we have laid aside our etheric body after passing
through the gate of death, we ourselves belong to the world of
the astral beings. With our own individuality, we are then among
the beings of the soul world. We are soul beings at that time:
beings of the soul world are our immediate environment. True,
we are also still related to the content of the elemental world,
inasmuch as we can kindle in it what evokes imaginations. The
elemental world, however, is in a certain sense outside us—or, as
one might also say, beneath us. It is something we use to communicate with the rest of the world. But we ourselves belong directly
to what I have now called the world of soul, and it is with the
beings of the soul world that we have our interchange. These
include other human beings who have also passed through the
gate of death and, after a few days, laid aside their etheric bodies.

Just as we constantly receive influences from the elemental
world, although we do not notice it, so too we constantly receive
influences directly into our astral body out of the soul world I
am now describing. The immediate, straightforward influences
that we thus receive can appear as *inspirations*. (We have already
spoken of the indirect influences via the etheric body.)

You will understand the character of these influences from
the soul world if I describe once more, in a few words, how it
appears to those who are spiritually trained, that is, to those who
are able to receive conscious *inspirations* from the spiritual
world. It appears as follows. Spiritual researchers can bring
these inspirations to consciousness only if they are able, so to
speak, to take into themselves some portion of the being who
wants to inspire them—some portion of the qualities, of the
inherent life tendency, of such a being.

Those who are spiritually trained to develop conscious relations with the dead, not only through the etheric body (imagination) but in this direct way through inspiration, must bear in their souls even more than simple interest or sympathy is able to call forth. They must, for a short while, at least, be able to transform themselves so as to receive into their own being something of the habits and character, the very human nature, of the one with whom they wish to communicate. These researchers must be able to enter the one who has died to such a degree that they could take on the person's habits and do what that person could do, and in the same way. They must also be able to feel and will as he or she could. It is the "could" that matters—the possibility.

This is to say that we must be able to live together with the dead even more intimately. For those who are spiritually trained there are many ways of coming close to the dead—provided, of course, that the dead person permits it. However, we must realize that the beings who belong to what we are now calling the world of soul are quite differently related to the world than we are in our physical bodies. Hence, there are certain quite definite conditions of exchange with such beings—including, among others, the dead, as long as these are still living as astral beings in their astral bodies. Here certain points deserve special attention.

You see, all that we develop for our lives in the physical body—our many and varied relationships to other people (I mean precisely those relationships that arise through earthly life)—all this acquires quite another kind of interest for the dead. Here on earth, we develop sympathies and antipathies. We must be clear about this. The sympathies and antipathies that we develop while living in the physical body are subject to the influences of our present form of life, which we owe to the physical body and to its conditions. These sympathies and antipathies are subject to the influences of our own vanity and of our egoism. Let us not fail to realize how many of the relationships that we develop with this or that human being result from vanity or egoism—or other things that depend on our physical and earthly life in this world. We love other people or we hate them.

As a rule, we actually take little notice of the true grounds of our loving and our hating—our sympathies and antipathies. In fact, often we avoid consciously noticing our sympathies and antipathies simply because if we did so, as a rule highly unpleasant truths would emerge. If, for instance, we followed up what was really behind our failure to love this or that human being, we would often have to ascribe so much prejudice, vanity, or other qualities to ourselves that it would frighten us. Therefore, we do not bring to full, conscious clarity why we hate this person or that. And the same is often true with love. Interests, sympathies, and antipathies evolve in ways that have significance only for our everyday life. Yet it is out of all this that we act. We arrange our life according to these interests, sympathies, and antipathies.

Now, it would be quite wrong to imagine that the dead can possibly have the same interest we on earth have in all the ephemeral sympathies and antipathies that arise under the influence of our physical and earthly lives. That would be utterly wrong. Truly, the dead are obliged to look at these things from quite another standpoint. Moreover, we may ask ourselves if we are not largely influenced in our estimate of our fellow human beings by these subjective feelings—by all that lies inherent in our subjective interests, our vanity, egoism, and the like. Let us not think for a moment that the dead can have any interest in such relationships between ourselves and other human beings, or in our actions arising from such interests. But we must also not imagine that the dead do not see what lives in our souls. For it really lives there, and the dead see it well enough. They share in it, too. But they see something else as well. The dead have a quite different way of judging people. The dead see people quite differently. One thing is of outstanding importance in how the dead see human beings here on earth. Let us not imagine that the dead do not have a keen, living interest in the world of human beings. They certainly do, for the world of human beings belongs to the whole cosmos. Our own lives belong to the cosmos. And just as we, even in the physical world, interest ourselves in the subordinate kingdoms, so the dead interest themselves intensely in the human world, and send their active impulses into it. *The dead work through the living into the earthly world.* We have just given an example of the way they go on working soon after their passage through the gate of death.

The dead see one thing above all, and that most clearly. Suppose, for example, that they see someone here following hateful impulses—hating this person or that, and with a merely personal intensity or purpose. The dead see this. At the same time, however, depending upon the whole manner of their vision and all that they are then able to know, they will observe quite clearly the part that Ahriman is playing in this case. The dead see how Ahriman impels us to hatred. The dead actually see Ahriman working upon the human being. On the other hand, if a person on earth is vain, the dead see Lucifer at work. That is the essential point. It is in connection with the world of Ahriman and Lucifer that the dead see the human beings who are here on earth. Consequently, what generally colors our judgment of people is quite eliminated for the dead. We see this or that human being, whom in one sense or another we must condemn. Whatever we find blameworthy, we ascribe to the human being. The dead do not ascribe it directly to the human being. They see how the person is misled by Lucifer or Ahriman. This brings about a toning down, so to speak, of the sharply differentiated feelings that in our physical and earthly life we generally extend toward this or that human being. To a far greater extent than on earth, a kind of universal human love arises in the dead. This does not mean that the dead cannot criticize—that is to say, that they cannot rightly see what is evil in evil. They see it well enough, but they are able to refer it to its origin, to its real inner connections.

What I have described here is not without its consequences, for it means that those with esoteric training cannot consciously come near one who is dead unless they truly free themselves from feelings of personal sympathy or antipathy toward individuals. Such researchers must not allow themselves to be dependent in their souls on personal feelings of sympathy or antipathy. You need only imagine it for a moment. Suppose that a trained clairvoyant was about to approach a dead human being—whoever that might be—so that the inspirations sent by the dead might find their way into the researcher's consciousness. Suppose, moreover, that the researcher on earth was pursuing another human being with a quite special hatred—hatred having its origin only in personal relationships. Then truly as our hand avoids fire, so would the dead avoid such a person who was capable of hatred for personal reasons. Such a person cannot approach the dead, for hatred works on the dead like fire. *To come into conscious relation with the dead we must be able to make ourselves like them—independent, in a sense, of personal sympathies and antipathies.*

Thus, you will understand what I now have to say. Bear in mind this whole relation of the dead to the living, insofar as it rests on inspirations. Remember that the inspirations are always there, even if they pass unnoticed. They are perpetually living in the human astral body, so that human beings on earth have relations with the dead in this direct way, too. Now, after all we have said, you will understand that these relationships depend on our whole mood and spirit in our lives here on earth. If our attitude to other people is hostile, if we are without interest or sympathy for our contemporaries—above all, if we do not have an unprejudiced interest in our fellows—then the dead cannot approach us as they long to do. They cannot properly transplant themselves into our souls, or, if they must do so, it is made difficult for them in one way or another and they can do it only with great suffering and pain. All in all, the living together of the dead with the living is complicated.

Thus, we continue to work when we pass through the gate of death, even directly, inasmuch as after death we inspire those who are living on the physical plane. And this is absolutely true. Especially in their inner habits and qualities, the way they think, feel, and develop inclinations, those living on earth at any given time are dependent to a great extent on those who have died and passed from the earth before them—those who were related to them during life, or to whom they themselves established a relation even after death, which may sometimes happen, though it is not so easy.

A certain part of the ordering of the world and of all of human progress depends on this working of the dead into the life of earthly human beings, inspiring them. Moreover, in their instinctive life people have an inkling that this is so and that it must be so. We can observe this if we consider for a moment ways of life that were formerly very widespread and are now dying out because humanity goes on to new forms of life in the course of evolution. In times gone by when, generally speaking, human beings divined far more of the reality of spiritual worlds, they were more deeply aware of what is necessary for life as a whole. They knew that the living need the dead—need to receive into their habits and customs the impulses from the dead. What, then, did they do? You need only think of former times, when it was generally customary for a father to take care that his son should inherit and carry on his business, so that the son went on working in the same sphere. Then, when the father was long dead, a bond of communication was created through the physical world itself because the son remained in the same channels of life. The son's activity and lifework being akin to his father's, the father was able to work on in him.

Many things in life were based on this principle. And if whole classes of society attached great value to the inheritance of this or that property within the class or within its several families, it was due to their divining this necessity. The life habits of those who live earlier must enter into the life habits of those who live later, but only when these life habits are so far ripened that they come forth after one has passed through the gate of death—for it is only then that they become mature.

These things are coming to an end, as you know. Such is the progress of the human race. We can already see a time when these inheritances, these conservative conditions, will no longer play a part. The physical bonds will no longer be there in the same way. To compensate for this, it is all the more necessary that people receive detailed spiritual-scientific knowledge that will lift the whole matter into their consciousness. Then they will be able to consciously connect their life with the life habits of former times—which we have to reckon with in order for life to go forward with continuity.

Since the beginning of the fifth post-Atlantean period we have been living in a time of transition. During this period, a more or less chaotic state has intervened. But the conditions will again arise when, through recognition of spiritual-scientific truths, people will connect their life and work in a far more conscious way with what has gone before them. Unconsciously, merely instinctively, they used to do so—of that there can be no doubt. But even what remains instinctive to this day must be transmuted into consciousness. Instinctively, for instance, people still teach like this— only we do not observe it. Those who study history from a spiritual perspective will soon notice it, if only they pay attention to the facts and not to the dreadful abstractions that prevail nowadays in the so-called humanistic branches of scholarship. If we look at the facts we can easily see that what is taught in a given epoch bears a certain character only because people attach themselves unconsciously, instinctively, to what the dead pour down into the present. Once you learn to truly study the educational ideas that are propounded in any given age by the leading spirits in education—not the charlatans but the true educators—you will soon see how these ideas have their origins in the ingrained habits of those who have recently died.

This is a far more intimate living together—for what affects the human astral body enters far more into one's inner life than what affects the etheric body. The communion that the dead themselves, as individualities, can enjoy with people on earth is far more intimate than what the etheric bodies have—or, for that matter, any other elemental beings. Hence you will see how one epoch in the life of humanity is always conditioned by the one that preceded it. The preceding time always goes on living in the time that follows.

In reality, strange though it may sound, it is only after our death that we become truly ripe enough to influence other people—I mean to influence them directly, working right into their inner being. To impress our own habits on anyone who is "of age" (spiritually speaking, not in the legal sense) is the very thing we should not do while we are on earth. Yet it is right and in accordance with the conditions of progressive human evolution that we do so after we have passed through the gate of death. Besides all the things that comprise the progress of karma and the general laws of incarnation, these influences occur. If you ask for the occult reasons why people are doing one thing or another this year, not in all cases, but certainly in many, you will find that they are doing so because impulses are flowing down to them from those who died twenty or thirty years ago, or even earlier. These are the hidden connections— the real concrete connections—between the physical and the spiritual world. It is not only for ourselves that something ripens and matures in what we carry with us through the gate of death. It is not only for ourselves, but for the world at large. And it is only from a given moment that it becomes truly ripe to work upon others. Then, however, it becomes riper and riper.

I beg you to observe that I am not speaking of externals here, but of inner, spiritual workings. A person may remember the habits of a dead father or grandfather and repeat them out of memory on the physical plane. That is not what I mean. That is a different matter. I mean the inspired influences—imperceptible to ordinary consciousness—that make themselves felt in our habits, in our most intimate character. Much in our life depends on our finding ourselves obliged, here or there, to free ourselves from the influences—even the well-meant ones—coming to us from the dead. Indeed, we gain much of our inner freedom by having to liberate ourselves in this way, in one direction or another. Inner soul conflicts, which a person is often unaware of, will grow intelligible to us when we view them in the light of spiritual knowledge of this kind. To use a trite expression, we may say that the past is rumbling on—the souls of the past go rumbling on—in our own inner lives.

These things are facts—the truths which we look into with spiritual vision. Unfortunately people have a peculiar relation to these truths, especially in modern life. It was not always so. Anyone who can study history in a spiritual way will know this. Today, people are afraid of these truths—they are afraid to face them. They have a nameless fear—not indeed conscious, but unconscious. Unconsciously, they are afraid to recognize the mysterious connections between soul and soul, not only in this world, but between here and the other world. It is this unconscious fear that holds people back in the outer world. And this is a part of what holds them back, instinctively, from spiritual science. They are afraid of knowing reality. They are unaware of how, by their unwillingness to know reality, they are disturbing and confusing the whole course of world evolution, and with it, needless to say, the life that will have to be lived through between death and a new birth, when these conditions must be seen.

Everything that evolves continuously ripens and matures. Therefore, what lives in us does not stop short at *inspiration*, but becomes *intuition* (in the true sense, as I use the word in *How to Know Higher Worlds*), which is still more mature. Now, intuition is only possible for a being that has a "spirit body" (to use this paradoxical expression). To work intuitively upon other beings— and, among others, upon those who are still incarnated here in the physical life—human beings must first have laid aside the astral body; that is to say, they must belong entirely to the spiritual world. That will happen only decades after death, as we know. But at that point one can work down on other people through *intuition*—no longer merely through *inspiration* as I described it just now. Not until then does the person who has passed through the gate of death as an I work, in the spiritual world, in a purely spiritual way into other I's. Before reaching this stage, the dead worked by inspiration into the astral body— or, through the etheric body, into the human etheric body (imagination). But those who have been dead for decades can also work directly as an I—although at the same time they can still work through the other vehicles, as described above. At this stage the human individuality grows sufficiently ripe to enter not just into people's habits but even into their views and ideas of life. To modern feeling, full of prejudice as it is, this may be an unpleasant truth—doubtless, very unpleasant. Nonetheless it is true. Our views and ideas, originating as they do in our I, are under constant influences from those long dead. Those who are long dead live in our way of looking at and conceiving of life. By this very means, the continuity of evolution is preserved—out of the spiritual world. It is a necessity, for otherwise the thread of people's ideas would constantly be broken.

Forgive me if I insert something personal at this point. I do so, may I say, for thoroughly objective reasons. For such a truth as this can only be made intelligible by concrete examples.

We really ought not bring forward our own personal opinions as views or ideas—however sincerely gained. Therefore, those who stand with full sincerity on the true ground of occultism—who are experienced in the premises of spiritual science—will not impose their own opinions on the world. On the contrary, such people will do all they can to avoid imposing their own opinions directly. For the opinions and the outlook one acquires under the influence of a personal way of feeling should not begin to work until thirty or forty years after one's death. Then it will work in this way: it will enter people's souls along the same paths that the impulses of the time spirits or archai do. Only then has it become so mature that it can work in harmony with the objective course of things.

Those who stand on the true ground of occultism must therefore avoid making personal proselytes, must avoid setting out to gain followers for their own personal views—as is the general custom nowadays. No sooner do people get an opinion of their own, than they hasten to make propaganda for it. That is what a real, practicing spiritual scientist cannot possibly want to do.

Let me now introduce the personal matter I mentioned. It was not chance, but something essential in my life, that led me to begin by writing and communicating to the world not my own views, but Goethe's. Goethe was the first thing I wrote about. At first I wrote entirely out of the spirit and sense of Goethe's worldview. I did not take my start from any living person, for even if that living person were myself, it could not possibly justify my teaching spiritual science in the comprehensive way I try to do. Placing my work like this into the objective course of world evolution was a necessary link in the chain. Therefore I did not write my own theory of knowledge but Goethe's (*A Theory of Knowledge Implicit in Goethe's Worldview*), and I continued for some time in the same vein.

Thus you see how human development proceeds. What we attain on earth ripens not only for the sake of our own lives as we advance on the paths of karma. It also ripens for the sake of the world. And so we continue to work for the world. After a certain time, we become ripe to send *imaginations* into the habits of human beings; then, after a further time, *inspirations*. And only after a longer time has elapsed do we grow ready and mature enough to send *intuitions* into the most intimate part of people's lives—into their views and ideas.

Let us not imagine that our views and ideas of life grow out of nothing—or that they arise anew in every age. They grow from the soil in which our own soul is rooted, and this soil is in truth identical with the sphere of activity of human beings who died long ago.

With this knowledge, I believe human life will receive the enrichment that it needs in accordance with the character and sense of our age and of the immediate future. Many old customs have grown rotten to the core. The new must be developed. But we cannot enter a new life without the impulses that grow in us through spiritual science. What matters are the feelings—feelings toward the world in its entirety, and all the other beings of the world—that we acquire through spiritual science. The mood of our lives will grow different through spiritual science. Through spiritual science, the supersensible worlds, in which we always live, become alive for us. We are and always have been living in them....

8

IN THE PHYSICAL WORLD, our actions seem to have limited consequences. It seems that what we do causes little pleasure or pain around us. The situation is otherwise in the world of the dead. There, everything causes either pleasure or pain. No act is without its echo. On earth there are the four kingdoms of mineral, plant, animal, and human. Among the dead, however, the lowest kingdom is that of the animal. It is the "soil" upon which the dead live. Therefore, the first task for one who has died is to acquire intimate, exact knowledge of this. This is necessary because, in communion with the whole hierarchy of cosmic beings, the dead must prepare for their next physical incarnation. In doing so, they are woven by a self-correcting process into pleasure and pain until, eventually, both soul and body are ready for the new incarnation. Acquaintance with the human kingdom is more limited, because the dead can contact only those with whom they are already linked. Such links can be made only on earth. Other souls whom one has not met on earth pass by unnoticed. This is one meaning of karma. It also points to the supreme significance of earthly life as the place where we develop connection— love. This has to do with soul life, because this connection refers to the interpenetration of soul lives in such a way that, after death, one soul can find itself in another.

After death, souls are as intimately related as we are with our own bodies on earth. In the spiritual world, souls are either inside or outside other souls. The same is true of their relationships to the beings of the hierarchies— angels, archangels, and so on. It is this interpenetration that makes communication possible. But there are dangers. What is higher life in the spiritual world can easily become a lower impulse when it is within us on earth. Therefore, to communicate with the dead requires a great personal purity, especially because the relationship with the dead is always through the blood or nervous system— for the dead live in the animal realm. Another difficulty lies in the fact that, in communication with the dead, the normal process of communication is reversed. On earth when we speak to another, we know who is speaking. But when we speak to the dead, what we say comes from them. And when they speak, this comes from our own soul. As Steiner says, when speaking with the dead "we must adapt ourselves to hear from them what we ourselves say and to receive from our own soul what they answer." In fact, the dead are always with us, around us, but we do not notice them because of this reversal. We think we have an idea, when perhaps it is inspired into us—whispered to us—by a loved one who has died. All of us are in constant communication with the dead in this way. To understand this, it is useful to concentrate on the "magic" moments of waking up and falling asleep. The time of falling asleep is especially favorable for turning to the dead to ask a question. The answer will come in the morning in the evanescent moment of awakening. Before this can happen, however, we must fill our thoughts with feeling; the question must be carried on the heart's current. The dead are always there and present with us, particularly those who died as children. These are especially with us and do not go away. Older people, on the other hand, sometimes go away, because they are drawn swiftly into the spiritual sphere. Therefore, funeral services for young children and old people should be different. These are very important matters that remind us of our communion with the spiritual world.

The Dead Are Always with Us

NUREMBERG, FEBRUARY 10, 1918

… Today we will again think of the life that takes its course between death and a new birth—the life that seems so far removed from the human being in the physical world. I will begin by simply narrating what spiritual investigation has found. These things can be understood if sufficient thought is applied to them. Their own power makes them comprehensible to the soul. Those who do not understand them should realize that they have not thought about them deeply enough. These things must be *investigated* by the methods of spiritual science, but they can be *understood* by constant study. They will then be confirmed by the facts that life itself confronts us with, provided life is rightly observed.

You will have realized from many of the lecture courses that study of the life between death and rebirth is fraught with difficulty, because its conditions are so entirely different from those of the life that can be pictured by the organs of the physical body here in the physical world. We therefore have to become familiar with utterly different conceptions.

We know that when we enter into relationship with the things in our physical environment, only a small proportion of the beings around us in the physical world react to our deeds—the manifestations of our will—in such a way that we realize our deeds cause *pleasure* or *pain*. Reactions of this kind take place in the animal and human kingdoms, but we are justified in thinking that the mineral world (including what is contained in air and water) and, essentially, the world of plants, are insensitive to what we call pleasure or pain as the result of our deeds. (Spiritually considered, of course, the matter is a little different, but that need not concern us at this point.)

In the environment of the dead all this is changed. Conditions in the environment of the so-called dead are such that everything—including what is done by the dead themselves—causes either pleasure or pain. The dead cannot do a single thing—they cannot, if I may speak pictorially, move a single limb—without pleasure or pain being caused by what is done. We must try to think our way into these conditions of existence. We must assimilate the thought that life between death and a new birth is so constituted that everything we do awakens an echo in the environment. During the whole period between death and a new birth we can do nothing—metaphorically speaking, we cannot even move—without causing pleasure or pain in our environment.

The mineral kingdom as we have it around us on the physical plane does not exist for the dead, nor does the world of plants. As you can gather from my book *Theosophy*, these kingdoms are present for the dead in an entirely different form. They are not present in the spiritual world in the form we are familiar with here—that is, as realms devoid of feeling.

The first of the kingdoms familiar to us on the physical plane that has significance for the dead, because it is comparable with what the dead have in their environment, is the animal kingdom. I do not, of course, mean individual animals as we know them on the physical plane, but the whole environment is such that its effects and influences are as if animals were there. The reaction of the environment is such that pleasure or pain proceeds from what is done. On the physical plane, we stand upon mineral soil. The dead analogously stand upon a "soil"—they live in an environment—that may be compared with animal nature. The dead, therefore, start their lives two kingdoms higher than we do on earth. On earth, we know the animal kingdom only from outside. Between death and a new birth, the first, most outer activity of life consists in acquiring more and more intimate and exact knowledge of the animal world. For it is in this life between death and a new birth that we must prepare all those forces that, working in from the cosmos, organize our own body. In the physical world we know nothing of these forces. Between death and a new birth we know that our body, down to its smallest particles, is formed out of the cosmos. We ourselves prepare this physical body, bringing together in it the whole of animal nature. We ourselves build our physical body.

To make the picture more exact, let us acquaint ourselves with an idea that is rather remote from current mentality. People today know that when a magnetic needle lies with one end pointing toward the north and the other toward the south, this is not caused by the needle itself. The earth as a whole is a cosmic magnet, one pole pointing toward the north and the other toward the south. It would be sheer nonsense to say that the direction is determined by forces contained in the magnetic needle. In the case of a seed or a germinating entity that develops into an animal or a human being, all the sciences and schools of thought deny the factor of cosmic influence. What would be described as nonsense in the case of the magnetic needle is accepted without further thought in the case of an egg forming inside the hen. But when the egg is forming inside the hen, the whole cosmos is, in fact, participating. What happens on earth merely provides the stimulus for the operation of cosmic forces. Everything that takes shape in the egg is an imprint of cosmic forces, and the hen herself is only a place, an abode, in which the cosmos, the whole world system, is working. It is the same in the case of the human being. This is a thought with which we must become familiar.

Between death and a new birth, we work in communion with beings of the higher hierarchies—with the whole system of forces permeating the cosmos. Between death and a new birth we are not inactive. We are always at work—but in the spiritual realm. The animal kingdom is the first sphere with which we become acquainted. This happens as follows. If we commit some error we immediately become aware of pain, of suffering, in the surroundings; if we do something right, we become aware of pleasure, of joy, in the environment. The dead work on and on, calling forth pleasure or pain, until finally their soul nature is such that it can descend and unite with what will live on earth as a physical body. Our soul being could never descend if it had not itself worked at the physical form.

It is the animal kingdom, then, that the dead come to know first. Next is the human kingdom. Mineral nature and the plant kingdom are absent. To use a familiar phrase, the dead's acquaintance with the human kingdom is limited. Between death and a new birth—and this begins immediately or soon after death—the dead have contact and can make links with only those human souls, whether still living on Earth or in the world beyond, with whom they have already been karmically connected on earth in the last or in an earlier incarnation. Other souls pass by; they do not come within their ken. The dead become aware of the animal realm as a totality, but only the human souls they have had some karmic connection with here on earth come within their purview, and with these they become more and more closely acquainted. You must not imagine that the number of these is small, for individual human beings have already passed through many lives on earth, and in each life many karmic connections are formed. A web is then spun of these that, in the spiritual world, extends over all the souls whom the dead have known in life. Only those with whom no acquaintance has been made remain outside the circle.

This indicates a truth that must be emphasized, namely, *the supreme importance of earthly life for the individual human being*. If we had no earthly lives we would be unable to form links with human souls in the spiritual world. The links are formed karmically on earth and then continue between death and a new birth. Those who can see into the spiritual world perceive how the dead gradually make more and more links—all of which are the outcome of karmic connections formed on earth.

Just as we may say that everything the dead do, even simple movements, causes pleasure or pain in the environment of the first kingdom they encounter—the animal kingdom—so we may say that everything that is experienced in the human realm in the other world is much more intimately connected with the life of *soul*. When the dead become acquainted with a soul, they come to know it as if they themselves were within it. After death, knowledge of other souls is as intimate as knowledge here on earth is of our own finger, head, or ear—we feel ourselves within the other soul. The connection is much more intimate than it can ever be on earth.

Human souls between death and a new birth enjoy two basic community experiences. They are either within other souls or outside them. Even in the case of souls already known, the dead are sometimes within and sometimes outside them. Meeting a soul consists in feeling at one with it, being within it. To be outside it means that it is not noticed, that the other soul does not become aware of it. If we look at an object here on earth, we perceive it; if we look away from it, we no longer perceive it. In the other world, when we are able to turn our attention to other souls we are actually within them. But when we are not in a position to do so, we are outside them.

What I have said gives an indication of the fundamental form of the soul's communion with other souls during the period between death and a new birth. In the same way, the human being is also within or outside the beings of the hierarchies, the angeloi, archangeloi, and so on. The higher the kingdoms, the more intensely one feels bound to them after death. One feels as though they were bearing one, sustaining one, with great power. The archangeloi are a mightier support than the angeloi, the archai mightier than the archangeloi, and so on.

People today still find it difficult to acquire knowledge of the spiritual world. But the difficulties would soon be resolved if a little more trouble were taken to become acquainted with its secrets. There are two approaches. One leads to complete certainty of the eternal in one's own being. This knowledge—that in human nature there is an eternal core of being that passes through birth and death—remote as it is to the modern mind, is comparatively easy to attain; and it will certainly be attained by those who have enough perseverance along the path described in my book *How to Know Higher Worlds* and in other writings. It is attained by treading the path I have described there. That is one approach to knowledge of the spiritual world. The other is through what may be called direct exchange with beings of the spiritual world. I shall now speak of the exchange that is possible between those still living on earth and the so-called dead.

Such communication is most certainly possible, but it presents greater difficulties than the first form of knowledge, which is easy to attain. Actual exchange with an individual who has died is possible, but difficult, because it demands scrupulous vigilance by the one who seeks to establish it. Control and discipline are necessary for this kind of communication with the spiritual world, because it is connected with a very important law. Impulses recognized as lower impulses in people on earth are, from the spiritual side, higher life. It may therefore easily happen that a human being who has not achieved true control of the self can experience the rising of lower impulses as the result of direct exchange with the dead. When we make contact with the spiritual world in the general sense, when we acquire knowledge about our own immortality as beings of soul and spirit, there can be no question of the ingress of anything impure. But when it is a matter of contact with individuals who have died, the relation with the individual dead—strange as it seems—is always a relation with the blood and nervous system. The dead enter those impulses that live themselves out in the system of blood and nerves. In this way lower impulses may be aroused. Naturally, this is a danger only for those who have not purified their nature through discipline and control. This must be said, for it is why communication with the dead is forbidden in the Old Testament. Such exchange is not sinful when it happens in the right way. The methods of modern spiritualism must, of course, be avoided. When the communication is of a spiritual nature it is not sinful, but if it is not accompanied by pure thoughts, it can easily lead to the stimulation of lower passions. It is not the dead who arouse these passions, but rather the element in which the dead *live*.

Consider this: the basic element in which the dead live is what we feel here as "animal" in quality and nature. The kingdom where the dead live can therefore easily be changed when it enters us. What is higher life in the other world can become lower impulses when it is within us on earth. It is very important to remember this. It must be emphasized here when we are speaking of communication between the living and the so-called dead. This is an occult fact. We shall find that it is precisely when we are speaking about such communication that the spiritual world can be described as it really is, for such experiences reveal that the spiritual world is completely different from the physical world.

To begin with, I will tell you something that may seem to have no meaning for you as long as you have not developed faculties of clairvoyance; but if you think it over you will realize that it concerns you closely. Those who are able to commune with the dead as the result of developed clairvoyance realize why it is so difficult for human beings to know anything about the dead through direct perception. Strange as it may seem, the whole form of exchange to which we are accustomed in the physical world has to be reversed when communication is established between the earth and the dead. In the physical world, when we speak to a human being from physical body to physical body, we know that the words come from ourselves; when the other person speaks to us, we know that the words come from him or her. The whole relationship is reversed when we are speaking with one who has died. The expression "when we are speaking" can truthfully be used, but the relationship is reversed. When we put a question to the dead, or say something to someone who has died, what we say comes from the dead person, comes to us from the dead. That soul inspires into our soul what we ask it, what we say. And when the one who has died answers us or says something to us, this comes out of our own soul. It is a process human beings in the physical world are quite unfamiliar with. We feel that what we say comes out of our own being. In order to establish communication with those who have died, we must adapt ourselves to hear from them what we ourselves say, and to receive from our own soul what they answer.

Abstractly described, the nature of the process is easy to grasp, but it is very difficult to become accustomed to the total reversal of the familiar form of communication. The dead are always there, always among us and around us, and the fact that they are not perceived is largely due to lack of understanding of this reversed form of communication. On the physical plane, we think that when anything comes out of our soul, it comes from us. We are far from being able to pay intimate enough attention to whether it is not, after all, perhaps being inspired into us from the spiritual environment. We prefer to connect it with experiences familiar to us on the physical plane, where something that comes to us from the environment is at once ascribed to the other person. This is the greatest error when it is a matter of communication with the dead.

I have spoken of one of the fundamental principles of communication between the so-called living and the so-called dead. If this example helps you to realize only one thing—that conditions are entirely reversed in the spiritual world—then you will have grasped a very significant concept, one constantly needed by those who aspire to become conscious of the spiritual world. The concept is extremely difficult to apply in actual, individual cases. For instance, to understand even the physical world, permeated as it is with the spiritual, it is essential to grasp this idea of complete reversal. And because modern science fails to grasp it, it is altogether unknown to general consciousness. That is why there is today no spiritual understanding of the physical world. One experiences this even with people who try very hard indeed to comprehend the world, and one is often obliged simply to accept the situation and leave it at that. Some years ago I was speaking to a large number of friends at a meeting in Berlin about the human physical organism, with special reference to some of Goethe's ideas. I tried to explain how the physical structure of the head can only be rightly understood when it is conceived as a complete transformation of the other part of the organism.[1] No one was able to understand at all that a bone in the arm would have to be turned inside out like a glove in order to produce a skull bone from it. It is a difficult concept, but one cannot really understand anatomy without such pictures. I mention this only parenthetically. What I have said today about communication with the dead is easier to understand.

What I have described to you is going on all the time. All of you sitting here now are in constant communication with the dead, only ordinary consciousness knows nothing of it because it lies in the subconscious. Clairvoyant consciousness does not evoke anything new into being. It merely brings up into consciousness what is present all the time in the spiritual world. All of you are in constant exchange with the dead.

We shall now consider how this exchange takes place in individual cases. When someone has died and we are left behind, we may ask, How do I approach the one who has died, so that he or

---

1. See also Rudolf Steiner, *Foundations of Human Experience*, lecture 10, Hudson, NY: Anthroposophic Press, 1997.

she is aware of me? How do they come near me again so that I can live in them?

These questions may well be asked, but they cannot be answered if we have recourse only to concepts familiar on the physical plane. On the physical plane, ordinary consciousness functions only from the time of waking until the time of falling asleep; but the other part of consciousness, the one that remains dim in ordinary life between falling asleep and waking, is just as important. When human beings are asleep, they are not, properly speaking, unconscious; consciousness is merely so dim that they experience nothing. But the whole human being—awake *and* asleep—must be considered when we study the connections of human beings with the spiritual world. Think of your own biography. You reflect upon the course of your life, but this reflection always has interruptions—you describe only what has happened in your waking hours. Life is punctuated: waking and sleeping, sleeping and waking. You are also there while you sleep. When you study the whole human being, both waking life and sleeping life must be taken into consideration.

A third thing must also be kept in mind regarding our exchange with the spiritual world. Besides waking life and sleeping life there is *a third state*, even more important for exchange with the spiritual world than the first two: *the state connected with the act of waking up and the act of going to sleep*. This third state lasts only a few brief seconds, for we immediately pass on into other conditions. However, if we develop a delicate sensitivity for these moments of waking and going to sleep we shall find that they shed great light on the spiritual world.

Although such customs are gradually disappearing, when we who are today older were still young, people in remote country places were wont to say that when you wake from sleep, it is not good to go immediately to a window where the light is streaming through—you should stay in the dark a while. Country folk used to have some knowledge about communication with the spiritual world, and they preferred not to come right into the bright daylight at the moment of waking, but to remain inwardly collected in order to preserve something of what sweeps with such power through the human soul at that moment. The sudden brightness of daylight is disturbing. In cities, of course, we can hardly avoid being disturbed. There we are disturbed not only by the daylight but also, even before waking, by the noise from the streets, the clanging of streetcar bells, and so forth. The whole of civilized life seems to conspire to hinder our communication with the spiritual world. This is not said to decry material civilization, but we must remember the facts.

The spiritual world approaches us powerfully again at the moment of going to sleep—but we fall asleep immediately and lose consciousness of what has passed through the soul. Exceptions do, of course, occur. These moments of waking and of going to sleep are of the utmost significance for communication with the so-called dead, as well as with other spiritual beings of the higher worlds. To understand what I have to say about this, however, you must familiarize yourselves with an idea that is not easy to apply on the physical plane and is therefore practically unknown.

It is this: *Spiritually, what is "past" has not really vanished but is still there.* In physical life people have this conception only in regard to space. If you stand in front of a tree and then go away and come back later to look at it, the tree has not disappeared; it is still there. The same is true for time in the spiritual world. If you experience something at one moment, it has passed away in the next as far as physical consciousness is concerned; spiritually conceived, however, it has not passed away. You can look back at it just as you looked back at the tree. Richard Wagner showed his knowledge of this in the remarkable words he put into his *Parzival:* "Time here becomes space." It is an occult fact that in the spiritual world there are distances that do not come to expression on the physical plane. That an event is past simply means that it is farther away from us. I beg you to remember this. For human beings on earth in the physical body, the moment of going to sleep is "past" when the moment of waking arrives. In the spiritual world, however, the moment of falling asleep has not gone; we are only a little farther distant from it at the moment of waking. *We encounter our dead at the moment of going to sleep and again at the moment of waking.* (As I said, this is happening all the time, only it usually remains in the subconscious.) As far as physical consciousness is concerned, these are two quite different moments in time; but for spiritual consciousness the one is only a little farther distant than the other. I want you to remember this in connection with what I am now going to say—otherwise you may find it difficult to understand.

As I told you, the moments of waking and going to sleep are particularly important for communication with those who have died. Through the whole of our life there are no such moments when we do not come into relation with the dead.

The moment of going to sleep is especially favorable for us to turn to the dead. Suppose we want to ask the dead something. We can carry it in our soul, holding it until the moment of going to sleep, for that is the time to bring our questions to the dead. Other opportunities exist, but this moment is the most favorable. When, for instance, we read to the dead we certainly draw near to them, but for direct communication it is best of all if we put our questions to them at the moment of going to sleep

On the other hand, the moment of waking is the most favorable for receiving what the dead have to communicate to us. And again, there is no one—did people but know it—who at the moment of waking does not bring with them countless tidings from the dead. In the subconscious region of the soul, we are always speaking with the dead. At the moment of going to sleep we put our questions to them, we say to them what, in the depths of the soul, we have to say. At the moment of waking the dead speak to us, give us the answers. But we must realize that these are only two different points and that, in the higher sense, these things that happen at different times for us are really simultaneous, just as on the physical plane two places are there simultaneously.

Some factors in life are favorable for exchange with the dead, others less so. We may therefore ask, What can really help us to establish conversation with the dead? The manner of our conversation cannot be the same as it is with those who are alive, for the dead neither hear nor take in this kind of speech. There is no question of being able to chatter with one who has died as we chatter with one another at tea or in cafes. What makes it possible to put questions to the dead or to communicate something to them is that we unite the life *of feeling* with our thoughts and ideas. Suppose a person has passed through the gate of death and you want your subconscious to communicate something to him or her in the evening. It need not be communicated consciously. You can prepare it at some time during the day. Then, if you go to bed at ten o'clock at night having prepared it, say, at noon, it passes over to the dead when you go to sleep. The question must, however, be put in a particular way; it must not merely be a thought or an idea, but must be imbued with feeling and with will. Your relationship with the dead must be one of the heart, of inner interest. You must remind yourself of your love for the person when he or she was alive and address yourself to that soul with real warmth of heart, not abstractly. This feeling can take such firm root in the soul that in the evening, at the moment of going to sleep, it becomes a question to the dead without your knowing it. Or you may try to realize vividly the nature of your particular interest in the one who has died. Think about your shared experiences; visualize actual moments when you were together, and then ask yourself, What was it about that person that attracted me, that particularly interested me? When was it that I was so deeply impressed, liked what he or she said, found it helpful and valuable? If you remind yourself of moments when you were strongly connected with the dead and were deeply interested in them, and then turn this into a desire to speak to them, to say something—if you develop the feeling with purity of heart and let the question arise out of the interest you took in them—then the question or the communication remains in your soul, and when you go to sleep it passes over to the dead. Ordinary consciousness as a rule will know little of what is happening, because sleep ensues immediately. But what has thus passed over often remains present in dreams.

In the case of most dreams we have of the dead, in actual content they are misleading. All that happens is that we interpret them incorrectly. We interpret them as messages from the dead, whereas they are nothing but the echoing of the questions or communications we ourselves have directed to the dead. We should not think that the dead are saying something to us in our dream, but should rather see in the dream something that goes out from our own soul to the dead. The dream is the echo of this. If we were sufficiently developed to be conscious of our question or communication to the dead at the moment of going to sleep, it would seem to us as though the dead themselves were speaking—hence the echo in the dream seems as if it were a message from them. In reality, it comes from ourselves. This becomes intelligible only when we understand the nature of clairvoyant connection with the dead. What the dead seem to say to us is really what we are saying to them.

The moment of waking is especially favorable for the dead to approach us. At the moment of waking, a great deal comes from the dead to every human being. A great deal of what we undertake in life is really inspired into us by the dead or by beings of the higher hierarchies, although we attribute it to ourselves, imagining that it comes from our own soul. The life of day draws near, the moment of waking passes quickly by, and we seldom pay heed to the intimate indications that arise out of our soul. And when we do, we are vain enough to attribute them to ourselves. Yet in all this—and in much else that comes out of our own soul—there lives what the dead have to say to us. It is indeed so: what the dead say to us seems to arise out of our own soul. If people knew what life truly is, this knowledge would engender a feeling of reverence and piety toward the spiritual world where we are always living, together with the dead with whom we are connected. We should realize that in much of what we do, the dead are working. The knowledge that around us, like the very air we breathe, there is a spiritual world, that the dead are around us, only we are not able to perceive them—this knowledge must be unfolded in spiritual science not as theory but so that it permeates the soul as inner life. The dead speak to us inwardly, but we interpret our own inner life incorrectly. If we understood it aright, we would know that in our inmost being we are united with the souls of the so-called dead.

Now whether a soul passes through the gate of death in relatively early years or later in life makes a great difference. The death of young children who have loved us is a very different thing from the death of people older than ourselves. Experience of the spiritual world shows that the secret of communion with children who have died can be expressed by saying that in the spiritual sense we do not lose them, they remain with us. When children die in early life they continue to be with us, spiritually with us. I would like to give this to you as a theme for meditation: when little children die they are not lost to us; we do not lose them, they stay with us spiritually. The opposite may be said of older people who die. Those who are older do not lose us. We do not lose little children; elderly people do not lose us. When elderly people die they are strongly drawn to the spiritual world, but this also gives them the power to work into the physical world so that it is easier for them to approach us. True, they withdraw much farther from the physical world than do children who remain near us, but they are endowed with higher faculties of perception than children who die young. Knowledge of different souls in the spiritual world reveals that those who died in old age are able to enter easily into souls on earth; they do not lose the souls on earth. And we do not lose little children, for they remain more or less within the sphere of earthly humanity.

The meaning of the difference can also be considered in another respect. We do not always have sufficient insight into the experiences of the soul on the physical plane. When friends die, we mourn and feel pain. I have often said that it is not the task of anthroposophy to offer people shallow consolation for their pain or try to talk them out of their sorrow when good friends pass away. One should grow strong enough to bear sorrow and not allow oneself to be talked out of it. But people do not distinguish whether the sorrow is caused by the death of a child or of one who is elderly. Spiritually perceived, there is a very great difference. When little children have died, the pain of those who remain behind is really a kind of compassion—no matter whether the children were their own or others they loved. Children remain with us, and because we have been united with them they convey their pain to our souls. We feel their pain—that they would still be here! Their pain is eased when we bear it with them. The child feels in us, shares its feeling with us, and it is good that it should be so; the pain is thereby ameliorated.

On the other hand, the pain we feel at the death of elderly people, whether relatives or friends, can be called egotistical pain. Elderly persons who have died do not lose us, and the feeling they have is therefore different from the feeling present in a child. Those who die in later life do not lose us. We here in life feel that we have lost them—the pain is therefore *ours;* it is egotistical pain. We do not share their feeling as we do in the case of children; we feel the pain for ourselves.

A clear distinction can therefore be made between these two forms of pain: egotistical pain in connection with the elderly; pain fraught with compassion in connection with children. Children live on in us and we actually feel what they feel. In reality, our own soul mourns only for those who die in the later years of their life.

Something like this can show us the immense significance of knowledge of the spiritual world. For you see, the divine service for the dead can be adapted in accordance with these truths. In the case of a child who has died, it will not be altogether appropriate to emphasize the individual aspect. Because the child lives on in us and remains with us, the service of remembrance should take a more universal form, giving the child, who is still near us, something that is wide and universal. Therefore in the case of a child, a simple ceremony in the service is preferable to a special funeral oration. The Catholic ritual is better here in one case, the Protestant in the other. The Catholic service includes no funeral oration but consists in ceremony, in ritual. It is general, universal, alike for all. And what can be alike for all is especially good for children. But in the case of one who has died in later years, the individual aspect is more important. The best funeral service here will be one in which the life of the individual is remembered. The Protestant service, with the oration referring to the life of the one who has died, will have great significance for the soul; the Catholic ritual will mean less in such a case.

The same distinction holds good for all our thought about those who have died. It is best for children when we induce a mood of feeling connected with them; we try to turn our thoughts to them, and these thoughts will draw near to them when we sleep. Such thoughts may be of a more general kind—ones, for example, that could be directed to all those who have passed through the gate of death. In the case of elderly people, we must direct our thoughts to remembrance of them as individuals, thinking about their life on earth and experiences we shared with them. To establish the right communication with older people, it is very important to visualize them as they actually were, to make their being come to life in ourselves—not only by remembering things they said that meant a great deal to us but by thinking of what they were as individuals and what their value was for the world. If we make these things inwardly alive, they will enable us to come into connection with an older person who has died and to have the right thoughts of remembrance. So you see, for the unfolding of true piety it is important to know what attitude should be taken toward those who have died in childhood and to those who have died in the later years of life.

Just think what it means at the present time, when so many human beings are dying comparatively early, to be able to say to oneself: They are really always present, they are not lost to the world. (I have spoken of this from other points of view, for such matters must always be considered from different angles.) If we succeed in becoming conscious of the spiritual world, one realization at least will light up in us out of the deep sorrow with which the present days are fraught: Because those who die young remain with us, a living spiritual life can arise through communion with the dead. A living spiritual life can and will arise, if only materialism is not allowed to become so strong that Ahriman is able to stretch out his claws and gain the victory over all human powers.

Many people may say, speaking purely of conditions on the physical plane, that what I have been indicating here seems very remote. They would prefer to be told definitely what they can do in the morning and evening to bring themselves into a right relation with the spiritual world. But this is not quite correct thinking. Where the spiritual world is concerned, the first essential is that we should develop thoughts about it. And even if it seems as though the dead are far away, while immediate life is close at hand, the very fact that we have such thoughts and that we allow our minds to dwell on things seemingly remote from external life, uplifts the soul, gives it spiritual strength and spiritual nourishment. Do not, therefore, be afraid of thinking these thoughts through again and again, continually bringing them to new life within the soul. *There is nothing more important for life, even for material life, than the strong and sure realization of communion with the spiritual world.*

If modern people had not lost their relationship with spiritual things to such an extent, these grave times would not have come upon us. Only a very few today have insight into this connection, although it will certainly be recognized in the future. People think nowadays that when human beings pass through the gate of death, their activity ceases as far as the physical world is concerned. But indeed it is not so! There is a living and perpetual exchange between the so-called dead and the so-called living. Those who have passed through the gate of death have not ceased to be present; it is only that our eyes have ceased to see them. They are there in very truth.

Our thoughts, our feelings, our impulses of will, are all connected with the dead. The words of the Gospel hold good for the dead as well: "The kingdom of the Spirit cometh not with observation" (that is to say, external observation); "neither shall they say, Lo here, lo there, for, behold, the kingdom of the Spirit is within you." We should not seek the dead through externalities but become conscious that they are always present. All historical life—all social life, all ethical life—proceeds by virtue of cooperation between the so-called living and the so-called dead. The whole of our being can be infinitely strengthened when we are not only conscious of our firm stand here in the physical world but are also filled with the inner realization of being able to say of the dead whom we have loved: they are with us, they are in our midst.

This, too, is part of a true knowledge and understanding of the spiritual world that must, as it were, be woven together from many different threads. We cannot say that we *know* the spiritual world until the way we think and speak about it comes from that world itself.

The dead are in our midst. These words in themselves are an affirmation of the spiritual world. Only the spiritual world itself can awaken within us the consciousness that in very truth the dead are with us.

9

IN THE FOLLOWING LECTURES, Steiner becomes simpler, more direct, and even more concrete. He begins with the assumption that the dead—along with the whole spiritual world—are present and participate in our world. He lays the foundations for an active community of earth and heaven, visible and invisible. First he affirms that this community—this interpenetration of spiritual and "physical"—already exists, and has always existed, despite the fact that we are presently unaware of it. In a certain sense, earlier human beings lived much closer to the spiritual worlds than we do. Whereas today we are closer to freedom, our physical organization is "coarser" and does not allow us—without intentional effort—to think, feel, or perceive to the degree that we could. A side effect of this is that we enter the spiritual world at death with many unfulfilled thoughts, feelings, and perceptions. Previously, human beings passed through the gates of death having accomplished most of what they were supposed to. Not so with us; we arrive with much to do. Above all, we arrive with the freedom to experience certain thoughts, feelings, and perceptions for the first time. This is an incentive to maintain and cultivate a relationship with our dead, so that their unfulfilled thoughts, feelings, and perceptions may pass through our souls into the world. Our

*task, therefore, is to draw these thoughts into our souls,
to open our souls to them. To do this, we must discipline
our soul lives so that we may share a common ground
with the dead. This means that we must begin to exercise control over our souls so that their natural forces do
not dissipate in idle, chattering thoughts, egotistic feelings, and so forth. Above all, we must learn to empty
ourselves and to wait for thoughts, insights, feelings to
arise from the soul depths, where we touch the universal
spirit—the cosmic world of thoughts—that we share
with the dead. Cultivating this inner quiet will help us
touch this universal, surging "sea," or "web," of
thought in which we and the earthly world are submerged. If we are able to cultivate the presence of this
world within us, we will share a common sphere with
the dead that they can enter. Once we become aware of
this, we can begin to notice the many other points at
which our lives touch this sphere. Chance encounters,
synchronicities, and seemingly accidental occurrences
begin to indicate another world. Too often, we forget to
look for the unconscious and unthought in the "outer"
world. In fact, there is an "underground thought" that
encompasses both inner and outer. Becoming aware of
this, our lives become richer, wider, deeper. Thereby, we
come closer to the dead. We learn to unite with them in
interest and love. We learn to wait for them to speak. We .
allow them to complete their lives on earth.*

Uniting with the Universal Spirit

BERLIN, MARCH 5, 1918

... From various facts brought before our souls by spiritual science, we know that the human spirit also goes through its own
evolution in the course of earthly evolution. We know further
that we can know *ourselves* only if we ask in a fruitful way: What is
our relationship in any incarnation—say, our present incarnation—to the spiritual world, to the spiritual realms? That is,
what common evolutionary stage has humanity attained at the
point when we ourselves live a particular incarnation?

We know that a more detailed observation of our common
human evolution brings us to the insight that in earlier times
and epochs what we have called "atavistic clairvoyance" was
poured out over humanity, and that the human soul was then, in
a certain way, closer to the spiritual worlds. But it was at the same
time further from its own freedom, its own free will, while we in
our age are closer to freedom but more shut off from the spiritual worlds. Anyone who knows the real nature of present-day
humanity must acknowledge that the old relation to the whole
spiritual world persists, unconsciously, in the really spiritual
aspect of human beings. People today are generally unable to be
consciously aware of it (there are exceptions) in the way that was
possible in earlier epochs. If we ask why people can no longer
bring this relationship to the spiritual world into consciousness—by nature, as I said, it is as strong as ever, though in a different mode—we find the reason is that we have passed the
midpoint of earthly evolution and are now in a descending current. Our physical organization (though this is not perceptible
to external anatomy and physiology) has become more "physical" than it was, so that during the time we spend between birth
(conception) and death, we are no longer organized to bring
fully to consciousness our connection with the spiritual world.
We must clearly understand that we experience very much more

subconsciously than we can generally be conscious of—and the more materialistic we are, the truer this is.

The implications of this go even further. And here I come to a very important point in the present development of humanity. *At present, generally speaking, human beings cannot think, perceive, or feel all that actually could be thought, perceived, and felt within them. We are gifted for far more intensive thoughts and perceptions than the coarse materiality of our organism allows us to achieve.* Consequently, we are not in a position to bring our capacities to complete development during our earthly lives. Whether we die young or old has very little influence on that. Whether young or old it is the rule that, because of the coarse substance of our organism, we cannot fully accomplish all that we could if our bodies were more finely organized. Thus, whether we are young or old when we pass through the gate of death, we all leave behind certain unexercised thoughts, feelings, and perceptions. These unprocessed thoughts, feelings, and perceptions are there, and when we pass through the gate of death, whether young or old, we feel an impulse to return to earthly life for further thinking, feeling, and perceiving.

Consider some of the implications of this. *After death, we become free to form certain thoughts, feelings, and perceptions for the first time.* We could have done much more on the earth if we could have fully realized all these thoughts, feelings, and perceptions during our physical lives. But we could not. It is a fact that in our present condition we could do far more on earth than we actually do. In earlier evolutionary times, the situation was different. The human organism was finer, a certain conscious looking into the spiritual world was present, and people could work out of the spirit. During those times, people could, as a rule, accomplish everything for which their gifts fitted them. Today, though we may be proud of our gifts, the facts are as I have described.

Since this is so, we can see how necessary it is today that what those who have died carry through the gate of death unprocessed should not be lost to earthly life. The only way to prevent this loss is by cultivating and maintaining a true relationship with the dead. We can do this by making the effort to become fully conscious—under the guidance of spiritual science—of our relationship to those among the dead with whom we are linked by karmic ties. If we do this, the unfulfilled thoughts of the dead pass through our souls into the world, and in this way we can allow these stronger thoughts—which are possible for the dead because they are free from the body—to work in our souls. Though we cannot bring our own thoughts to full development, these thoughts can be effective.

We can see from this that the course of events that brought us materialism should make us realize how absolutely necessary it is for us now and in the near future to seek a true relationship with the spirits of the dead. The only question is, *How can we draw these thoughts, perceptions, and feelings from the realm of the dead into our own souls?*

I have already spoken of this from different points of view. In the last lecture I mentioned two important moments that should be well observed: the moments of going to sleep and of waking up. Today, I will describe in greater detail a few things connected with this.

The dead cannot enter directly the world we inhabit in our ordinary waking lives—the world that we perceive from outside, that touches our desires, and in which we act through our will. Once the dead have passed through the gate of death, they are removed from this world. Yet we can have a world in common with them if, spurred on by spiritual science, we make the effort—which is difficult in our materialistic times—to discipline our thinking and our outer life, and not to allow them their customary free course. We can develop certain faculties that give us a common ground with the spirits who have passed through the gate of death. There are, of course, a great many hindrances at the present time to finding this common ground. The first hindrance is that we are, as a rule, too extravagant, too lavish with our thought life. I might even say: we are excessive in our thought life.

What exactly do I mean by this? Today people live almost exclusively under the influence of the German saying, "Thoughts pay no toll." That is to say, one can allow almost anything to gush out in thoughts. Just remember that speaking is an image of thought life. Consider therefore what sort of thought life is involved when people chatter and wander from subject to subject, allowing thoughts to flash up at will. This means that we are squandering the force that gives us thinking! We do this all the time. We are endlessly extravagant, excessive in our thought life. We allow ourselves any thought whatsoever. We want something that pleases us, or we let it go for something else. In short, we don't want to keep our thoughts under control. How unpleasant it is sometimes when people begin to talk and we listen for a minute or two—and then they change the subject. We want to keep to the original topic—indeed, it may be important. So we have to remind ourselves, What was it we were talking about? Such things happen every day. Just when the talk ought to be serious, we have to struggle to remember how it began. This dissipation of thought force prevents us from receiving the thoughts that come from the depths of soul life and are not our own, but are rather thoughts we have in common with the spiritual realm—the universal ruling Spirit. The impulse to fly as we like from thought to thought does not allow us to wait receptively for thoughts to arise from the depths of the soul—to wait for *insight*, if I may so express it. This attitude, however, is something we need to cultivate, especially in our time. We really need to create the disposition in our soul that allows us to wait watchfully, until from far down in the soul thoughts arise that clearly distinguish themselves as *given*, not of our own making.

We must not suppose that the creation of such a mood can occur overnight. But when we cultivate it, when we really take the trouble simply to be watchful and, having driven out arbitrary thoughts, wait for inspiration, the mood gradually develops. Then it becomes possible to receive thoughts from the depths of the soul, from a wider world than our own ego. If we really develop this capacity, we shall soon see that the world does not consist only of what we see and hear and perceive with our outer senses—and the combinations we build up through our reason—but that there is also an objective web of thoughts. Very few people today know this through personal experience.

Yet this experience of a universal web of thought, within which the soul is actually immersed, is not some kind of special occult experience. It is something that all of us can have if we develop the mood I have described. Anyone who has had this experience will express it something like this: "In everyday life I stand in the world that I perceive with my senses and assemble with the help of my reason; but then I reach a point when it is as if, standing on the shore of sense existence, I plunge into the sea and swim in the surging water. Standing on the shore I can plunge into the surging sea of thought. Then I am really as though in a surging sea." At this point, one has the feeling (or at least the inkling) of a life that is stronger and more intense than the life of dreams. Yet the boundary separating this life from the sense world is similar in kind to the boundary between the sense world and the life of dreams.

We can, if we like, refer to such experiences as dreams, but they are not dreams! For the world into which we plunge, this world of surging thoughts that are not our thoughts but thoughts we are submerged in, is the world out of which our physical sense world arises, out of which it condenses, so to speak. Our physical sense world is like blocks of ice floating in water: the water is all around; the ice congeals and floats in it. Just as the ice consists of the same substance as the water (only it is brought into a different physical condition), so our physical sense world arises from this surging, undulating sea of thought. That is its true origin. Physics speaks of "ether," of whirling atoms, only because it does not know of this primordial substance. Shakespeare is nearer to it when he has one of his characters say, in effect, "We are such stuff as dreams are made of." People give themselves too easily to all kinds of deceptions in this respect. They want to find a crude atomic world behind physical reality, but if we are to speak of anything at all behind physical reality, we must speak of an objective web of thought, an objective thought world. However, we can arrive at this only if we stop letting our thoughts go to waste and instead develop the mood that comes when we can wait for what is popularly called "inspiration."

It is not so difficult for those who study spiritual science to develop this mood. The way of thinking that one must develop to do spiritual science leads the soul toward it. When we study spiritual science seriously, we feel the need to develop this intimate web of thought within ourselves. It is this web of thought that provides us with the common sphere where we and the so-called dead are both present, we on one side, they on the other. The web is the common ground where we can "meet" the dead. The dead cannot enter the world that we perceive with our senses and build up with our reason, but they can enter the world that I have just described.

There is a second way to find common ground with the dead, which I spoke of last year.[1] It depends on noticing the finer, more intimate connections that arise in our lives. I gave an example to be found in psychological literature: Schubert calls attention to it.[2] It is taken from old literature, but such examples can still often be found in life. A man was accustomed to taking a certain daily walk. One day, when he reached a certain spot, he had an impulse to step to the side and stand still, and the thought came to him whether it was right to waste time with this walk. At that moment, a boulder that had split from the cliff above him fell on the road and would certainly have struck him had his thought not caused him to turn aside.

This is a crude experience, which anyone would notice if it occurred. But similar experiences of a subtler kind press into

---

1. Lectures of December 9 and 10, 1917. In *Geschichtliche Notwendigkeit und Freiheit, Schicksalseinwirkungen aus der Welt der Toten*, GA179, "Historical Necessity and Free Will." (Typescript only.)

2. Gotthilf Heinrich Schubert (1780–1860), doctor and natural scientist.

our ordinary lives every day. As a rule we do not notice them. We consider only what actually happens, not what might have happened had it not been averted. We do not reckon with what happens when we are detained at home and go out for a walk a quarter of an hour later than we intended. Often, in such cases, we would notice something very significant if only we were ready to reflect how different things would have been if we had not been detained and had left the house a quarter of an hour earlier.

Try to observe systematically in your own life what might have happened had you not been delayed a few minutes by somebody coming in, though at the time, perhaps, you were very angry at being detained. Things are constantly impinging on our lives, perhaps making them turn out differently than they might have according to our original plans. We seek a "causal connection" between events in life. We do not reflect upon life with that subtle discernment that would reveal the breaking of a probable chain of events, so that an atmosphere of possibilities continuously surrounds us.

If we pay attention to this, then, if we are delayed by ten minutes in doing something we have been accustomed to do at midday, we will have a feeling that what we do at that time is often— not always—under the influence not just of what happened before, but also of countless other things that have not happened, from which we have been held back. By thinking of what is possible in life—not only in the outer world of sense—we are led to the impression that seeking the connection of what follows with what has gone before is a very one-sided way of looking at life. If we truly ask ourselves such questions, we arouse something within us that would otherwise remain dormant in our mind. We begin, as it were, to read between the lines of life. We come to know life as multifaceted. We come to see ourselves, so to speak, in the midst of our environment, and we see how it forms us and leads us forward incrementally. This is something we usually observe far too little. We consider, at most, only the inner driving forces that lead us from stage to stage.

Let us now consider some simple ordinary instance that may show how we connect the outer world with our inner being only in a very fragmentary way.

Turn your attention to the way you usually become aware of waking in the morning. If you think about it, you will find that you have a very vague notion of how you make yourself get up in the morning; perhaps even the concept of it is quite nebulous. Try, however, to reflect for a few days in succession on the thought that drives you out of bed. Try to grasp this thought in full clarity. For example, yesterday I got up because I heard the coffee being prepared in the next room: this gave me the impulse to get up. Today, it was something else. What was the *external* cause? That is the point to be quite clear about.

Usually, we forget to look for *ourselves* in the outer world. Therefore, we find so little of ourselves there. Anyone who gives even a little attention to such things will easily develop a mood that people today have such a holy terror of—I should say, an *unholy* terror—a mood that compels us to realize that there is at least an *underground thought* at the basis of our life that does not enter our ordinary lives. We enter a room, for instance, or go somewhere, but we seldom ask ourselves how the place changes when we enter it.

At times, other people may notice or have an idea of this, but even that is not very widespread today. I do not know how many people have any perception of the fact that when a group is in a room, one person is often twice as strongly present as another; one person is strongly there, another weakly.

This is something that depends on imponderables. We may easily experience the following. Someone is at a social gathering; he or she enters quietly and glides out again—you have the feeling that an angel flitted in and out. Another person's presence is so powerful that he or she is not present only with two physical feet, as it were, but with all sorts of invisible feet. The other people, however, do not as a rule notice this, although it is quite perceptible. The actual individual may not notice it at all. We do not usually hear the undertone arising from the change called forth by our presence. We keep to ourselves and do not inquire of our surroundings what change our presence produces. Yet an inkling of the echo of this presence in our surroundings is something we can come to feel. Just think how our outer lives would gain in intimacy if we not only peopled a place with our presence but learned to feel how the place was changed by our being there.

That is only one example. Similar examples could be drawn from all situations in life. In other words, it is quite possible— not by constantly treading on our own toes but in a quite healthy way—to become concretely aware of our surroundings *so that we feel the difference we make in them.* If we could do this, we would learn to acquire the beginnings of a sensitivity to karma. Indeed, if we could perceive fully what comes about through our deeds or presence—if we always saw the reflection of our own deeds and existence in our surroundings—then we would feel our karma, for karma is woven of this experience.

Here, I will point only to the enrichment of life that comes from cultivating such intimacies. By learning to read between the lines, we learn to look at life in such a way that we are consciously aware—and aware with our *conscience*—that we are there. Through this awareness, we do something to create a realm that we can enjoy in common with the dead. And when we develop this inner mood, which looks up to the two pillars I have described—a conscious mode of life and an economical (not extravagant) habit of thought—then we shall achieve what is necessary, now and in the future, for successfully drawing near the dead.

If we then form thoughts and connect them with a dead person, aiming not merely at a union of thoughts, but at a union of feeling and interest; if we carry our thoughts further into life situations we shared with that person, so that a tone of feeling plays between us; if we relate our thoughts to occasions when we were concerned with how the person thought, lived, and acted, and with the interest we aroused in him or her—then we can use such occasions *to carry the conversation further,* as it were.

If we then allow these thoughts to rest quietly, so that we pass into a kind of meditation, and bring our thoughts, as it were, to the altar of inner spiritual life, then a moment will come when we receive an answer from the dead: when the dead can again reach an understanding with us. We need only build a bridge between the thoughts we unfold toward the dead person and those by which he or she can return to us. For this returning it will be especially useful to build up in the deepest part of our souls a picture of that individual essential soul being. This is something quite foreign to the present time, for, as I have said, people pass one another by, often coming together in the most intimate spheres of life and parting again without knowing one another. This coming to know another person does not depend on analysis. Those who feel themselves being analyzed by someone living with them feel, if they are sensitive, as though they have received a blow. It is of no significance to analyze one another. The best knowledge of another is gained through harmony of heart. There is no need for analysis.

I started by saying that the cultivation of relations with the so-called dead is especially needed today because, not from choice, but simply through the evolution of humanity, we live in an epoch of materialism. Because we are not able to cultivate fully all our capacities for thought, feeling, and perception before we die, because something remains undeveloped when we pass through the gate of death, it is necessary for the living to maintain the right connection with the dead, so that ordinary life may be enriched. If only we could bring into human hearts today the fact that life is impoverished when the dead are forgotten! But the right way of thinking about the dead can be developed only by those who are in some way connected with them by karma.

When we strive for direct communication with the dead, similar to communication with the living—if we cultivate communication with the dead in this way—the dead are really present, and their thoughts, not completed in their own lifetime, will work into this life. All this certainly makes a very

exacting demand on our age. However, if one is convinced by
spiritual facts, it must be said that our social, ethical, and religious lives would be endlessly enriched if the living allowed
themselves to be advised by the dead. Today, people do not
want to consult even those who have reached a mature age.
Nowadays, it is thought to be quite right for members of a town
or state council to be as young as possible, since at that age—in
their own opinion—they are already mature enough for anything. In the days when there was a better knowledge of
human nature, a person would have had to reach a certain age
before serving on any council. Now people have to wait until
others are dead to receive advice from them! Nevertheless, our
epoch in particular ought to be willing to heed the counsel of
the dead. Improvement will come only when people are willing to listen to their advice....

10

THE DEAD ALREADY LIVE the future conditions of human existence, which Steiner calls "Jupiter" existence. This makes their functioning somewhat more difficult to understand than the spiritual beings whose nature we can understand (in a certain sense) by reading descriptions of them. Nevertheless, communion with the dead is possible and, since we are also preparing for our future conditions, such communication is part of our evolutionary task. From this point of view, the first capacity to be acquired is a "feeling of community" with everything that exists. This feeling of community with the world must become a concrete experience in our lives. We must come to realize that we leave our mark on all that we encounter, and that we remain connected in our subconscious with everything with which we come into contact. This fact also underlies karma; it provides the basis for our general feeling of community with the world. We are able to have this feeling, because we have left our mark everywhere. As we become aware of this, we also become conscious of the invisible bond that unites all things. This feeling of community with everything is fundamental for both Jupiter existence and the life of the dead. For the most part, we lack any real sense of this today. We live primarily for ourselves. We have no sense that the welfare of the individual, when it has nothing to do with the welfare of the community, has no

*justification. This must become the fundamental prin-
ciple of ethics: we are all connected. We must begin to
understand the sense in which humanity constitutes a
single organism. If we can begin to understand this—
to develop a sense of community—we can begin to live
with others as if they were ourselves. The ability to
attune so closely to another that we can think, feel, and
imagine acting as they do is a great aid in establishing
the larger community of the living and the dead. One
way to do this is to reexperience a shared event from the
other's point of view. Only from this place of community can the dead bring themselves into our consciousness, for they can speak only toward this "place of
community." Of course, it is necessary to hear what they
speak, as they speak it. For this, Rudolf Steiner tells us
we must pay attention to the "air" between us and the
dead. There must be a medium, an intermediary. The
creation of this medium can begin with the mood of
gratitude. Subconsciously, we already experience this
sense of gratitude for every impression life brings us.
Subconsciously, we receive each impression as a gift. We
must pay attention to this sense of gratitude beneath the
surface of our consciousness. As we do this, we begin to
realize that the sense of gratitude is linked to the awareness that we are dreaming all the time; beneath waking
life, dream life continues. And through this dream element, the dead can begin to speak. They speak into the
"intimate, subconscious perceptions that occur on their*

own," for which we must be grateful, and which, in a
sense, we discover through the practice of gratitude
itself. Ultimately, in fact, we are led to the conviction that
all of life is a gift. Within our conviction that life is a
gift, the dead find a sure and common ground with us.
Hence, if we cannot find and develop the feeling of grat-
itude the dead cannot find us.

The Feeling of Community
and the Experience
of Gratitude

BERLIN, MARCH 19, 1918

...We always have a relationship to the spiritual world and we always have a certain relationship with those among the dead who are karmically united with us. Nevertheless, it is one thing to speak of the "reality" of such a relationship, and another to speak of the degree of awareness we may have in relation to it. It is important for everyone—even those who feel quite remote from any awareness of such a relationship—to experience what those who have this consciousness speak of, because they are realities that always surround us.

We must clearly understand, however, that the relationship between the so-called living and the so-called dead is in some ways more difficult to bring to awareness than is our relationship to other beings of the spiritual world. Through seeing inwardly, it is easier to become aware of beings of the higher hierarchies, and even to find them distinctly revealed, than to become aware of a definitive relationship with those who have died — that is, to become truly conscious of them in the right way.

This is because between death and rebirth we pass through states that are very different from our life's relationships in the physical world. Just look at the course of lectures on the life between death and rebirth. You can see that, in speaking of life after death, we must use thoughts and concepts that are quite different from those we apply to the physical world.[1] Why must they be so different? Between death and rebirth, we anticipate, as it were, certain conditions that will manifest as conditions of life only during the earth's next embodiment (the phase of cosmic evolution termed *Jupiter*). During our evolutionary stage, a person's experiences between death and rebirth anticipate the life conditions of the Jupiter stage of evolution, though in a form more subtle and spiritualized. In our present earthly lives, we retain something of the earth's earlier Moon, Sun, and Saturn embodiments; likewise, during our life between death and rebirth, we receive something that is part of the future. The beings of the higher hierarchies on the other hand (to the degree that we can examine them with human perception) are naturally united, immediately and presently, with the whole spiritual world as it now passes through a particular form. In the future they will reveal the future. Although this may sound contradictory, it is a fact.

It sounds paradoxical because we must ask, How can the beings of the higher hierarchies actively affect the dead if the dead already bear something of the future within themselves. Of course, the beings of the higher hierarchies also carry something of the future within themselves and are able to shape it. But they also shape something that is immediately characteristic of the present. Therefore, a perception of what the higher hierarchies accomplish constitutes a preparation for becoming

---

1. Rudolf Steiner, *The Inner Nature of Man and the Life between Death and Rebirth*, London: Rudolf Steiner Press, 1994.

aware of communication with those who have died. Not until we have brought about a more or less conscious perception in our soul of the beings of the higher hierarchies will it be possible for us gradually to become conscious, through our faculties of perception and feeling, of anything having to do with communication with the dead. I do not mean that we must become aware of the higher hierarchies in a clairvoyant way. But we must understand what flows into existence from them, to the degree that spiritual science makes this possible. In all these things, it is our *understanding* that is primary. If we take the trouble to understand the hierarchies through spiritual science, conditions of existence can certainly arise that call up something like a union of the so-called living with the so-called dead. If we wish to understand this, however, we must remember that the spiritual world (in which human beings dwell between death and rebirth) has its own special conditions of existence—conditions we can scarcely imagine in our ordinary earthly lives. They sound strange and paradoxical when presented to us as part of a general picture.

Mostly, we must remember that one who wishes to experience such things with awareness must acquire something we might call a *feeling of community* with everything in existence. A requirement for our continued spiritual evolution—from our own disastrous time on—is that we gradually develop this *feeling of community* with all that exists. A lower variation of this feeling is well-established in the human subconscious. We must not, however, chatter pantheistically about some "universal spirit." We must not speak of some general feeling of unity; we must be clear, concrete, and specific about how to speak of it and how it is gradually established in the soul, because this feeling of unity is an *experience* in life.

We often hear that criminals (in whom instinctive subconsciousness works very strongly) have a peculiar urge after committing a crime; they are drawn back to the scene of the crime. A vague feeling drives them to return. This phenomenon reveals a common human trait. When we have accomplished something, regardless of how unimportant it seems, some part of what we have learned during the process remains in us. Some of the forces with which we acted remain connected with the I. This cannot be put any other way, though the way I put it, of course, is only a kind of imagination. We cannot avoid forming certain connections with all the beings we meet and the things we take up (not only physical things, naturally). I am speaking of the things we have some relationship to in life. We each leave our distinctive mark on everything we encounter, and a feeling of connection with those things we have contacted through our actions remains in our subconscious. For criminals, this is expressed abnormally, because their subconscious flashes up very instinctively into ordinary consciousness. But all of us sense in our subconscious that we must return to those places we have encountered through our activities.

This, too, is basic to our karma, which arises from it. From this subconscious feeling, at first only nebulous, we have a general feeling of community with the world. We feel this way because we leave our mark everywhere. We can comprehend this feeling, sense it, and perceive it. First, however, we must pay attention to certain intimacies of life. For example, when about to cross a street, we must try to really go into the idea: I am now crossing a street. Then once we have walked across the street, we continue to imagine ourselves crossing it. By continued exercises like this we evoke, from the depths of our soul, a general feeling of community with the world. As consciousness of this feeling of community grows more concrete, it will continue to develop so that, eventually, one thinks, *There really is a connection, though invisible, between all things—a connection like that between the members of a single organism.* Just as the finger, the earlobes, and indeed every part of our organism are connected with each other, there is also a connection between everything and every event in our world.

Modern earthly humanity does not yet have a fully valid consciousness of this feeling of community with all things, an organic penetration into phenomena; it remains unconscious. But in the Jupiter stage of evolution, this feeling will be fundamental, and we are preparing for this as we pass gradually from the fifth to the sixth post-Atlantean era. But this feeling of community must be cultivated now and in the immediate future; it must begin to provide morals and ethics with a definite foundation, morals much more actively related to daily life than today.

I mean, for example, that many people today think nothing of enriching themselves at the expense of others. Not only do they live like this—with no moral self-criticism—but they simply do not give it a thought. If people were to reflect upon it, they would discover that they live far more at the cost of others than they ever realized. In fact, every one of us lives at the expense of others. In the future, the consciousness will arise that living life at the expense of others has the same effect on a community that an organ has on the body when it develops inappropriately at the expense of another organ. People will realize that individual welfare is really impossible apart from the welfare of the community. Today, of course, there is no inkling of this, but it must gradually become the fundamental principle of true human ethics. Today, people all strive for their own welfare, never thinking that, essentially, individual welfare is possible only in common with that of everyone else. Thus, there is a connection between the feeling of community I have mentioned and the feeling that the life of the whole community is an organism.

The feeling of the whole community as an organism can be enhanced greatly and lead to an intimate feeling of community with all that surrounds us. By enhancing this intimate feeling, we gradually gain the ability to perceive what I described in the previous lecture as the light shining out beyond death into our evolution between death and rebirth—a light we perceive and with which we build our karma.[2] I want to give a mere hint of this. When we develop this feeling of community, we can do something else as well—we can live with the idiosyncrasies, situations,

---

2. That lecture was given in Berlin on March 5, 1918, and is unavailable in English.

thoughts, and actions of others as though they were our own. This is related to a certain difficulty in the soul life, one of attuning our thoughts so closely to another that whatever the other does, thinks, and feels is felt as our own experience. And we are ready to reach the discarnate individual only when we are able to think back fruitfully to what we had in common with the one to whom we were karmically united. This can happen only when we are able to reexperience what we experienced in common with that other soul, even the slightest detail, and to think of it as one thinks when one has this feeling of community.

We can picture it this way: we think of something that took place between ourselves and one who has died—how we sat at a table with that person, or whatever, no matter how insignificant. But the possibility of entering this experience in the right way—so that we get through to the reality—will only come to our soul when it is truly suffused with that feeling of community. It will lack the necessary strength otherwise. We must understand that the dead can bring themselves into our consciousness only from a place over which we have cast this "feeling of community." We can imagine this spatially. However, we must, of course, remain aware that we are forming only a image of it, but that this image is a picture of a reality.

Going back to what I said before, we visualize a situation in which we were together with the one who died, how we sat at table with that person or how we walked together. Turn your whole soul life toward this thought. If in thought we can develop a soul communion with the dead that is in harmony with the "feeling of community," then our gaze toward the spiritual world can find its way from these thoughts to the reality, just as our thoughts find the reality to which they are directed. If you allow these loving thoughts of the dead person to permeate your soul, then your inward gaze can encounter that soul's gaze. In this way the one who has died can speak to you. But that speech can come only from the place toward which you direct your feeling of community with that person. This is how these things are connected. We learn to feel our karma, so to speak, when we gain an idea of how we leave behind everywhere the stamp of our thoughts; by learning to identify ourselves with such ideas, we develop the feeling that brings us increasingly conscious union with those who have died. Thus they are finally able to speak to us.

The other requirement is that we should be able to hear what is said and really perceive it when it occurs. We must, above all, pay attention to what exists as air, so to speak, between us and the dead, so that they can speak to us across it. To use a physical analogy, if the space between us were airless, you would be unable to hear me; air acts as a medium. Likewise, there must be something between us and the dead before they can approach us; there must be "spiritual air." We can speak now about the nature of this spiritual air in which we live with the dead. What does it consist of?

To understand this we must recall what I said in other connections about how human memory works, because these matters are all related. Conventional psychology speaks of human memory in one way. For example, I now receive an impression from the external world. It evokes a concept in me, and somehow that concept goes into my subconscious, where it is forgotten. But then a particular occasion arises, it returns from the subconscious, and I remember. Almost all psychologists believe that a concept arises in us in response to an impression that was quickly forgotten, having sunk into the subconscious until an incident recalls it; then we "remember." We think we have recalled the concept that we formed initially. This is complete nonsense. It is a bit of nonsense taught in almost all psychology, but nonsense nonetheless. What this describes does not take place at all.

When we receive an impression through an outer experience and remember it later, it is not at all the same concept we first formed that rises within us. As we form the concept, a second subconscious process is taking place. It does not come to consciousness during the outer experience, but it takes place nonetheless. And through a course of events (which we will not speak of just

now), what takes place in our organism today but remains unconscious will take place again tomorrow. Today the outer impressions evoked the concept, and tomorrow the process, which has
continued to work below, evokes a new concept. A concept I have
today passes away and is gone; it no longer stirs my subconscious.
But tomorrow if that same concept arises from my memory, it is
because there is something in me that evokes that same concept.
Now, however, it is generated subconsciously. If we imagine that
concepts are taken into the subconscious, move about there, and
finally emerge from the soul, we should be able to recall what
happens if we write out something that we want to remember
three days later. Do we remain in the notebook and emerge from
it after three days? The notebook contains only signs, and memory contains only signs that evoke a repetition of what we experienced, though certainly in a weaker form.[3]

People who memorize or otherwise try to instill in their mind
something they want to retain—those who "cram," as we called
it when we were young—know quite well that perception alone
is not enough. Sometimes people must resort to external aids
when committing something to memory. Let us observe ourselves when we try to "cram." Let us see what efforts we make to
aid the unconscious activity that comes into it. We want to find a
way to help the subconscious. Here we have two very different
processes—committing something to memory and forming an
immediate concept of it. If we study people and observe their
character, we soon find that even here we are concerned with
two kinds of people. There are those who grasp things quickly
but have a terrible memory, and there are those whose comprehension is slow but who have a good memory and especially
strong faculties of imagination and judgment. These two things
may be found side by side, and spiritual science must make the
truth of the matter clear.

---

3. For more on the nature of memory, see *An Outline of Esoteric Science*
(pages 39–44) and *Anthroposophy and the Inner Life* (especially lecture 9).

From the time we wake up in the early morning until we fall asleep, we continually perceive something of the world. And when we perceive anything in life, we are more or less conscious of attraction or aversion toward the objects of our perception, and we are usually satisfied once we have grasped something. The activity that leads on to memory, however, is far more extensive than the activity needed to comprehend an impression. Memory takes place at a far more subconscious level in the soul.

This subconscious process, proceeding by itself, often contradicts in a remarkable way what happens consciously. We may feel an aversion toward an impression. The subconscious does not feel that antipathy but usually has feelings that are very different from those of ordinary consciousness. The subconscious develops a remarkable feeling toward all impressions. A phrase from the physical world and applied to the spiritual can be no more than figurative, but here it is appropriate to say that the subconscious develops a certain feeling of "gratitude" toward every impression, regardless of its nature. It is not inaccurate to say that, while your conscious impression of someone may be highly unpleasant—a person may hurl insults in your face— your subconscious impression will still be a certain feeling of gratitude. The simple reason is that anything in life that approaches the deeper aspect of our being, including unpleasant experiences, enriches our life, really enriches it. This has no connection with the way we consciously conduct ourselves toward outer impressions. How we consciously respond to anything has nothing to do with what takes place subconsciously; in the subconscious, everything leads to a certain feeling of thankfulness—there we receive every impression as a gift for which we must be grateful.

It is extraordinarily important to pay attention to these happenings below the threshold of consciousness. This activity that breaks into a feeling of thankfulness works in a similar way to the effect of an impression that comes to us from the outer world and passes into memory; it goes along side by side with the concept.

We can be consciously aware of these things only if we have a distinct feeling that all the time we are awake we are also dreaming. In my public lecture, I said that in our feeling and will we continue to sleep and dream even in waking life. So long as we allow the world to work upon us, we are continually forming our impressions and concepts, but beneath all this we dream about everything, and this dream life is far richer than we think. It is only eclipsed by our conscious concepts, as is a weak light by a stronger.

We can experiment in coming to understand these relationships by paying attention to various intimacies of life. Try the following experiment: suppose you are lying asleep on a sofa and then wake up. Of course you do not observe yourself at that moment, because immediately the world makes various impressions upon you; but it may happen that you lie quiet for a time after waking. Then you may observe that you perceived something before you awoke—you can notice this particularly well if someone had knocked at the door and did not repeat the knock. You can confirm by asking, but when you woke up you *knew* that something had happened; it was apparent from the whole situation.

When we observe something in this way, we are not far from recognizing what spiritual science can verify — that we perceive unconsciously a far wider range of our environment than is possible consciously. It is quite true that if we are walking along a street and meet someone just coming around the corner, we may feel that we had seen the person just before he or she appeared. Quite often we may have a feeling of having seen something happen before it actually occurs. It is indeed a fact that first we have a psychic, spiritual connection with what we later perceive; only we are deafened, as it were, by the later sense perceptions and do not observe what goes on in the intimacies of soul life.

This again is something that takes place of itself subconsciously, like the formation of memory or the feeling of thankfulness toward all surrounding phenomena. The dead can speak to us only through the element that pervades the dreams that are

For &
Lou

interwoven with our life. The dead speak into these intimate, subconscious perceptions that occur on their own. And it is possible for us, given the right conditions, to share with the dead the same spiritual-psychic air. If they wish to speak to us, it is necessary that we take into our consciousness something of the feeling of gratitude for all that reveals itself to us. If there is none of this feeling within us, if we are not able to thank the world for enabling us to live, for enriching our life continually with new impressions, if we cannot deepen our soul by often realizing that our entire life is a gift, then the dead will not find a common air with us, for they can speak with us only through this feeling of gratitude. Otherwise there is a wall between us and them.

Being with souls on the other side

We can see how many obstacles there are to communication with the dead, for, as we know from other connections, it depends on our being karmically united with them. We cannot arouse in ourselves this feeling of gratitude if, having lost them, we wish them back in life; we should be thankful that we had them with us quite irrespective of the fact that we have them no longer. Thus, if we do not have this feeling of gratitude for the beings we wish to approach, they do not find us; or at least they cannot speak to us. The very feelings we so often have toward our nearest dead are a hindrance to their speaking to us. The dead who are not karmically united with us usually have more difficulty in speaking to us; but with those nearest to us, we may feel too little gratitude that they have been something to us in life. We should not cling to the idea that we have them no more, for that is an ungrateful feeling in the wider sense of life. If we clearly understand that the feeling of having lost our dead weighs them down, we will keep in mind the whole import of this. When we lose people we love, we must be able to raise ourselves to a feeling of thankfulness that we have had them; we must be able to think selflessly of what they were to us until their death, and not of what we feel now that we have them no more. The better we can feel what they were to us during their life, the sooner will it be possible for them to speak to us—to speak to us through the common air of gratitude.

11:25. 21
conv. Lane's a
Soviet housekeeping
independence. Kevin -
bi-polar? Usu
thinks non-lasting
Lou called NB
if he not
here why

In order to enter more and more consciously into the world
whence this all comes, many other things are necessary. Suppose you have lost a child. The necessary feeling of companionship can be brought about by picturing to yourself how you sat
and played with the child in such a way that the game was as
interesting to you as it was to him or her. When you can do this,
you have the appropriate feeling of companionship—for playing with a child has meaning only if one is as much a playmate as
the child is. Thus, if we picture ourselves playing with the child
and bring the picture to life, the place is created upon which
both of our gazes can fall. If we are able to grasp what the dead
say, we are in conscious union with them. This, too, can be
brought about by many things.

For many people, thinking is remarkably easy. You will say,
That is not true! Still, there are some who find it very easy; if
people find it difficult, that is really a different feeling. The
very people who most regard thinking as easy, find true
thought most difficult. That is because their thinking is lazy. I
mean that most people take their thinking lightly—one cannot
say *how* lightly—because it is so easy for them to think. All one
can say is that they just think; they do not acquire a single new
idea—that might be too difficult. They merely think; they form
their concepts, then they have them and are content to live
with them. Then other things come along, for example, spiritual science. Spiritual science is not avoided by so many people
because it is difficult to understand, but because a certain
effort is needed to take hold of its ideas; and most people shy
away from this. Anyone who progresses in spiritual science
gradually observes that to comprehend the thoughts it com-
prises requires an application of will, just as much as in weight-
lifting. But people do not want that; they want to think easily.
Those who progress in thinking find themselves thinking more
and more strenuously, more and more laboriously, as it were,
because they learn that to really assimilate a thought, they
must make efforts. Nothing is more favorable for penetrating
the spiritual world than the experience of finding it harder

and harder to grasp the relevant thoughts. Best of all for progress in spiritual science is for people to find they can no longer apply the standards of easy thinking that are customary in daily life, so that they say to themselves: Thinking of this kind is a really exhausting exercise, it takes as much effort as threshing with a flail!

Such a feeling can only be indicated, but it can develop, and this is good and favorable. Many people are so quick with their thinking that it is only necessary to mention a particular point and they grasp its whole context; they always have a ready answer. What would drawing-room conversations amount to if thinking were difficult! We can, however, observe that as we gradually become acquainted with the inner relationships of things, it becomes more difficult to chatter and be ready with an answer; for that comes from easy thinking. When individuals advance in knowledge they become more Socratic, so that they have to strain every nerve to gain the right to express an opinion.

This feeling, that efforts of will go into the grasping of thoughts, is related to another feeling we often have when we commit something to memory by "cramming"—and fail to take in what we should. We can experience the relationship between these two things—the difficulty of retaining something in the memory and the difficulty of exerting an effort of will in order to understand something. We can, however, exercise ourselves in this; we can apply what may be called conscientiousness, a feeling of responsibility toward our thinking. It often happens that when, from a certain experience of life, a person says, for instance, "So-and-so is a good man," the hearer instantly retorts, "An awfully good man." Just think how often a reply is not positive, but comparative. There is of course no reason at all why the answer should be comparative; it comes only from not knowing in the least what to think. We have a feeling that we ought to have had some experience and that we ought to speak of it. Of course, such a demand must not be pressed too far, or in many drawing rooms a great silence would set in.

Still, this feeling—which springs from a sense of responsibility toward thinking and from a recognition that thinking is difficult—opens the way toward the possibility and capacity for receiving inspirations. For an inspiration does not come in the way that thoughts spring up in most people; it always comes when it is as difficult as anything else we find difficult. We must first learn to experience thoughts as difficult, to feel that retaining memories is different from mere thinking. If we do so, we will be able to get a feeling for that weak, dreamlike welling-up of thoughts that do not really want to stay, but would rather vanish—thoughts that are difficult to grasp. We can reinforce ourselves by developing a sense of really living with the thoughts. We must clearly realize what goes on in our soul when we intend, for example, to go somewhere—and get there. As a rule we do not think about this, but we should reflect on what has taken place in the world as a result of our having accomplished our purpose and attained what we had in mind. We should also reflect on what takes place in our soul. Often this comes to expression quite strikingly. When mountaineers, for instance, have to exert themselves strenuously to reach a summit and, finally arriving, exclaim breathlessly, "Thank God, I am here!" we feel how the emotions have responded. In this way, we can acquire an even finer perception, and this delicate perception lives on in the intimacy of the soul.

When one begins to recall a shared situation with a friend who has died, trying to unite in thinking and feeling with that friend, the feeling of being on a kind of journey arises. Then a moment comes when one feels as though pausing for a rest after a long walk. This pause can be of tremendous help toward the inspiration such a thought can offer. We can also prepare for inspiration through thoughts by recollecting the *whole person*, not just the aspect generally expressed in that person's life. Doing this leads naturally to a stronger and more intimate form of such an experience. Those who succeed in bringing into their consciousness the feeling of *gratitude*—which would otherwise remain unconscious—will immediately notice that, unlike ordinary gratitude, this gratitude works in such a way that one can unite with the whole person, at least as far as the arms and hands.

Here, I must remind you of what I have already said—about how ordinary concepts are grasped by the brain, but more intimate ideas pass through it as through a sieve, because the hands and arms are in fact organs for apprehending them. One can experience this. Of course, we need not express it externally, but when faced with certain impressions in life, we feel that this gratitude and similar feelings—wonder and awe, for example—can be experienced only through the arms. An unconscious impulse to participate in these impressions stirs in the arms and hands. Such fragmentary expressions of gratitude become evident when people are motivated to clasp their hands together in response to the beauty of nature or, at other times, to fold their hands. Everything that happens unconsciously is expressed in life only in a fragmentary way. We can remain physically unmoved in response to this "desire of the hands and arms to be a part of our outer expression" and move only our etheric hands and arms. As we become more conscious of this and feel outer expressions sympathetically in our own limbs, we develop a feeling that may be expressed this way: When I see red, I am inclined to move my hands in a certain way, because those movements belong to that color; if I see blue, I tend to make other movements.

The more conscious we become of this, the more we find ourselves developing a feeling for inspirations and impressions that should reach the soul and be retained. When we surrender to playing with children, we lose ourselves in the impression—but we also find ourselves. Then comes the inspiration, if we have prepared ourselves and made our whole being ready to receive the impression; if, when we absorb ourselves in our thoughts with the dead, we are able to bring this absorption into relation with a feeling of solidarity or fellowship; and if, when we emerge from absorption, we can unite this feeling with a true experience of the whole person—I mean an experience of gratitude that is felt to run right down into the arms and hands. Then the real spiritual existence, where the dead live between death and rebirth, communicates with the living in such a way that we can say: *We find the dead when we can meet in a common spiritual place with a common thought that they also perceive—when we can meet in this shared thought with a feeling of full companionship.* The feeling of gratitude is the medium that makes this possible; for the dead speak to the living out of the space woven by the feeling of community, through the air that is created from the feeling of universal gratitude toward the world.

φ common ground
φ gratitude
φ trust

11

UNDERLYING THE SOUL QUALITIES we have already uncovered—universal gratitude for the experiences of life and a sense of community with the world around us—there is an even more basic factor. This other aspect is universal trust, which might also be called faith, or confidence in life. This is the rock-bottom, fundamental conviction that life, no matter what, is always good and always has something to give us. Such basic trust leads us to the spirit. Opening to trust, we open to perceptions of the spiritual world weaving in this world. Underlying gratitude, solidarity with all existence, and so forth, this trust in all life and in humanity and the earth provides the basic medium whereby the dead can communicate with us. Such trust, in fact, forms the basis in the soul of all spiritual cognition, while at the same time renewing the soul, making it healthy and in love with life, full of hope and expectation.

*subconscious
feeling in
the soul*

Trust in Life and
the Rejuvenation of the Soul

BERLIN, MARCH 26, 1918

For the sake of continuity we will first briefly go over some of the points in the previous lecture.

We found that when we have something to do with relationships between incarnate and discarnate souls, the chief thing is to keep one's spiritual eye, as it were, on the "air" or psychic atmosphere that joins the living and the dead so that a relationship can take place. We found, too, that there must be certain dispositions of soul among the living, since these in a way build a bridge to the realms of the so-called dead. Such soul moods always imply that a certain element is present in the soul, and when this element manifests in the corresponding feeling among the living, relations with the dead can come about.

We went on to say that this shared atmosphere is created by the living through two kinds of feeling. The first may be called *a feeling of universal gratitude for all the experiences of life.* As I told you, the relation of the soul to its environment is partly conscious, and partly subconscious. Everyone knows the conscious part: on this level we respond with sympathy or antipathy, and with ordinary sense perceptions, to whatever we encounter in life. Subconsciously, however, below the level of consciousness, we develop a better and nobler feeling than any feeling we are able to elicit consciously. This feeling can be described only by saying that in our subconscious soul we always know that we must be grateful for every experience of life, even the smallest. When we meet difficult experiences, they may certainly strike a painful note, but in a wider view of existence we can be grateful for them in the lower (not the upper) soul, thankful that our life is unceasingly supplied with gifts from the universe. This is something that exists as a real subconscious feeling in the soul.

The other kind of feeling arises when we feel that we unite our own "I" with every being we have anything to do with in life. Our actions embrace other beings, even inanimate beings. And wherever we have done anything, wherever our being has been united with another in action, something remains behind. This remainder establishes a permanent relationship between our being and everything we have ever been connected with. This feeling of kinship is the foundation for a deeper feeling, one generally unrecognized by the upper consciousness or soul—*a feeling of community or solidarity with the surrounding world.*

These two feelings—of gratitude, and of solidarity or community with the environment one is karmically united with—can be brought more and more to conscious fruition.

We can raise up into our soul what lives in these feelings and perceptions; and to the extent that we do this, we prepare ourselves to build a bridge to the souls who live between death and rebirth. The thoughts of these souls can find their way to us only through the realm of the feeling of gratitude that we develop; and we can find the way to them only when we have become accustomed, at least to some extent, to nurturing a real feeling of community. Our being able to feel gratitude toward the universe makes it possible for a mood of gratitude to arise in our soul when we wish to enter into a relationship with the dead. And, because we have cultivated this mood of gratitude, because we are able to feel it, the way for the dead to reach us is opened; and because we can feel that our being lives in an organic community of which it is a part, just as our finger forms a part of our body, we become ripe to feel the same gratitude to the dead when they are no longer present in the physical body, and through this feeling we can reach them with our thoughts. Only when we have acquired something of a mood of gratitude, a feeling of community, can we begin to apply these feelings in given cases.

These experiences are not the only ones. Subconscious perceptions and moods are of many kinds. Everything that we develop in the soul helps to open a path to the world where the dead live between death and rebirth. For instance, there is a very definite feeling that is always present in the subconscious and can be gradually brought into consciousness, a feeling we may put alongside the feeling of gratitude. It is a feeling we lose to the degree that we fall into materialism—although to a certain extent it is always there in the subconscious and is never rooted out, even by the strongest materialism. The enrichment, enhancement, and ennobling of life depend on such feelings being raised into consciousness from the subconscious. The feeling I refer to may be called a universal trust, faith, or confidence in the life that flows through and past us— trust in life! From a materialistic standpoint, this mood of trust in life is very difficult to find. It resembles gratitude for life, but is a different feeling; it exists alongside gratitude. It consists in an unshakable mood in the soul that life, however it may approach us, has under all circumstances something to give us, so that we can never fall into thinking that life could have nothing more to give us. True, we pass through difficult, painful experiences, but in the wider context of life these experiences appear as precisely those that do the most to enrich and strengthen us for life. The chief thing is that this enduring feeling, always present in our lower soul, should be raised a little into the upper soul: *"Life—you lift and bear me; you make sure that I move forward."*

If something were done in education to foster such a mood, a tremendous amount would be gained. It would be good to plan our education so as to show, by individual examples, that life deserves our trust—just *because* it is often hard to get through. When we consider life from such a standpoint—when we ask, Does life deserve our trust?—we find much that we would not otherwise find. Such a mood should not be considered superficially. It should not lead to finding everything in life bright and good. On the contrary, in some cases having trust in life may lead us to sharp criticism of wicked, foolish things. When we have no trust in life we may often avoid criticizing what is bad and foolish, because we prefer to ignore things we have no trust in. It is not a matter of having trust in particular things; that belongs to another realm. One can have confidence in one thing and not in another, according to circumstances. The point is for us to have trust in life as a whole, for the whole content of life. If we can draw from the subconscious some of the trust that is always there, the way is opened to the spiritual, to observing the wise guidance and ordering of life. If we can affirm, not in theory but with perceptive feeling, that life's manifestations, following one upon the other, mean something for us when they draw us into them, and have something to do with us that we can trust, then we are preparing ourselves gradually and truly to perceive the spiritual activities that work and weave in things. Those who lack this trust in life shut themselves off from these perceptions.

Let us now apply this to the relations between the living and the dead. When we develop this attitude of trust, we make it possible for the dead to find their way to us with their thoughts; for thoughts from the dead can, as it were, sail to us on this mood of trust. When we have confidence in life, faith in it, we are able to bring the soul into a condition such that inspirations—which are thoughts sent to us by the dead—can appear. Gratitude for life and trust in life belong together in a certain way. If we do not have this general trust in life, in the world, we cannot acquire sufficient trust in anyone to reach out beyond death—all we have is, so to speak, the memory of our trust. We must realize that if our feelings are to meet with the dead, who are no longer in their bodies, these feelings must be different from the perceptions and feelings that go out to someone in a physical body. True, trusting those who are in the physical body will be useful for the conditions after death; but this trust needs to be strengthened by a general, all-embracing trust, for the dead live under different conditions, and it is not enough to recall the trust we bore toward them during life. We need to call forth freshly renewed trust or confidence in *one who can no longer inspire that trust through physical presence.* To do this we must, as it were, ray out into the world something that has nothing to do with physical things. The all-embracing trust, confidence, and faith in life that I described have nothing to do with physical things.

Just as *trust* goes together with *gratitude*, so does the feeling of community, of solidarity, go with something that is always present in the lower soul and can be called up into consciousness. This, too, should receive more consideration than it does, particularly in the educational systems of our materialistic age. A great deal depends upon this. If human beings are to take their right place in the world during the present time cycle, they must develop a faculty that today must be cultivated not instinctively, but from knowledge of the spiritual world. We might say that we need to draw up from the lower soul something that in earlier times arose out of atavistic clairvoyance and did not then need to be cultivated. A few sparse remnants of it remain, but they are gradually passing away, together with everything else that stems from ancient times. In this connection, what we need now is to be able to refresh and rejuvenate again and again, from the springs of life itself, our *feelings* for whatever we encounter. We can spend our lives in such a way that after a certain age we begin to feel more or less tired, because we are losing the power of spontaneous participation in life and are not able to bring enough zest to it for its phenomena to give us joy. Compare the two extremes, the seizing and acceptance of experience in early youth and the weary acceptance of life in later age, and think how many disappointments are connected with this. There is a difference in whether we are able to let our soul forces take part in a continual resurrection, so that each morning is a new experience, or whether in the course of life we grow weary of its offerings.

It is particularly important in our time to take these facts into consideration, since they should influence education. Our judgment of earlier epochs is framed in the context of modern history, which is really a *fable convenue* of a peculiarly distorted kind. People do not realize that upbringing and education have been so organized in the last few centuries that what should be gained from them in later life is not gained. The most we have to show for the pains spent on our education is a memory. We remember what we learned, what was said to us. Indeed, as a rule, we are content merely to remember. No attention is paid to the fact that among the many secrets underlying human life, one important secret is relevant here. I have already spoken of it in previous lectures from another point of view.

The human being is a manifold being; here we will consider the human being as twofold. This twofoldness is expressed directly in our outward bodily form, which reveals a distinction between the head and the rest of us....

I have introduced this twofold nature in order to explain the outcome of this duality. Our soul life, which develops under the restrictions of our bodily nature, is included within this duality. We have not only the organic development of the head and that of the rest of the body, but also two different rates, two different velocities, *in the development of the soul.* The development of the head is comparatively rapid; that of the rest of the organism—we will call it the development of the heart—is about three or four times slower. The rule for the head is that it generally completes its development by about the twentieth year. In regard to the head, we are old at twenty—it is only because we obtain nourishment from the rest of the organism, which develops three or four times more slowly, that we continue our life agreeably. The development of the head is quick; that of the heart, which means the rest of the organism, is three or four times slower. We live our earthly life in this duality. In childhood and youth, our head organism can absorb a great deal; therefore we study during that time. But what is then received must be continually renewed and refreshed, must be constantly encompassed by the slower development rate of the other organs....

All this is intended to throw light—only from a certain point of view, of course—on something that the lower soul always feels but that is so difficult to bring up into the higher soul at the present time. It points to something that the human soul desires and will increasingly long for as time goes on: the fact that the soul needs something with which to continually renew its forces, so that we do not grow weary with the course of life, but will always be full of hope and able to feel that each new day is like the first day we consciously experienced. For this to happen we must, in a sense, not need to grow old. Indeed, it is very necessary that we do not need to grow old. If today we see how many comparatively young people are dreadfully old and how few regard each day as a new experience given to them, as to a lively child, we know what a spiritual culture must achieve and contribute in this realm.

Ultimately the feeling I refer to—the feeling of never, never losing hope in life—is the feeling that enables us to experience a right relationship between the living and the so-called dead. Otherwise, the facts that should establish our relationship to a dead person remain too strongly embedded in memory. We can remember what we experienced with our dead friends during life. But if we are unable to feel that we can always bring these experiences freshly to life when a friend is physically absent, then our feelings and perceptions will not be strong enough to experience the new relationship—for our friend is now present only as a spiritual being and must act as a spiritual being. If we have grown so deadened that we can no longer revive anything of the hopefulness of life, we will not be able to feel that this complete transformation has taken place. Formerly our dead friends could help themselves by coming to meet us in life; now the spirit alone can help. We can meet our friends, however, if we develop this feeling for the perpetual renewal of life forces, so that our hopes for life always remain fresh.

Here I want to make a remark that may seem strange to you. A healthy life—healthy particularly in the ways we develop here— will never lead people, unless their consciousness is clouded, to look on life as something they are weary of and sated by. Rather, a healthily fulfilled life will lead us, even in later years, to wish to greet each day as fresh and new. A healthy attitude will never induce an old person to think, "Thank God my life is behind me," but rather, "I would like to go back forty or fifty years and live it all through again!" And it is healthy when people have acquired the wisdom to take comfort from the thought that they cannot go back and repeat past actions in *this* life, but that in another life they will be able to improve on them. That is a healthy attitude: to regret nothing one has been through—and, if wisdom is needed to accept that, not to crave it in this life but to be able to wait for it in another. That is the trust that is built on true confidence and hope in life, actively sustained.

These, then, are the feelings that properly inspire life and at the same time create a bridge between the living here and the living there: gratitude toward the life that comes to meet us here; trust in its experiences; an intimate feeling of fellowship, solidarity; and the faculty of making hope active in life through continually refreshed life forces. These are the inner ethical impulses that, rightly felt, can furnish the very best social ethics, for ethics, like history, can be grasped only in the subconscious realm.

Another question about the relationship of the living to the dead frequently arises: What is the real difference in the relationship between two persons when they are both incarnated in physical bodies and when only one of them is, or when neither is? I want to say something important about this from a particular point of view.

When, with the aid of spiritual science, we observe the two highest members of the human being, the I and the soul life or astral body, we must say that they are not as yet far enough advanced for us to rely on them alone for power to maintain ourselves independently of others. I have often pointed out that the I is the youngest, the baby, among the members of the human organism, whereas the astral body is somewhat older, though dating only from the Moon evolution. If we were here with one another, each only as I-being and astral body, we would be together as though in a sort of primordial jelly. Our entities would merge into each other. We would not be separate and would not know how to distinguish ourselves from each other.

There would be no possibility of knowing whether a hand or a leg were one's own or another's (of course it would all be quite different—these comparisons cannot really be drawn). We could not even properly recognize our feelings as our own. The fact that we perceive ourselves as separate beings depends on our having been drawn out of a fluid continuum—that is how we must picture it for a certain early period—in the form of drops, in such a way that the individual souls did not run together again; we must imagine each soul drop enclosed as though in a piece of sponge. Something like that really occurred. Only because human beings are in etheric and physical bodies are we separated from one another, properly separated. In sleep we are kept separate only by a strong longing for our physical bodies. This longing, which draws us ardently to the physical body, divides us in sleep; otherwise we would drift through one another all night long. It would probably be much against the grain of sensitive minds if they knew how strongly they come into connection with other beings in their neighborhood. This, however, is not so very bad in comparison with what might happen if this ardent longing for the physical body did not exist as long as we are physically incarnate.

We might now ask, What divides one soul from other souls during the time between death and rebirth? Well, just as we, with our I and astral body, belong to a physical and etheric body between birth and death, so after death, until rebirth, we are part of quite definite starry patterns, no two of them identical. Each one of us belongs to a quite distinct pattern. It is out of this instinct that we speak of a person's "star." The whole starry structure, if we take first its physical projection, is globular on the periphery, but we can divide it in the most varied ways. The regions overlap, but each appertains to another. Expressed spiritually, we might say that each region belongs to a different group of archangels and angels. Just as the souls of people here on earth draw them together, so between death and rebirth each soul belongs to a particular starry pattern, to a particular group of angels and archangels: the soul is drawn there. The reason this is so—but only apparently, for we must not now go further into this mystery—is that on earth each soul has its own physical body. You will wonder why I say "apparently," but research does surprisingly reveal how each soul belongs to a particular starry pattern, and how the patterns overlap. Let us think of a particular group of angels and archangels. In life between death and rebirth, thousands of angels and archangels belong to one soul. Imagine only one of all these thousands taken away and replaced by another, and we have the region of the next soul.

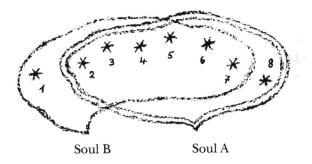

Soul B   Soul A

In this diagram two souls have, with one exception in each case, the same stars; but no two souls have identical structures. Thus human beings are individualized between death and rebirth by each having a special starry pattern. From this we can see how the separation of souls between death and rebirth is effected. In the physical world, as we know, it is effected by the physical body. We live in our physical body as though in a sheath; we observe the world from it, and everything must reach us through it. All that comes into the human soul between death and rebirth with regard to the relation between the astral body and the I, is connected with a certain starry region in a way similar to the connection of the astral body and the I with the physical body during life on earth. This explains how the separation between souls occurs between death and rebirth.

We have seen in these considerations how we can work upon our soul to form certain feelings and perceptions, so that a bridge of communication can be formed between the so-called dead and the living. What has been said is also well suited to calling up thoughts—one might call them perceptive thoughts or thought-filled perceptions—that in their turn can have a share in creating the bridge. This will occur through our seeking more and more, when we experience something, to form a kind of perception that can call up in the soul the impulse to ask ourselves, How would my dead friend experience what I am experiencing at this moment? By creating the imagination that the dead friend is experiencing the event side by side with us and making this a really living feeling, we can form some impression of how communication arises between the dead and the living, on the one hand, and on the other between the dead themselves, if we also consider how the various starry regions are related to our own souls or to each other. In this way we can gain a feeling for the influences that play from soul to soul because of their relation to certain starry regions.

If we concentrate upon an immediate interest mindful of the presence of the dead, and feel the dead living close beside us, then from such things as I have discussed today we become more and more conscious that the dead really do approach us. The soul will develop an awareness of this. But we must have confidence that these things really are so, for if we lack confidence and are impatient with life, another truth prevails—the good effects that confidence can bring are driven away by impatience; the enlightenment that comes through confidence is darkened by impatience. Nothing is worse than letting impatience conjure up a mist before the soul.

12

TO COMMUNICATE WITH THE DEAD, as we have learned, we need to speak the language of the dead. This language, Steiner tells us here, is a language of verbs—everything is related to activity and movement—not nouns. The dead do not understand nouns. Their world is one of openness and connection. They do not understand anything that is closed off. Rather, they live in a "heart" world: an image world of weaving, interconnecting feeling.

The Language of the Heart

LONDON, AUGUST 30, 1922

...I would like to begin by pointing out that while it was important for the earliest initiates to look up into the spiritual world from which humanity descended and clothed itself with an earthly body, and while for later initiates such things as I characterized by pointing to Greek portrayals of a descent into the underworld were important, *it is the obligation of modern initiation, as I have already said, to seek as knowledge the rhythmical relationship of heaven and earth.*

This can only be achieved if we consider the following. Certainly, we must know heaven, and certainly we must know the earth. But then we must also look at human beings—in whom, among all the beings around us, heaven and earth work together to create a unity. We must look at the human beings—

and that means we must look at them with our sun-eye, with our heart-eye, with the whole human eye.

The human being! Humanity contains infinitely more secrets than the worlds that we can perceive with our external organs of perception, that we can explain with an intellect bound to the senses. The task of present-day initiation knowledge is to come to know the human being spiritually. I would like to say that initiation science wants to come to know everything for this reason: in order to understand the human being through knowledge of the whole world, through knowledge of the whole cosmos.

Compare the situation of the present-day initiate with the situation of the ancient initiate. Because of all the abilities that existed in the soul of ancient humanity, the initiate could awaken memories of the time before the descent into an earthly body. Initiation, therefore, for the ancients was an awakening of cosmic memories. Then, for the Greeks, initiation meant looking into nature. Modern initiates want to know the human being directly as a spiritual being. For this we must now acquire the ability to set ourselves free from the grasp of earth, from the ties connecting us with the world. I would like to repeat an example that I have just recently mentioned.

Achieving a relationship to the souls who have passed through the gate of death, who have left the earth, either recently or long ago, is one of the most difficult tasks of initiation knowledge. However, it *is* possible to achieve such a relationship by awakening forces that lie deeper in the soul.

Here we must understand clearly, however, that we have to accustom ourselves, through exercises, to the language we must speak with the dead. This language is, I would like to say, in a certain sense a child of human language. But we would go completely astray if we thought that our earthly human language could help us to cultivate communication with the dead. The first thing we become aware of is that the dead are only able to understand for a short time what lives as nouns in the language of earth. What is expressed as a thing, a closed-off thing, the characterization of a noun, is no longer present in the language of the dead. In the language of the dead everything is related to activity and movement. For this reason we find that some time after the human being has passed through the gate of death, *they have a real feeling only for verbs.* In order to communicate with the dead we must in some cases direct a question to them, formulating it in such a way that it is understandable to them. Then, if we know how to pay attention, the answer comes after a while. Usually several nights must pass before the deceased person can give us an answer to our questions. But we must first find our way into the language of the deceased; finally, the language appears for us, the language the dead actually have, the language the deceased have had to live into after death, distancing themselves from the earth with their entire soul life. We find our way into a language that is not at all formed according to earthly conditions, but is rather a language arising from feelings, from the heart. It is a kind of language of the heart. Here, language is formed in the way vowels or feeling sounds are formed in human language. For example, when we are amazed we say "Ah!" or when we want to lead ourselves back to ourselves we speak the "ee" sound. Only in such instances do the sounds and sound combinations receive their due, their real meaning. And beginning with such instances, language becomes something that no longer sounds bound to the speech organ. It is transformed into what I have just described, a language of the heart. When we have learned this transformed language, the forces that rise from the flowers give us information about humankind and we ourselves begin to speak with what comes from the flowers. When we enter into the tulip blossom with our soul forces we express, in the imagination of the tulip, what is expressed here on the earth in the formation of words. We grow again into the spiritual aspect of everything.

From the example of language just characterized, you see that human beings grow into entirely different conditions of existence when they have gone through the gate of death. You see,

we really know very little about a human being if we only know
his or her external side; the modern science of initiation must
know the other side. This begins with language. Even the
human body, as it is described if you read the relevant literature,
becomes something else for us. The body becomes a world in
itself when we grow into the science of initiation....

13

In this late lecture, Rudolf Steiner speaks of "following the dead in their destinies"—the original meaning of "memento mori" ("remember you must die"). The souls of those who have died are interwoven with and are part of the spiritual world. As the individuality continues its journey and the incarnation just completed on earth is handed over to continue its work in the spiritual world, the hierarchies of divine-spiritual beings receive the fruits of earthly life and transmute them so that they, too, can continue to work for cosmic human evolution. It is important, Rudolf Steiner suggests, that we bear witness to this process with prayers that are "simple and good, wonderful and beautiful."

— May the Angels, Archangels, and Archai (Principalities) weaving in the Ether receive the human being's Web of Destiny.

— May the righteous consequences of human earthly life die into the realm of Being in the astral feeling of the Cosmos: in the Exusiai (Powers), Dynamis (Virtues), Kyriotetes (Dominions).

— May the justly transmuted fruits of earthly life be resurrected in the Thrones, the Cherubim, and the Seraphim, as their Deeds of Being.

Memento Mori

DORNACH, JULY 4, 1924

2·28·22

... In earthly life, as we have seen, the inner experience of karma is instinctive. It takes its course beneath the surface of consciousness; but the moment we pass through the gate of death we become objectively conscious, during the first few days, of all the experiences we first underwent on earth. We have them before us in ever expanding pictures, and what we thus behold as a great tableau of our life also contains all that took place instinctively in the working of our karma.

When we pass through the gate of death and our life is unfolded, ever expanding, before our eyes, it includes all that was instinctive—the web of karma—which we were unconscious of in life. We do not actually see it in the first days after death. But what we would otherwise perceive only in pale images of memory, we now behold vividly as a living configuration. Nor do we fail to perceive that something more is contained in it than ordinary memory. And, if with the vision made possible by initiation, we look on all that we have before us at this stage, we can describe it as follows.

Once we have passed through the gate of death, having possessed ordinary consciousness during earthly life, we see life spread out before us as a mighty panorama. But we see it only "from in front." Initiation vision also sees it from the other side— "from behind," as it were. Ordinary human consciousness sees it only from one side. But initiation vision sees it "from behind," so that the whole web of karmic relationships springs forth. This web of karmic relationships arises, to begin with, from the thoughts that lived within the will during a person's earthly life. But something else immediately enters into it.

I have often emphasized that the thoughts we experience *consciously* during our earthly life are dead thoughts. But the thoughts that are woven into our karma, the thoughts that now emerge, are *living*. Living thoughts spring forth on the other side, as it were, of the panorama of our life. And now—this is a fact of

[handwritten: 3rd H]

[handwritten: Angels Archangels Archai receive the web of destiny.]

untold significance—now the beings of the third hierarchy draw near, and receive what is springing forth from the "other side" of the panorama. Angels, archangels, and archai draw it into themselves; they breathe it in.

This takes place during the time when we ascend on our way upward, after death, to the edge of the Moon sphere.

Thereafter we enter the Moon sphere, and our backward journey through life begins. As we know, this lasts for a third of the time we spent on earth, or, more accurately, for the same length of time that we spent in sleep while on earth.

...We may now ask ourselves, How does our state of ordinary sleep relate to the state in which we find ourselves immediately after death? Normally when we go to sleep, we are, as beings of soul and spirit, only in our astral body and our I. We do not have our etheric body with us, for this has remained behind in the bed. Hence, our thoughts remain dead; they have no active power, they are mere pictures. But when we pass through the gate of death, to begin with we take our etheric body with us, and the etheric body begins to expand. Now the etheric body has a life-giving quality, not only for physical existence, but for thoughts themselves. Therefore, since we have brought the etheric body with us, our thoughts can become alive. The etheric body, as it frees itself, carries forth our living thoughts to the angels, archangels, and archai, who in their Divine Grace receive these thoughts.

This, if I may so describe it, is the first act that is unfolded in the life between death and a new birth. Beyond the threshold of death, the beings of the third hierarchy approach what loosens itself from the human being—all that is entrusted to our etheric body as it dissolves away. The beings of the third hierarchy receive it into their care. And we, as human beings on the earth, can utter a simple and good, a wonderful and beautiful prayer, when we think of the connection of life and death, or of one who has passed through the gate of death, by saying, *"Angels, Archangels, and Archai weaving in the Ether receive the human being's Web of Destiny."*

When we say these words we turn our eyes to a real spiritual fact. Much depends upon whether human beings on the earth *think* the spiritual facts or not: whether they simply accompany the dead with thoughts that remain behind on the earth, or accompany them on their further path with thoughts that are a true image of what takes place in that other realm they have entered.

This, my dear friends, seems so infinitely desirable to initiation science: that we shall have thoughts in earthly life that are a true image of real spiritual happenings. By merely thinking of theories enumerating so many higher members of the human being and the like, we cannot achieve union with the spiritual world. We can do so only by thinking the realities enacted there.

Therefore, human hearts should be ready to hear once more what human hearts *did* hear in the old ages of initiation, in the ancient Mysteries, when the words were called out impressively, again and again, to those about to be initiated: *"Accompany the dead in their further destinies."* "Memento mori" is all that is left of it now, a more or less abstract exhortation that no longer deeply affects human beings, for it no longer expands our consciousness into a life that is more living than this life in the world of the senses.

We can see the reception of the human web of destiny by angels, archangels, and archai unfolding as follows. There is the impression that this web "lives and moves and has its being" in a bluish-violet ethereal atmosphere—lives and weaves in the bluish-violet atmosphere of the ether.

Once the etheric body is dissolved, that is, when the thoughts have been breathed in by the angels, archangels, and archai, then, after a few days, discarnate souls enter that backward course of life I have described to you. There they experience their deeds, impulses of will, tendencies of thought—they experience how they worked on other people to whom they did either good or evil. They enter right into the minds and feelings of those others. They do not live in their own mind. With the clear consciousness that it is their concern, they undergo all that took place in the depths of the souls of the other human beings with whom they entered into any kind of karmic relationship—to whom they did anything whatever, good or ill. And once again we can see how what human beings experience there is *received.* They experience it in full reality—a reality more real than sensory reality between

... the just consequence of his earthly
life dies into the realm of
being

birth and death. They experience a reality in which they stand more fully, more glowingly than in any reality of earthly life here below.

But if we look at it once more from the "other side" with the vision and insight of initiation, we see all that the human being experiences being *received* into the essence, the reality and being of the kyriotetes, dynamis, and exusiai. These spiritual beings draw into themselves, as it were, the "negative" of the human deeds. This wondrous process unfolds before the initiate's vision. The consequences of human actions, transformed in righteousness and justice, are taken up into the exusiai, dynamis, and kyriotetes.

Now, seeing all this transports those who have this vision into such a consciousness that they know they are in the center of the Sun, the center of our whole planetary system. They behold what is now taking place from the Sun. They see a lilac-colored living and weaving—the exusiai, dynamis, and kyriotetes absorbing the human deeds, transformed into righteousness, in the living and weaving of a pale violet, lilac-colored astral atmosphere.

Here we have the truth: the aspect of the Sun that appears to us on Earth is only the one side. Here on Earth the Sun is seen from the periphery while, from the center, the Sun is seen as the field of action for the living spiritual deeds of exusiai, dynamis, and kyriotetes. There it is all spiritual action, spiritual happening. There we find the other side, as it were, of the pictures of the earthly life we experienced consciously here between birth and death.

Once again we can think truly of what is happening there. We must think of the word *verwesen*, usually used to mean "fade" or "die," or the process of destruction and passing from existence. In its true and original meaning, *verwesen* means "to carry the real being away" (as when we say "to forgive" or "to forego," which really means a "giving away" in devotion).

Thinking thus we may say, "*In Exusiai, Dynamis, and Kyriotetes, in the astral feeling of the Cosmos, the righteous consequences of human earthly life die into the realm of Being.*"

Finally, this too is accomplished. The one who has died has now lived through a third of the time of the past earthly life. Journeying backward, the soul feels itself once more at the starting point of earthly life—in the spaces of the Spirit—at the moment before entry into the past earthly life. And now, we may say, the discarnate soul enters through the center of the sun into the real "spirit Land." There, earthly deeds—transformed into divine righteousness—are received into the activity of the first hierarchy. They come into the domain of seraphim, cherubim, and thrones. As the dead step out into this new kingdom, they feel: *"All that took place through me on Earth is now being received by Seraphim, Cherubim and Thrones, into their own active Being."*

Consider well what this means, my dear friends. We are thinking truly of what happens to the dead in their further life after death, when we cherish the thought that the web of destiny, which the departed one wove here on earth, is caught up, to begin with, by the angels, archangels, and archai. In the next part of the life between death and new birth, they bear it into the kingdom of exusiai, dynamis, and kyriotetes. These in turn are gathered in and woven around by the beings of the first hierarchy. And in the process, ever and again, human action upon earth is received into the being—into the deeds of being, into the living action—of the thrones and cherubim and seraphim.

Thus, to the first and the second saying we must now add the third: *"In Thrones and Cherubim and Seraphim, as their Deeds of Being, the justly transmuted human 'fruits of the earthly life' are resurrected."*

Thus we can turn the gaze of initiation upon what is going on perpetually in the spiritual world. Here on earth we have the unfolding of human life and action with human beings' instincts of karma, their ceaseless weaving of destiny—a weaving more or less similar to the weaving of thought. Looking up into the spiritual worlds, we see there what were once human earthly deeds—having passed through angeloi, archangeloi, archai, exusiai, dynamis, and kyriotetes—being received by the thrones, cherubim, and seraphim, and expanding as their heavenly deeds above.

1. Angels, Archangels, and Archai weaving in the Ether receive the human being's Web of Destiny.

2. In Exusiai, Dynamis, Kyriotetes, in the astral feeling of the Cosmos, the righteous consequences of human earthly life die into the realm of Being.

3. In Thrones, Cherubim, and Seraphim, as their Deeds of Being, the justly transmuted fruits of earthly life are resurrected.

This is a succession of spiritual facts infinitely sublime and significant especially for our present age. For the dominion of Michael has now begun, and in this historic moment for the world it is as though we could behold the deeds of those who lived upon earth before the end of the Kali Yuga, in the 1880s and 1890s.[1] What was then enacted in human beings on earth has now been received by thrones, cherubim, and seraphim. Yet never was the spiritual contrast of light so great as it is today, in the realm of these spiritual facts.

In the 1880s one could look upward and see how the deeds of people of the period of revolution in the middle of the nineteenth century were received by thrones, cherubim, and seraphim. But as one looked, a kind of dark cloud settled over the middle of the nineteenth century. What one then saw passing into the realm of seraphim, cherubim, and thrones lit up only a very little.

But today, when we look back to all that took place at the end of the nineteenth century—human deeds, people's relationships to one another—having seen it clearly only a short time ago, it vanishes away. We still saw it clearly a moment ago—then all that took place in that declining age of the Kali Yuga—wafted away like thought masses before our eyes. We saw what was worked out in destiny among the human beings of the end of the Kali Yuga, and then it vanished, and we beheld in clear, radiant light what became of it as it passed heavenward.

This bears witness to the immense importance of what is presently taking place in the transmutation of the earthly deeds of human beings into the heavenly deeds of souls.

What we experience as our destiny or karma takes place for us, within and about us, from earthly life to earthly life. But in the heavenly worlds the consequences of what we did and experienced on earth go on working—and they work on even into the

---

1. See Rudolf Steiner, *The Archangel Michael*, Hudson, NY: Anthroposophic Press, 1994.

historic shaping of this earthly life. For there are many things that are not grasped or controlled by the individual human being here upon earth.

My dear friends, you must take this statement in its full weight and importance. The individual experiences his or her destiny. But as soon as two human beings are working together, something more arises—*more* than resolution of their individual destinies. Something takes place between the two that transcends the individual experiences of either. Ordinary consciousness does not perceive the connection between what happens among human beings and what goes on in the spiritual worlds above. For ordinary consciousness, the connection is most clearly established when sacred spiritual actions are brought into this physical world of sense—as when in sacred cult or ritual, human beings consciously transform their physical actions so as to make them actions of the spiritual world at the same time.

But in a far wider sphere, all that happens between human beings is *more* than what the individual experiences as destiny. Everything that is not merely individual destiny, but is brought about by the feeling together and working together of individuals on earth, is forever in connection with the deeds of seraphim and cherubim and thrones above. Into the latter flow the deeds of human beings in their mutual connection with one another, as well as individual earthly human lives.

Most important at this point is the wider range of vision that opens out for the initiate. For today, as we look upward we behold the heavenly deeds and consequences of what took place on earth in the late 1870s through the 1890s. And it is as though a fine spiritual rain were falling, falling to the earth, moistening human souls, impelling them to many things that arise historically in our time, in the relations between one human being and another.

Once more we can see how what was enacted here on earth by human beings of the 1870s through the 1890s exists again today in living mirror images of thought—through seraphim, cherubim, and thrones.

When one sees through these things, one must repeatedly think, Here I am speaking with a human being of today. What he or she says to me out of commonly accepted opinion—not from personal emotions or inner impulses but simply as a person of this age—often seems as if it is connected with human beings who lived in the 1870s through the 1890s of the last century. Indeed, it is so. We see many human beings today as though they were in a meeting of departed spirits, surrounded by human beings who are busily at work on them. But in reality they are only the afterimages, rained down from heaven, of what lived through human beings upon earth in the last third of the nineteenth century.

Thus in a spiritual sense the shades—the real ghosts, I would say—of a former age are roaming about in a later age. This is one of the more intimate workings of karma, which are indeed widely present in the world though they frequently remain unnoticed even by the most occult of occultists. One would fain whisper to many today when they utter some stereotyped opinion, "That was said to you by this person or that, of the last third of the nineteenth century...."

PART THREE

"Experience"

14

THE PRESENCE AND CONTINUING EXISTENCE of
those who have passed through the gate of death was
brought home to Rudolf Steiner very early in life. For
instance, in an autobiographical lecture on February 4,
1913, in Berlin, he spoke of himself in the third person
and recounted the following incident.

First Experience with the Dead

Something else struck the boy. One day, he was sitting in the waiting room [of his father's railroad station], all alone on a bench. There was a stove in one corner, and a certain distance from it in the opposite wall was a door. The boy could see both the door and the stove from the corner where he sat. He was still very young. As he sat there, the door opened. He must have found it quite natural that a person, a woman, came through the door, someone who, although he had never seen her before, looked extraordinarily like a member of his family. The woman came through the door, walked into the middle of the room, and, gesturing, spoke words that might be rendered as, "Try to do as much as you can for me—both now and later!" She stayed for a while, making gestures that once seen can never vanish from the soul, then went to the stove, and disappeared into it.

The event made a deep impression upon the boy but he could not speak of it to anyone in his family, for he knew that had he done so, he would have been scolded severely for his silly superstition.

Now, after this event, the following occurred. The next day, his father, ordinarily a very cheerful man, grew very sad, and the boy could see that he knew something he did not wish to talk about. After a few days had passed and another family member had encountered something similar, it became clear what had happened. In a place that—according to the thinking of the time—was quite far from the railroad station, a close family relation had committed suicide in the very hour when the figure had appeared to the small boy in the waiting room. The boy had never seen that relative, nor had he heard much about her, because (this should be emphasized) in a certain way he was somewhat unaffected by the stories told in his surroundings. They went in one ear and out the other, and he actually did not hear much of what was said. Thus, he did not know much about the woman who had committed suicide. The event made a strong impression on the boy, for there could be no doubt that it was her spirit that had visited him and asked him to help her in the time following death. Moreover, the connections of this spiritual event with the events on the physical plane just described revealed themselves quite clearly in the following days.

Now, someone who experiences something like this in early childhood and tries to understand it according to the soul's disposition knows—if the event is experienced consciously—how one lives in the spiritual worlds... After this event, soul life began to develop in the boy that fully revealed to him not only the outer world of trees and mountains that speak to the human soul, but also the worlds behind them. From that time on, the boy lived with the spirits of nature, which can be observed quite particularly in such a region; he lived with the creative beings behind things, and he allowed them to work upon him in the same way as he allowed the outer world to work upon him.

15

In his AUTOBIOGRAPHY, writing of his time in Weimar (1894), Rudolf Steiner tells of how two people who had passed through the gate of death helped him create his main philosophical work, INTUITIVE THINKING AS A SPIRITUAL PATH: A PHILOSOPHY OF FREEDOM.

An Example of Working with the Dead

... My friendship with Heinrich Frankel led to something else. Frankel introduced me to his family—he had a very charming wife and sister-in-law. Through them, I met yet another family.

Then something occurred that was like a replica of the remarkable destiny connection I had once encountered in Vienna, where I had been intimately associated with a family. I never saw the head of the family, but I became so close to him in soul and spirit that when he died I could give the funeral address as if for my nearest friend. Through his family, the whole spiritual nature of this man stood before my soul in full reality.

Now I entered into practically the same relationship with the father of the family I met indirectly through the liberal politician Frankel. The father of this family had died a short while before, and the widow lived piously in thoughts of her husband. It happened that I was leaving the place where I had been staying in Weimar, and that I took lodgings with this family. There I saw the library of the deceased, who had been a person of wide interests, but just like that other man in Vienna, he had avoided contact with people. Like the other man, too, he had lived in a "world of his own," regarded by others as an "odd character."

I experienced these two men—whom I did not meet in physical life—in the same way. It was as if they entered my destiny "behind the scenes of existence." In Vienna a beautiful bond had developed between me and the family of the one who was to me "known yet unknown," while in Weimar an even more significant bond arose between me and the family of this other man who was "known" to me in the same way.

I know that most people will regard what I must now say about these two "known yet unknown" persons as sheer fantasy—for it concerns the way I was privileged to come into close contact with these two human souls in the cosmic region where they were after they had gone through the gate of death.

Everyone has the unquestionable right to be uninterested in statements about this region, but to treat them as mere fantasy is a different matter. I must emphasize to anyone who does so that I have always approached spiritual knowledge in the same state of clear consciousness as is necessary for the pursuit of such exact branches of knowledge as mathematics or analytical mechanics. Therefore no one can reproach me for making superficial statements or lacking in responsibility and knowledge when I state the following.

The powers of spiritual sight that I then possessed enabled me to enter into a close relationship with these two souls after their earthly deaths. Their disposition after death was different from that of other souls. Normally, life after death is *at first* closely related to earthly life; only slowly and gradually does it become like the life we experience in the purely spiritual sphere where our existence continues until our next earthly life.

Both of these "known yet unknown" souls were thoroughly at home in the materialistic ideas of their age. Both had conceptually assimilated and elaborated the natural-scientific way of thinking. The second, with whom I became connected in Weimar, had even studied Billroth and similar scientific thinkers.

On the other hand, both had remained distant from any spiritual view of the world during earthly life. No doubt, both would have rejected any views of a spiritual kind they might have met because, according to the habits of thought of the time, the facts seemed to demand the prevailing natural-scientific way of thinking.

But both these men were really bound up with materialism only in their life of thought. Neither led a materialistic life, which would have been logical according to their materialistic thinking and was predominant all around them. "Odd characters in the eyes of the world," these men lived on a more primitive level than was customary or appropriate to their means. Thus they did not carry over into the spiritual world—as fruits for their spiritual individualities—any materialism affecting the life of the *will*, but only the result of materialistic *thinking*. Naturally, on the whole, all of this took place in the subconsciousness of these two souls.

And I was now able to see that, after death, the fruit of materialistic thinking as such does not alienate human beings from the divine-spiritual world. Such alienation occurs only when the fruit of materialism enters the sphere of the will. After death, the spirit of both men—the one I became connected with in Vienna as well as the one I came to know in Weimar—shone with wonderful light, and their souls were filled with images of those spiritual beings who are bound up with the creation of the world. In their last earthly life, their acquaintance with ideas that had enabled them to think more exactly about material phenomena helped them to gain a discriminating relationship to the world after death to a degree that would have been impossible had those ideas remained alien to them.

The significance of scientific thinking revealed itself to me directly from the spiritual world in the two souls who had thus entered my destined path. I could see that in itself this thinking need not cause us to turn away from a worldview that acknowledges the spirit. It had done so in the case of the two personalities in question because they had found no opportunity during their earthly life to raise scientific thinking to the sphere where experience of the spirit begins. After death, however, they fully accomplished this. I saw then that scientific thinking could be raised into this sphere even during earthly life—if one gathers sufficient inner courage and strength. And, by witnessing an event of greatest significance in the spiritual world, I saw that humanity *had to* develop scientific thinking. In earlier times, thinking was so constituted that it could unite the human soul with the spirit of the supersensible world. Thinking could lead human beings—if they practiced self-knowledge, which is the foundation of *all* knowledge—to become aware of themselves as the image of a divine-spiritual world to which they belonged; but that thinking could never have enabled them to experience themselves as independent, self-contained spiritual beings. Therefore, humanity had to progress to the point of being able to grasp a world of ideas that is kindled *not* by spirit, but by matter: a world of ideas that is indeed spiritual, but is not *derived* from the spirit.

It is impossible for human beings to kindle in themselves such a world of ideas in the spiritual world where they live between death and a new birth. This must be done in earthly life, for only there does one meet a material form of existence.

Through these two souls I was able to recognize what human beings gain for their life as a whole, including spiritual life after death, by developing scientific thinking. But I saw others as well whose life of will had taken hold of the consequences of abstract scientific thinking; these alienated themselves from the world of spirit. Scientific thinking had caused them to live less in their humanity than would have been the case *without* it.

The two souls had seemed odd "in the eyes of the world" because they refused instinctively to lose their humanity during earthly life. They assimilated scientific thinking in full measure because they wished to reach the stage in humanity's spiritual development that cannot be attained without it.

Had I met these two souls as physical personalities in earthly life, it might well not have been possible for me to attain this

insight through them. Great sensitivity of spiritual sight was
needed to behold the two individualities within the spiritual
world where their inner natures—and through these—much
else were to be revealed to me. This sensitivity of spiritual sight is
easily blunted when experiences of the physical world conceal
or at least impair what is to be experienced purely spiritually.

The unique way these two souls entered my life made me realize even then that this was something predetermined for my
path of knowledge.

There was nothing spiritistic in my relation to souls in the
spiritual world. A relation to the spiritual world had no value for
me unless it was based on the direct spiritual perception I later
spoke of publicly in my anthroposophical writings. Besides, all
the members of the family in Vienna, as well as those of the family in Weimar, were far too sound to have a mediumistic relationship with the dead.

Whenever I came across it, I was always interested even in the
kind of seeking that comes to expression in spiritualism. Spiritualism today is a false path to the spirit followed by souls who
seek the spirit in an outer way—even by means of experi-
ments—because they have lost all feeling for a real, true, genuine path. One who has an objective interest in spiritism and no
desire to use it as a means of research is best able to assess it and
recognize its wrong direction and misguided aims. My own spiritual investigations always followed paths far removed from
spiritism in any form. But one could, particularly in Weimar,
have interesting discussions with spiritualists, for at one time
there was a strong desire among artists to seek a relation to the
spirit in this way.

Through the two souls—Eunike was the name of the one who
had lived in Weimar—I gained a deeper insight for the content
of my *Intuitive Thinking as a Spiritual Path: A Philosophy of Freedom.*[1] This book is first of all the result of my philosophical

1. Hudson, NY: Anthroposophic Press, 1995.

endeavor during the eighties; secondly, it is a result of my direct insight into the spiritual world generally. Thirdly, its content was enhanced through witnessing the spiritual experiences of these two souls. In them, I perceived the step forward in evolution that humanity owes to the scientific view of the world, but they also revealed the fear sensitive souls experience of letting this worldview influence their will. These souls shrank back from the ethical consequences of such a worldview.

In *Intuitive Thinking as a Spiritual Path* I therefore attempted to present the power that leads from scientific ideas—which are ethically neutral—into the sphere of moral impulses. I attempted to show that because we no longer live in ideas that simply stream into us from the spirit but in ideas kindled by physical existence, we experience ourselves consciously as self-contained, spiritually-oriented beings, and that this experience enables us to develop *intuition* for morality out of our *own self*. This means that morality lights up within the independent individuality—as individual ethical impulses—just as do ideas concerning the outer world.

The two souls had not advanced to such moral intuition. This was why they shrank back (unconsciously) from life; they saw life only in relation to scientific ideas that were not developed to reach beyond the sphere of matter....

16

GÜNTHER WAGNER, the founder of the Pelikan Products firm in Hanover, was an early theosophist, a member of the German Theosophical Society in Berlin from 1895, and one of the founders of the German Theosophical Section. Among the first of Rudolf Steiner's esoteric students, he was followed in this by his wife, Anna, who died shortly after joining the Esoteric Section, on December 27, 1905. On her death, Steiner wrote to him: "It is easy to interpret everything that is linked to our destiny as a karmic debt. But that is nowise always the case. True though it is that karma is a real and all-embracing law, it is equally true that karmic blows can insert themselves into the chain of our relationships simply as a primal cause. Blows of fate that strike us are not always the result of past events; often they are new entries in our book of life that will only find their recompense in the future." In the following letter, written by Rudolf Steiner in 1905 to Paula Stryczek, a dear friend of Anna Wagner with whom she had a daughterly relationship, we find one of the first instances of Steiner's addressing in detail the question of our relationship to those who have died. Steiner is here advising her about how to help Gunther Wagner through his grief. It stands as a first introduction to working with the meditations.

Advice on Meditation

When loved ones pass over into the other worlds, it is vitally important that we send them our thoughts and feelings, without allowing the thought to arise that we wish to have them back. The latter makes existence in the sphere into which they must pass more difficult for the departed. We should send the *love* that we give them—and not the *pain* that we feel—into the worlds where they are. Do not misunderstand me; we should not become hardened or indifferent. Yet it ought to be possible for us to view the dead with the thought, "*May my love go with you! You are surrounded by it.*" To my knowledge, a feeling such as this is like a winged garment that carries loved ones upward, whereas the feelings of many people when they mourn—which we may express as "Ah, if only you were still with us"—become an obstacle to them.

The above is a *general* indication of how we should compose our feelings when a loved one has left us.

In your particular case, may I now give you the following advice. I will write down for you thoughts that I have not yet quite formulated in very good German. They are based on an ancient occult tradition for such a situation.

Compose yourself inwardly three times a day, one of which should be immediately before you go to sleep at night. In this way, you will take these thoughts over with you into the spiritual world. It would be best therefore if you were to fall asleep with the thought:

> May my love be the sheaths
> That now surround you—
> Cooling all warmth,
> Warming all coldness—
> Interwoven with sacrifice!
> Live, borne by love,
> Light-endowed, upward!

It is important that you have the right feeling toward the words "warmth" and "coldness." Physical "warmth" and "coldness" are not what is meant, but something like "warmth of feeling" and "coldness of feeling," though it is not at all easy for a person clothed in a physical body to have any idea of what these qualities mean to a discmbodied soul. Such souls have to become aware that the astral body, which they still have around them, is effective, though it cannot make use of the physical organs. Much of what human beings strive for here on earth is given by our physical organs, which are no longer there. This lack of the physical organs is similar—but only *similar*—to a feeling of burning thirst transferred onto the soul. These are the strong feelings of "burning thirst" experienced after a person has left the body. And it is just the same with what the will desires to do. The will is accustomed to using the physical organs, but it no longer has them. This "privation" approximates to a feeling of coldness in the soul. It is precisely with regard to these feelings that the living can help the so-called dead; for these feelings do not *merely* result from a person's individual life, but are connected to the mysteries of incarnation. It is therefore possible to aid someone who has died.

Now there is something else I would ask of you. Let a few thoughts about our Herr Wagner precede the above sentences. They should contain something of the following content: "Until now, you [Anna]were surrounded by faithful love. This still surrounds you unchanged. May it hold you fast in the power of the spirit, as it has previously illuminated you in the visible present."

This is all that I wanted to write to you today. I am at present burdened with so much work on the physical plane that, for the moment, I cannot say anything more of *special* importance—apart from the above general statements. The physical overshadows spiritual experience. Of course, you may feel free to communicate what I have written to anyone you yourself feel it is right to tell. I would wish that the hearts of many people are turned toward this dear person.

17

*THE MEDITATIONS GIVEN by Rudolf Steiner to connect
with the dead were not given arbitrarily. Each, though
having a general application, arose from his own particular experience of the specific needs and circumstances of
the moment. Similarly, whenever Steiner gave a burial or
a cremation address—which he often did—and spoke
verses uniting with the dead, these too arose from the
experience of the moment. Steiner rarely spoke personally
about such matters. In the following lecture, however, he
does give some indication of how, in specific cases, his
connection with the dead occurred. As a background to
the meditations, these indications are invaluable.*

The Importance of Self-Knowledge
in the Life after Death

BERLIN, FEBRUARY 22, 1915

First, let us recall all those who are at the front, in the great
arena of contemporary events:

> Spirits of your souls, guardian angels,
> May your wings bring
> Our souls' prayer of love
> To earthly human beings
> Entrusted to your care,

So that, united with your might,
Our prayer may stream full of help
To souls who seek for it in love.

Let us recall, too, those who, because of these events, have already passed through the gate of death:

Spirits of your souls, guardian angels,
May your wings bring
Our souls' prayer of love
To those human beings of the spheres
Entrusted to your care
So that, united with your might,
Our prayer may stream helpfully
To those souls who seek it in love.

This evening, I would like to offer some thoughts concerning knowledge of the relationship between our physical world and the spiritual world, which I will connect to somewhat more private events within our own movement. Such a thing is possible, of course, within an intimate, closed circle like this. I know above all that I must be ready to accept responsibility for these statements to those who were our fellow members during their physical lives and who will remain so in their next lives, and who bear some relationship to the facts I want to speak of today.

Several weeks ago, my dear friends, as brought to pass by karma, I was asked to speak at the cremation of several cherished friends, since I happened to be staying in the region where this cremation was taking place. Another element was involved as well, for it was directly suggested to me that I might receive certain remarkable impressions concerning the existence of these individuals in the spiritual world, since they had passed through the gate of death only a few days before.

I have often said that whether one receives impressions of this or that fact of the spiritual world depends upon a variety of factors. Above all, it depends upon how possible it is to form a true inner connection, a strong inner connection, with the souls concerned. It may be that at times one operates in the belief that a very special relationship must be established with this or that soul, yet such is not always the case. With many souls, what is experienced soon makes one realize that such a connection is in fact not so difficult to achieve after all.

Now, my dear friends, in the three cases I would like to speak of now, the most intense need arose to receive impressions concerning the very being of these souls directly after their death. I would like to state that in these cases the urging arose all by itself. To be sure, one can certainly talk about a great variety of things at a funeral service, but in these three cases the inner necessity arose to establish a vital connection with the being of the souls in question—to somehow clothe in words the essence of these souls during the course of the cremation ceremony.

It was not, however, as if I had exactly intended to characterize the inner being of these particular souls at the service, but rather this emerged as a need for clarification, for illumination. I certainly do not wish to say that it must be so in all cases, but in this instance the impulse to characterize the essence of one of these souls after death actually came to me from the spiritual world—not as a spiritual law, but as something I personally experienced. I had no need to choose the words; the words appeared, the words came. And we will see later, my dear friends, just why this was so, for several indications can be given about the further life of this particular soul after death.

For all this to be properly understood, I must first make some comments about the special nature of such experiences. When we wish to receive impressions here in the physical world, we place ourselves directly in the presence of things. We construct thoughts according to how we see, hear, or feel things. We know that it is we ourselves who create these thoughts. However, when we have to do with a soul who has passed through the gate of death, we notice at once that all we ourselves create, be it in thought or in word, actually distances us from the being in question—that it then becomes necessary to give ourselves over completely to what is forming itself within us. In order to describe these impressions in words, we must have the inner capacity for allowing the words to create themselves in us—for we ourselves can contribute nothing to the process whereby they are actually revealed. We must be able to listen inwardly to the words, and when we do so we come to know with certainty that these words are not spoken out of one's own self, but out of the being who has passed through the gate of death.

That was the case when, several weeks ago, an elderly member of ours departed the physical plane here—an older member who over many long years had deeply and wholeheartedly settled herself into our movement and who brought to life in her feeling and in her warmth the kinds of ideas and concepts that our spiritual science can offer. With enormous devotion, this individuality identified in her soul with all that works and weaves throughout our spiritual science.

It now became a matter of somehow surrendering oneself to the impressions proceeding from this soul. And, remarkably, a few hours after her physical death, certain words in fact arose, not just word impressions, but actual audible words which expressed themselves in a manner characteristic of the departed soul. The only possible response to these words was simply to offer one's very best effort to interpret clearly what the departed soul was speaking from its innermost being—for one must certainly call such communication "speaking." And those were in fact the words that I spoke at the cremation. They were not my words, as I said, but those—and I beg you to consider carefully the words I use now—which issued from this particular soul who had passed through death:

Into cosmic distances I shall bear
My feeling heart, so that it may be warmed
In the fire of the sacred powers

In cosmic thoughts I shall weave
My own thinking, so that it may become clear
In the light of life's eternal becoming

In depths of soul I shall dip
Devoted contemplation,
So that it may become strong
For the true goals of human striving

In God's tranquillity I shall strive
Through life's struggles and cares,
Preparing my self for its higher self

Seeking the peace of joyful labors,
Sensing cosmic being in my own being
Thus I would fain fulfil
The duty of being human;

Then I may live in expectation
Going toward the soul-star
That gives me my place in the spirit realm.

Then, speaking the words again at the end of the funeral oration, without intending it, I felt compelled to revise them so:

Then may I live in expectation
Going toward my star of destiny
That gives me my place in the spirit realm.

Well, it was clear what this was. It was an attempt by the particular individual to so impress into her own being all that she had taken up throughout the years of spiritual-scientific thought, ideas, and sentiments, that these ideas, these sentiments, could become forces to shape and mold her being after death. So, this individual made use of the ideas and conceptions of spiritual science in order somehow to inscribe, to imprint, her own inner being in such a way that it could then truly progress spiritually in the world beyond death.

Shortly thereafter we lost another friend of our movement, another member, from the physical plane. And again the great need was present to define this member's essential being. But it could not be done as it was in the previous case. In that instance,

I was fully able to say, because of how the words were formed, that a soul who had passed through the gate of death was expressing what it was feeling and what it wished to become; it was articulating itself. This second case was such that I had somehow to place my own soul in the presence of the soul in question and spiritually observe it. Then that soul too proclaimed itself, but it spoke in words which actually drew the material for its self-characterization out of the observing soul itself. Thus, what the soul of the deceased did there provided an impulse to express what I had now come to feel about that being, now that it had passed through the gate of death. And the following words arose, which I then had to voice at the cremation ceremony:

> You stepped amongst us
> And, from the quiet power of your eyes,
> The trembling sweetness of your being
> Spoke—
> Serenity, ensouled and alive,
> Flowed in the waves
> With which your glance
> Would bear your inner weaving
> To people and things.
> And this being ensouled
> Your voice with eloquence—
> More by the nature of the word
> Than in the word itself—
> Revealing what lay hidden
> In the beauty of your soul
> And revealing too,
> Wordlessly,
> The devoted love
> Of sympathetic listeners:
> This being, of noble, silent beauty
> Announced the "World-Soul-Creation"
> To hearts perceptive and receptive.

Thus, with the speaking of these words at the beginning and the end of the funeral address, the cremation began. And it was actually possible to observe, my dear friends, that at this moment—that is to say, not the moment of the spoken words but rather the moment when the heat of the oven took hold of the body—there occurred a kind of first instant of consciousness after death. What I mean by "instant of conscious" is this: Immediately after death a review takes place of what appears in the etheric body as a life panorama. However, this passes away after several days. In this case, it became necessary to have a fairly long delay between the time of death and the cremation, during precisely that special time of the panorama. Death occurred at six o'clock on Wednesday evening, and the cremation did not take place until the following Monday at eleven o'clock. Thus the pictures of the life tableau had already begun to fade away. Therefore, the first moment of any real consciousness following the panorama occurred when the heat of the fiery oven embraced the body. And in that moment, it was very clearly demonstrated that the manner of perception, the whole way of perceiving the world for such a newly-become spiritual being, is quite different from that of the human soul while it is in the physical body.

In the physical world we perceive things in space as remaining stationary when we ourselves move away from them. If I perceive a chair that is standing here, and then move a bit further away and look around, the chair is still there. I can look back at it. If I go further, the chair still remains there; it stays where it is. This is not true for events, which play themselves out in time. These events, passing by us in time, do not stay put. An event that has happened to us is gone, and when we look back at it we can do so only in memory. Only our past connects us with the event. This is not so for the spiritual being. It sees the events as remaining there, just as here we see things in space as remaining there.

Such was the first impression that the soul I have been speaking of had of the burial service and all that was said and done there. The service had already been over for some five or ten minutes, but for the deceased it was still there; it remained there as only things in space remain for physical human beings. And the first conscious impression was the looking back upon what had been spoken there, and most of all upon the words which were now resonating—upon the words that I have just read.

What Richard Wagner said out of deep intuition is really true: "Time becomes space." That is, what is past is not past in spiritual experience, but remains there, as things remain in space for physical human beings. And so, the first conscious impression after death was of the service and what was spoken there. This case was such that I could not call the life review and the contemplation of what had occurred during the burial ceremony an ultimate illumination of consciousness, for afterward the twilight state, which I am going to speak about, set in again, and only after some time did the consciousness light up once more. Once again, slowly and gradually, illumination of the consciousness returns. It takes months for it to be complete enough so that we can say that the deceased is now completely surrounded by the spiritual world. But later, precisely through this later brightening of the consciousness, the intense need arose within the individual to look back upon this first moment over and over again, and fix it clearly in her eye. And, as I will explain, this is in total harmony with what can be known about the whole behavior of the human being after death.

A third case, one that will touch our dear Berlin members especially deeply, is the instance of our recently deceased friend and fellow member Fritz Mitscher. Fritz Mitscher entered death's door shortly before the completion of his thirtieth year. He would have been thirty years old on February 26.

When I turned my thoughts toward Fritz Mitscher's being after his death, impulses arose above all in my own soul, the observing soul. These proceeded from his very intense dedication to our spiritual movement. He was in this regard an altogether exemplary individual, exemplary in the sense that, while his nature tended toward scholastic achievement, he developed more and more, out of a deep inner need, the capacity to place all the learning he strove to acquire in the service of our spiritual scientific movement. Thus he was precisely one of those individuals who are so essential to the progress of our spiritual scientific worldview. This is greatly needed in the present day, so that external scientific endeavors can be made use of by the soul in such a way that they stream into the knowledge gained from the spiritual world with which we so concern ourselves. And that quickened the youthful soul of Fritz Mitscher. Thus one has to feel, having also observed him here during his life on earth, that he is on a very, very proper path in regard to our movement.

Our friends will remember something I said years ago on the occasion of another death—that individuals such as this, who have passed early through the gate of death after having, to a certain extent, taken into themselves what physical science is able to offer at the present time, prove to be significant coworkers after death for our spiritual movement. Our movement is assuredly not dependent solely upon those souls who remain here in the body. If we did not have the strength of souls who have passed with earthly knowledge through the gate of death and remain connected with the power of will that streams into our movement, we would most certainly be unable in this present materialistic time to maintain the hope—which we must cherish in sufficient measure for it to be truly justified—that we will progress further.

Thus, something proceeded then out of Fritz Mitscher's soul that no words can express other than these I wish to read to you now, which I also spoke at the cremation:

A hope, delighting us,
You entered the field
Where earthly flowers of the spirit
May be revealed to the seeker
Through the power of soul being.

At the root of all your striving
Lay the purest love of truth;
To create out of the spirit light
Was the profound life goal
You ceaselessly strove for.

You nurtured your beautiful gifts,
Unconfused by cosmic contradiction,
The true servant of truth
On the bright path of spirit knowledge,
You turned your steps.

You practiced your organs of the spirit
Courageously and stubbornly
So that they pushed away error
From both sides of your path—
Giving you the space for creation of the truth.

You were forming your own self
To reveal the purest light,
Letting the sun force of the soul
Shine powerfully within you—
This was your life's joys and cares.

Other cares, other joys,
Hardly touched your soul,
Because cognition of the truth
Seemed to give life meaning
And a value that was real.

A hope, delighting us,
You entered the field
Where earthly flowers of the spirit
May be revealed to the seeker
Through the power of soul being.

Painful loss, most deeply felt,
You now vanish from the field
Where the earthly seeds of the spirit
Ripened in the womb of soul being
To become awareness for the spheres.

Feel our loving gaze directed
To the heights where you are facing now
A new and different task.
From those high spirit realms
Lend your strength to those you left behind.

Hear the prayer of our souls;
There speaks our truth and faith:
To fulfil our task on earth we need
Powers great from lands where spirits dwell,
Strength that comes from friends who have died.

Hope, delighting us,
Painful loss, deeply felt,
Let us hope that in far-nearness,
Never lost to us, you will guide our lives
As a soul star in the spirit realm.

Such words, my dear friends, have been so shaped that they
must be viewed as arising out of identification with the soul
which has gone through death. These words—even when not
articulated by the soul itself, even when only a suggestion issu-
ing from the soul—emerge through the forces which come
forth from the soul as a demand to be repeated precisely, down
to the very last one, just as they had been given. I had absolutely no other words in mind than those that I have just read
to you.

Afterward something I found extremely startling happened
to me. During the night following the funeral, the soul of Fritz
Mitscher, not yet communicating out of his consciousness but

certainly out of his being, made a kind of response to what had
been spoken at the funeral. The following words came from this
soul which had passed through death:

> I was forming my own self
> To reveal the purest light,
> Letting the sun force of my soul
> Shine powerfully within me—
> This was my life's joys and cares.
>
> Other cares, other joys,
> Hardly touched my soul,
> Because cognition of the truth
> Seemed to give life meaning
> And a value that was real.

It did not occur to me in the least when I was writing these
verses down that each "you" and "your" could be changed into
"me" and "my." They simply came alive for me:

> You were forming your own self
> To reveal the purest light,
> Letting the sun force of the soul
> Shine powerfully within you—
> This was your life's joys and cares.
>
> Other cares, other joys,
> Hardly touched your soul,
> Because cognition of the truth
> Seemed to give life meaning
> And a value that was real.

The words had now actually been transposed in that way,
which they could be without any need to alter a thing grammat-
ically, so that "you yourself" and "streams inwardly to you mightily" become "me myself" and "streams inwardly to me mightily,"
and so forth.

So, we have here a remarkable connection between what had been spoken here and the soul who had gone through the gate of death, a connection that demonstrates how what had been said actually came back out of the soul, not as a simple echo but instead altered to a certain extent in its meaning.

I would also like to observe that, as these words were expressing themselves, a certain feeling actually passed through my soul that set a basic tone like an urging, making me feel a kind of obligation to give this soul a special mission as it passed through the gate of death.

We know, of course, how much opposes our spiritual movement in today's materialistic time—how little the world today is suited for this spiritual movement. And when one comes to see what it is possible to accomplish in an earthly body, one can truly say that help is needed! And it was this feeling which found its way to expression in the words:

Hear the prayer of our souls;
There speaks our truth and faith:
To fulfil our task on earth we need
Powers great from lands where spirits dwell,
Strength that comes from friends who have died.

Thus, calling upon this soul to use the seeds which it had acquired here for the further advancement of our spiritual scientific movement seemed to me to be necessary and appropriate in this particular case.

So, we now see in these three cases of people so close to us that in spite of all the differences, something similar obtains. The similarity is that within the observing soul—strongly impelled through karma to observe, because it had to speak at the cremation ceremony—thoughts were stimulated about the inner being of these three souls, and therefore the need arose to speak, to articulate this inner being.

Concerning the first individual of whom I spoke (you know, of course, in what spirit I say these things—only to serve understanding, not in any way to flatter myself), I had actually come to know her on the physical plane as well, after she had joined the society. One indeed witnesses certain things that take place while individuals are here in our society, but our friends will know that it is not my custom to make any particular inquiries about the life situations of specific individuals, or ask about what they have experienced during their physical lives here.

So, it was less for my personal satisfaction than for the sake of understanding that I characterized this personality further in a small funeral address—how she had lived out her life here on earth according to the nature of her soul. In this I had nothing before me except the soul after death—not just the words that the soul had expressed, which I read at the beginning, but the actual soul as it was, with its unique characteristics, after death. I had nothing else before me.

I really knew very little about what had happened to her before she joined our society, and also not especially much of her life here, apart from meetings and such or those other occasions when I now and then have contact with our members. I knew nothing more. Nevertheless, in this particular case I felt myself obliged, as if in obedience to an inner demand, to speak at the funeral about certain life situations, certain relationships which had had a bearing upon her whole life (and she had lived to an advanced age)—her relationship with her children and to her work in life. And, as I said, I did not feel a personal satisfaction but rather the satisfaction of having gained understanding when her relatives said to me that they had really and truly recognized this particular individual from what had been said there, for every word characterized her perfectly. Thus a picture of an individual life during the course of physical existence had been formed by observing the condensed results of that life after they had been drawn together in the soul. What is especially interesting for our understanding, however, is that in this soul we perceive the intense need after death to concentrate one's spiritual gaze upon one's own life.

Now, it is certainly not to my credit to be able to characterize the personal life of this particular individual. Rather, the process was such that, although the individual was not conscious at the time, she nevertheless directed her soul being—directed those forces which would later become conscious—upon her own life and her own experiencing, thereby preparing herself for her later conscious life after death. And what I was made to say could be seen in the thought pictures which arose as she directed her soul toward her own experiences. Therefore, it fell to me to describe what the individual was unconsciously thinking about herself after death. What is important to us about this, what needs to be emphasized, is that the individual after death felt this intense need, unconsciously, to direct her gaze upon her own being.

With the second individual, who had to some extent been awakened as the heat took hold of the body, this need showed itself later in her uniquely characteristic conduct during a kind of sporadic reawakening. As I mentioned, she had the need to somehow reach back to, to turn again to, her own inner being and to the words which had been used to characterize it. And indeed in the speech—if one can call speech what expresses itself in the relationships between souls, whether in the body or already spiritual beings, already dead—to the extent that one can speak of such communication, I must truly say that when I was able to witness a later reawakening of this individual, I sensed a kind of joyful feeling that I had been able to express those words which had revealed themselves to me. And thus it was shown that there had really been a true working together with the dead. One can understand from this that the soul of this person—figuratively speaking, of course—expressed itself somewhat in this way: "It's good that this is here. It's good that this is in this place." Such a feeling revealed itself in the second awakening, as if the deceased were showing that a kind of strengthening is provided there in the spiritual world through this expression in human words here on the physical earth. It was for her something that she needed, and it was therefore good that through the physical, earthly word it became more fixed than she herself was able to fix it. That is to say, the need existed in her to make this fast, and it was a relief to her that it had been strengthened in this way.

In the case of our dear friend Fritz Mitscher we can see very clearly that in the night following the cremation he directly connected with and made use of what had been said here in order to make his own being clear to himself—in order to bring himself to true comprehension of his own being.

Thus, in all three cases we have a contemplation of the individual's own being. Unquestionably, such things move our souls and our hearts above all because of their purely human value, their truly human significance. But we gain spiritual knowledge from the real world only when it wishes, through grace, to offer itself to us. We cannot compel it; we must await it. And it is precisely through such things as these that we can see how remarkably karmic relationships work.

One day after the second of the individuals referred to had died in Zurich, I myself was in that city. We were passing by a bookshop and I noticed a book which I had read years before. I believed the book was still in my so-called library, but that was in such disorder due to my custom of living in many different places in unusual circumstances that it would not have been easy for me to find it there. Indeed, perhaps it was no longer in my library at all.

In any case, years before, I had read the book by the Viennese philosopher Dr. Ernst Mach, and now a secondhand copy was for sale right there in the bookshop. I wanted to read it again, or at least look through it. On the third page something came to my eye which I had lost sight of long ago, namely, a most interesting observation by Ernst Mach concerning human self-knowledge, about the difficulty of self-knowledge for human beings. I quote almost word for word from the notes on page three of the *Analysis of Sensations* by Ernst Mach, university professor: "Once as a young man I was walking along the street and happened to encounter a person about whom I had the feeling, What an unpleasant, obnoxious face this man has. And then I was not a little shocked to discover that it was my own face that greeted me, looking back at me from out of a mirror."

So, he had been walking along the street, and a mirror located opposite him had cast his own reflection back to him. And as he saw himself, he thought, What kind of man with such an unpleasant, obnoxious face encounters me here? And Mach immediately adds another similar observation concerning our inadequate self-knowledge. He writes: "I was returning one day tired from an excursion and got on a bus. I noticed another man enter opposite me and thought, What a dilapidated schoolmaster is boarding here! And then I saw that it was myself. The mirror in the bus had shown me my own portrait." And Professor Mach then adds, "Thus, I knew my professional image better than my actual one."

That is something like a pointing finger—how truly difficult real human self-knowledge is in contrast to our purely outward form. One has no idea how one appears in three dimensions, even when one is a university professor, as can be seen in this very candid example.

It is indeed interesting that precisely this illustration can be applied in our three cases, for it demonstrates that lack of self-knowledge need not be too great a hindrance to what human beings have to accomplish in the physical body here on earth. One can be a famous professor and still have as little self-knowledge as the man has expressed. But I mention this example because it is remarkable that it came to my attention out of physical life just as the soul was being guided anew to take notice of how the deceased feels the need to understand, to examine, its own being. That is to say, here in the physical world we can actually get along well enough without self-knowledge for as far as the purely material dimensions of our lives are concerned. However, understanding of the spiritual world cannot be gained without self-knowledge. For wholly external, material circumstances, one can manage without self-knowledge. But as soon as the soul has passed through the gate of death, self-knowledge is absolutely the primary thing that it requires, and this is shown in particular by the experiences I have presented. Self-knowledge is the starting point from which everything else must proceed.

You see, the materialistic thinker is usually stuck on the question of whether or not consciousness actually remains after death. However, spiritual research reveals that after the soul has passed through the gate of death it suffers from no insufficiency of consciousness at all; instead it actually has too much consciousness. That a kind of awakening occurs only later is not due to the fact that one needs to acquire a new consciousness after death, but because one has too blinding a consciousness already—too much consciousness, which must first gradually be reduced. Human beings have too much consciousness—an overwhelming consciousness—after death, and must first somehow orient themselves in this world of overpowering awareness. And to the degree that they gradually succeed in this, they become less conscious than they were before. They must first diminish their consciousness, as we must subdue sunlight when it is too strong.

So, the task one faces is a gradual restraining of consciousness. Therefore we cannot speak of an awakening as in the physical world, but rather of a recovery from the superabundance of consciousness to the degree that it becomes bearable, depending upon what we have experienced here in the physical world. In addition, something else is necessary. To be able to find one's way around in this deluge of light-consciousness after death, self-knowledge as a starting point is essential; it is essential that we be able to look back upon our own being in order to somehow find the guidelines needed to orient us in the spiritual world. Lack of self-knowledge is the true hindrance to consciousness after death. We must find our own self in the overflowing light. And now we can see why the need arises to characterize the dead: in order to aid them in the process of finding themselves.

That is revealed to us as a kind of universal knowledge through such intimate and moving experiences. After death, after the etheric life panorama has disappeared, a gradual development takes place whereby we come to know our own concluded life on earth, which we perceive gradually dawning out of the spiritual worlds. For, once the panorama is over, that is our sole task after death. We will be surrounded completely by what exists in the spiritual world. But what we must come to know first of all is our own being. And to this end ideas come to us for our very great benefit that we can know only from spiritual science, because they give us the means to orient ourselves. Thus we can see that what arose as self-criticism in our first case was made possible only through what that soul had received from spiritual science. She was able so to contemplate her own being that these words could emerge:

> In cosmic thoughts I shall weave
> My own thinking, so that it may become clear
> In the light of life's eternal becoming.

What the soul is applying here to the characterization of its own being has been distilled out of all that is offered in spiritual science. Or,

> In depths of soul I shall dip
> Devoted contemplation,
> So that it may become strong
> For the true goals of human striving.

However, our real desire is that these things be used to raise our spiritual-scientific movement out of the merely theoretical and into something of living comprehension for the soul, a kind of moving stream in which we truly exist and weave and have our being. Then we will know what is taking place all around us in the spiritual world just as we know that all around us in the physical world is the air we breathe. This is indeed possible, even if it is denied by the uninstructed. It is the future destiny of humankind: to know in some measure that, just as the air exists for and around the physical body, the spiritual world is all-surrounding and can be experienced by the soul. And just as the air interacts with the body, the spiritual world interacts with the soul, forms the soul, weaves the soul, penetrates it with its essence.

It is, in fact, possible for us to indicate in detail the destiny of the soul after death in individual cases. And, I would like to say, such things will be even more intimately set forth in our time precisely because, through the momentous and grievous events of the present, death is directing its breath throughout the world, and our age demands unnumbered victims. Thus a special challenge arises for us in dealing with the issue of death in our present day.

So, my dear friends, we know that the human being, in passing through the gate of death, gives the physical body over to the earth, to the elements of the earth, and that the astral body and the I withdraw from the physical body. We have seen in our second case that at the time of cremation the etheric body had already been laid aside as well; after some days the etheric body departs. Now, so many human beings in the present day are passing through the gate of death in the fullest bloom of life that we are endlessly concerned with one particular question. We can ask ourselves this question by transposing a purely physical concept into the spiritual, where it obtains far more than in the physical: What happens to the etheric body of one who has passed through the gate of death once it has separated after some days from the physical body? How does such a young etheric body fare? A person who moves through the gate of death at the age of thirty-five or thirty, or twenty-five or twenty, or even younger, sets aside the etheric body, of course, but it is an etheric body which could still have served physical life for decades—which would still have possessed strength for decades. As dictated by karma, the use of these forces is denied the deceased, but the forces remain in the person nonetheless. Here in physical life they would have been able to function for decades more. The physicist thinks, correctly, that here on earth no energy is lost; it is transformed. In the land of the spirit, this is truer still. The forces of a youth fallen upon the battlefield here, which could still have maintained the physical life for decades, do not pass simply into nothingness; they abide. And now we can say, prompted precisely by the events of our time, that these forces pass over into the being of the folk soul of that particular people. These forces of the etheric body are taken in by and act within the whole folk soul. These are true spiritual forces which continue to exist aside from the human being, aside from what is borne in the I and the astral body and the individuality throughout the time between death and new birth.

What this really means will best be understood only in the future—that within the folk soul these forces too are present, that they are active as forces, not as beings, within all that this folk soul will unfold. And, I would like to add, they will be the most fruitful, the most sun-radiant forces there.

Here I would like to offer another example which is close to us. It may at first seem to have little to do with the events of the time, but the manner in which it occurred and what resulted from it can nevertheless give us an insight into all those instances when an unconsumed etheric body is put aside after death has brought conclusion to a youthful life.

In autumn we experienced the passing of the seven-year-old child of one of our members. The death of this child happened in a most singular way. He was a lovely boy and an unusually spiritual child for his age—a lovely, good, and very spiritually aware child. Well, he met his death by being in a certain spot at precisely the instant when a furniture truck overturned, crushing him so that he was suffocated—at a place where probably no truck had ever driven before or since, but only at this particular moment. Moreover, one can ascertain by objective fact that this child was in that place at precisely the time the truck overturned because of a variety of circumstances which are called accidental in the external, materialistic view of the world. The boy was picking up some kitchen utensils for his mother and had left a little late on that particular evening because he had been delayed. Had he gone five minutes earlier he would have long since been past the spot where the truck overturned. Furthermore, he left by another door than was ordinarily his custom—just this once by another door! Had he left by the usual door, he would have passed by the truck on the right. The truck overturned toward the opposite side.

When one truly follows this whole case from a karmic, spiritual-scientific point of view, one can completely confirm that the rational logic that one employs correctly in the outer physical world is bankrupt and useless here.

I have often used another example to illustrate this further— the example of a man who is walking along a river and falls into the water at precisely the spot where a stone is lying. External observation will naturally assume that the man stumbled over the stone, fell into the water, and thereby met his death; the obvious conclusion would also be that he drowned. But if an autopsy were to be performed, it would be ascertained that the man had suffered a stroke and because of that had fallen into the water dead—that he had in fact fallen into the water because he was dead, not that he was dead because he had fallen into the water. Cause and effect have been mistakenly reversed.

We find such judgments in science at every turn, where cause and effect are confused. That which seems to be established by logic in external life can be utterly false. Thus, using external observation, the death of little Theodor Faiss could, of course, also be described as an unfortunate accident! In truth, however, the karma of the child was such that, to put it plainly, the I ordered up the truck; the truck overturned so that the child's karma might be fulfilled. And here we have a particularly youthful etheric body. This child too could surely have become a man and could have lived to be seventy years old. The forces in the etheric body, which would have sufficed for seventy years, passed through the gate of death after only seven.

All this played itself out in Dornach. The father was in the army and was not present when it all occurred; he in fact died shortly thereafter from wounds received in the war. This whole event took place in the immediate vicinity of our building, and since that time we have had in the aura of the Dornach building the forces of the etheric body of this child. And anyone who has work to do for this building and is able to perceive the spiritual forces that preside over it finds the forces of this child within. Thus, quite apart from the astral body and the I that passed over into the spiritual world in order to work in the life between death and rebirth, the etheric body remained behind and united itself with the entire spiritual aura of the Dornach building. Such insights are bound up with deep, meaningful feelings, for they are not ideas to be dryly received as if they were numerical constructs, but ideas to be received with a loving, thankful soul. And so, bearing such knowledge in mind, it goes without saying that when I myself have something to do for the Dornach building, I never for one instant allow myself to lose sight of the fact that these forces are working with me, that these forces are helping me. Thereby, theoretical knowledge unites itself with real life.

My dear friends, keeping such knowledge in mind while countless unfulfilled etheric bodies here on earth are passing through the gate of death will help us clearly imagine now what will happen when the sun of peace rises again after the dusk of the present war. Then these forces, these etheric forces of those who have passed through the gate of death, the gate of suffering, will truly be present and will seek to unite themselves with those souls who are working here on earth for the progress and the well-being of the world. However, for this to happen there will have to be people on earth who have understanding for these things, who can be conscious of the fact that above in the spiritual world, within those etheric bodies left behind, are those who made their sacrifice to the time. They wish to work here on earth. But their labors can truly bear fruit only if there are receptive souls here who wish to unite themselves in thought with what comes to them from out of the spiritual world. So it is eternally important for the fruits of this our great but difficult and painful time that a spirit-affirming knowledge bring forth thoughts which can unite with the thoughts descending from the etheric bodies of the deceased. Thus we must receive from these trying circumstances, which stand in the sign of suffering and death but also in the sign of greatness, the exhortation that they lead us to a higher time more inclined toward the spiritual than the past time has been. It must not come to pass that those who have sacrificed themselves in order to work for the progress of the earth and its well-being have to look down upon a world in which they find no chance to become involved because the souls are not there to send back to them the receptive thoughts they need. For this reason we must grasp spiritual science as something living and as something that is necessary for the time which will come about precisely because of the events of our day. And that is what I have summed up again and again, in the meaning and the spirit of our thinking, with the words:

> Out of courage shown in battle,
> Out of the blood shed in war,
> Out of the grief of those who are left,
> Out of the people's deeds of sacrifice
> Spirit fruits will come to grow
> If souls with knowledge of the spirit
> Turn their mind to spirit realms.

[Translated by Thomas Ehrhardt.]

18

FOR MANY YEARS, Rudolf Steiner gave out meditations to help those left behind remain connected to those who had died. These are specific indications, given to particular individuals in particular circumstances. Adapted, they are of universal application. Here are some of them.

Meditations

translated by Christopher Bamford

May my love *be* for you
In the spirit-realm.
May my seeking soul
Find your soul.
May *my* thinking of *your* being
Ease your cold,
Ease your heat.
In this way, we shall be united:
I with you,
You with me.

(GA 261/268, undatable)

In the light
Of cosmic thoughts
The soul weaves
That unites with me on earth.

(GA 261/268, notebook entry, 1924)

To bind soul to soul
I shall send the faithful love
We found
Into the fields of spirit.
If you turn your soul
From the lands of spirit light,
Seeking to see what you seek in me,
You will find my thinking
Through love.

(GA 261/268, notebook entry, 1916)

In the worlds,
Where the kernel
Of your being's soul
Now sojourns,
I send *love* to you—
To cool your heat
To warm your coldness.
If you find me in *feeling*
I shall always be near to you.

(GA 261/269, undatable)

May my heart-love reach to soul-love,
May my love's warmth shine to spirit-light.
Thus, I draw near to you,
Thinking spiritual thoughts *with* you,
Feeling cosmic love *in* you,
Willing in spirit *through* you—
Weaving with you
One in experience.

(GA 261/268, to Rudolf Hahn, for his wife, Marie, September 1918.)

May my heart's warm life
Stream to your soul,
To warm your coldness
To soothe your heat.
May *my* thoughts live in *your* thoughts—
And your thoughts in my thoughts—
In the spiritual worlds.

(GA 261/268, notebook entry, 1924)

May my soul's love *strive* to you
May my love's meaning *stream* to you.
May they *bear* you
May they *hold* you
In the heights of *hope*,
In the spheres of *love*.

(GA 261/268, undatable)

May our love follow you,
O soul,
Living there in spirit,
Seeing your earthly life;
Seeing yourself cognized as spirit.
And what appears to you
In the land of souls to be yourself
Thinking—
Accept our love
So that we may feel ourselves in you
And you may find in *our* souls,
What lives with you in faithfulness.

(GA 261/268, for the death of Marie Hahn, September 1918)

I see you
In the spiritual world
In which you are.
May my love
Alleviate your heat
Alleviate your cold.
It breaks through to you
And helps you
To find the way
Through the spirit's darkness
To the spirit's light.

(GA 261/268, undatable)

As the golden stars shine forth
From the blue depths of spirit,
So from my depths of my soul
The strong upholding powers stream forth.

[Drawing: Yellow Stars on a Blue Ground]

*(GA 268, to Hermine Stein, on the death of her son Friedrich,
fallen in battle, March 22, 1915)*

Faithfully
I will follow your soul
Through the gate of death
Into the light-engendering
time-places—
With *love*, I will ease spirit coldness for you,
With *knowing*, I will untangle spirit light for you,
With *thinking*, I will linger with you.

*(GA 261, for Gertrud Noss,
on the death of her son Fritz Mitscher, February 1915)*

May my soul follow you
Into the realm of spirit,
Follow you with the same love
It was able to nurture
In the realm of earth
When my eye could still behold you,
May it ease your warmth, ease your cold—
Thus we live united,
Unseparated, through the door of spirit.

(GA 261, for Gertrud Noss,
on the death of her son Fritz Mitscher, February 1915)

Feel how we gaze lovingly
Into heights that now
Call you to other work.
May your power reach out
From spirit-realms
To the friends you left behind.

Hear our souls' request
Sent to you in confidence:
We need here, for our earthly work,
Strong power from spirit lands—
We thank our friends now dead for this.

A hope that makes us happy,
A loss that pains us deeply:
Let us hope that you light our lives,
Far-and-near, unlost,
A soul-star in the spiritual firmament.

(GA 261, for Fritz Mitscher, Basel,
February 5, 1915)

May the eyes of your soul look
Into my thoughts' deeper power—
That is my will.
May my will meet your will
   in the Father's power
     in the Son's grace
      in the Spirit's light.

(GA 261, given to William Scott Pyle
after the death of Edith Maryon)

1. Your will was weak
2. Strengthen your will
3. I send you
Warmth for your cold
4. I send you
Light for your darkness
5. My love to you
6. My thoughts to you
7. Go—become—further.

(GA 268, to Franz Gerner,
for a friend lost through suicide, undatable)

O Soul in the land of soul
Seek Christ's grace
That brings you aid,
Aid from spirit lands,
And gives peace
To those spirits
Who, experiencing no peace,
Want to despair.

(GA 268, for a mother for her son who took his life)

Companion of my life,
Help the steps,
My thoughts,
Go to you,
To bring them to him,
I ask your soul, my spouse—

(GA 268, to the same mother,
to turn to her early deceased husband, undatable)

My thoughts stream
Heartwarming
Into your soul's sleep.
Experience them in your I
Now free.
I will be with you.
And bring out of your life,
From earth existence,
What you need for spirit remembering.

(GA 268, for Margaret Bockholt,
after the death of her father, January 1924)

With you, my soul
Seeks you, intuitively
My soul is with you
And lives your task
With you.
Thus we are
United karmically
For all time.

(GA 268, for Gertrud and Wilhelm v. Heydebrand,
after the short life of one of their children, 1911/1912)

To you
In love
On Christ's Ways
Seek my heart
Live
In my thoughts
As I live in your soul.

*(GA 268, to a mother
after the death of her small child, June 1921)*

You were ours
And you will be ours
As the light of the spirit
Now streams from your soul eyes
Filled with devotion.

It will be your thoughts'
Noble power
To seek in spirit worlds
The love that faithfully
We keep for you.

(GA 268, notebook entry, 1917)

Divinity in my soul
I will give you space
In my conscious being:
You connect me to all
That the power of destiny brings me,
You never set me apart
From what you have given me
To love:
Your spirit guards mine
For it is yours also:
So I will guard with you,

Through you, in you,
What you have agreed
with those who are your's—
I will be strong, and know
That it is wisdom.

(GA 261, for Mrs. Roemer,
after the death of her son, Christmas 1919)

In the beginning was the Word
And I myself was in the Word
And the Word was in God.
With the Word I myself was in God
And the Word was a God.
And a God saw me in the Word
And the Word should live in my soul.

(GA 268, for M. Corre,
at the death of his father, undatable)

CODA: *The Dead Speak*

I am not on the earth as soul
but only in water, air, and fire;

In my fire I am in the planets
and the sun.

In my sun-being I am the
sky of the fixed stars—

I am not on the earth as soul
but in Light, Word, and Life;

In my life I am within
the being of the sun and the planets, in the Spirit
of Wisdom.

In my wisdom being I am in the
Spirit of Love—

(GA 268, notebook entry, New Year 1917/1918)

No barrier can separate
What, united in the spirit,
preserves
The light-shining
Love-streaming
Eternal soul bond:
Thus I am in your thoughts
Thus may you be in mine.

(GA 268, sketch)

I was united with you,
Remain united in me.
We shall speak together
In the language of eternal being.
We will be active
Where deeds become events,
We will weave in the Spirit
Where human thoughts are woven
In the Word of eternal Thoughts.

(GA 268, address for Georga Wiese, January 11, 1924)

Acknowledgments to the Rudolf Steiner-Nachlassverwaltung, Dornach, Switzerland, for the following:

1. From: "Das gegenseitige In-Beziehung-Treten zwischen den Lebenden und den sogenannten Toten" in *Okkulte Untersuchungen über das Leben zwischen Tod und neuer Geburt: Die lebendige Wechselwirkung zwischen Lebenden und Toten* (GA 140). English: *Occult Research into Life between Death and a New Birth*. Translated by R. Hofrichter (revised). New York: Anthroposophic Press, 1949.

2. From: "Über den Verkehr mit den Toten" in *Okkulte Untersuchungen über das Leben zwischen Tod und neuer Geburt: Die lebendige Wechselwirkung zwischen Lebenden und Toten* (GA 140). English: *Life Between Death and Rebirth*. Translation by R. M. Querido (revised). New York: Anthroposophic Press, 1968.

3. From: "Die lebendige Wechselwirkung zwischen Lebenden und Toten" in *Okkulte Untersuchungen über das Leben zwischen Tod und neuer Geburt: Die lebendige Wechselwirkung zwischen Lebenden und Toten* (GA 140). English: *Links Between the Living and the Dead*. Translation by D. S. Osmond and Charles Davy (revised). London: Anthroposophical Publishing Company, 1973.

4. From: "Das Hereinwirken der geistigen Welt in unser Dasein" in *Wie erwirbt man sich Verständnis für die Geistige Welt* (GA 154), lecture 5. English: *The Presence of the Dead on the Spiritual Path*. Translation by Christian von Arnim (revised). Hudson, NY: Anthroposophic Press, 1990.

5. From: "Die Geisteswissenschaft als Zusammenfassung von Wissenschaft, Intelligenz und hellsichtiger Forschung," lecture 6 in *Wie erwirbt man sich Verständnis für die Geistige Welt* (GA 154). English: *The Presence of the Dead on the Spiritual Path*. Translation by Christian von Arnim (revised). Hudson, NY: Anthroposophic Press, 1990.

6. From: *Menschenschicksale und Völkerschicksale* (GA 157). *The Forming of Destiny and Life after Death*. Translator unknown. Blauvelt, NY: Garber Communications, 1989.

7. From: "Die Verbindung zwischen Lebenden und Toten," lecture 7 in *Die Verbindung zwischen Lebenden und Toten* (GA 168). English "On the Connection of the Living and the Dead" in *Life Beyond Death*, selected lectures by Rudolf Steiner. Translation by M. Barton (revised). London: Rudolf Steiner Press, 1995.

8. From: "Der Tod als Lebenswandlung," lecture 2 in *Der Tod als Lebenswandlung* (GA 182). English: *The Dead Are With Us*. Translation revised. London: Rudolf Steiner Press, 1964.

9. From: "Die Verbindung der Lebenden mit den Toten. Wirklichkeits-gemässes Denken," lecture 4 in *Erdensterben und Weltenleben* (GA 181). English: *Earthly Death and Cosmic Life*. Revised translation. London: Rudolf Steiner Press, 1964.

10. From: "Gemeinsamskeitsgefühl und Dankbarkeitsempfinden, eine Brücke zu den Toten," lecture 7 in *Erdensterben und Weltenleben* (GA 181). English: *Earthly Death and Cosmic Life*. Revised translation. London: Rudolf Steiner Press, 1964.

11. From: "Vertrauen zum Leben und seelische Verjüngung, eine Brücke zu den Toten," lecture 7 in *Erdensterben und Weltenleben* (GA 181). English: *Earthly Death and Cosmic Life*. Revised translation. London: Rudolf Steiner Press, 1964.

12. From: *Das Geheimnis der Trinität* (GA 214). English: *The Mystery of the Trinity*, lecture 4, "The Other Side of Human Existence." Translation by James H. Hindes (revised). Hudson, NY: Anthroposophic Press, 1991.

13. From: *Esoterische Betrachtungen kärmischer Zusammenhänge, III. Die kärmis-chen Zusammenhänge der anthroposophischen Bewegung*, lecture 2. English: *Karmic Relationships*, volume III, lecture 2. Translation by George Adams (revised). London: Rudolf Steiner Press, 1977.

14. From: "Skizze eines Lebensabrisses (1861-1893)" in *Briefe I (1881-1891)*. English: *Self-Education: Autobiographical Reflections 1861–1893*. Translated by A. Wulsin (revised). Spring Valley, NY, Mercury Press, 1985.

15. From: *Mein Lebensgang*, chapter 20. English: *Autobiography: Chapters in the Course of My Life*. Hudson: New York Anthroposophic Press, 1999.

16. From: *Zur Geschichte und aus den Inhalten der ersten Abteilung der Eso-terischen Schule 1904–1914* (GA 264). English: *From the History & Contents of the First Section of the Esoteric School 1904–1914*. Translated by John Wood. Hudson, NY: Anthroposophic Press, 1998.

17. From: "Persönlich-Übersinnliches" in *Menschenschicksale und Völker-schicksale* (GA 157), lecture 7. English: *Destinies of Individuals and of Nations*. Translated by Thomas Ehrhardt. New York: Anthroposophic Press, 1986.

18. From *Unsere Toten: Ansprachen, Gedenkworte und Meditationssprüche 1906-1924* (GA 261) and *Mantrische Sprüche: Seelenübungen II* (GA 268).

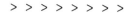

PUBLISHER'S NOTE: In order to focus on the motif of the relationship between the living and those who have died, the parts of the lectures that are not directly related to this theme have been omitted. This is indicated by ellipses in the text.

Further Reading

RELATED WORKS BY RUDOLF STEINER

Angels: Selected Lectures by Rudolf Steiner, Anna Meuss (ed.). London: Rudolf Steiner Press, 1996.

Anthroposophical Leading Thoughts. London: Rudolf Steiner Press, 1973.

Anthroposophy (A Fragment): A New Foundation for the Study of Human Nature. Hudson, NY: Anthroposophic Press, 1996.

Anthroposophy and the Inner Life. Bristol, UK: Rudolf Steiner Press, 1994.

At the Gates of Spiritual Science. London: Rudolf Steiner Press, 1986.

A Way of Self Knowledge (including *The Threshold of the Spiritual World*). Hudson, NY: Anthroposophic Press, 1999.

A Western Approach to Reincarnation and Karma: Selected Lectures and Writings by Rudolf Steiner, René Querido (ed.). Hudson, NY: Anthroposophic Press, 1996.

Between Death and Rebirth. London: Rudolf Steiner Press, 1975.

Cosmic and Human Metamorphoses. Blauvelt, NY: Garber Communications, 1989.

The Destinies of Individuals and of Nations. London: Rudolf Steiner Press, 1986.

Earthly Death and Cosmic Life. London: Rudolf Steiner Press, 1964.

The Forming of Destiny and Life after Death. Blauvelt, New York: Garber Communications, 1989.

How to Know Higher Worlds. Hudson, NY: Anthroposophic Press, 1994.

History of Spiritism and the History of Hypnotism and Somnambulism. New York: Anthroposophic Press, 1943.

The Inner Nature of Man and the Life between Death and a New Birth. London: Rudolf Steiner Press, 1994.

Karmic Relationships. 8 volumes. London: Rudolf Steiner Press, current.

Life between Death and Rebirth. Hudson, NY: Anthroposophic Press, 1989.

Life beyond Death, Frank Teichmann, (ed.). London: Rudolf Steiner Press, 1995.

Man in the Light of Occultism, Theosophy, and Philosophy. London: Rudolf Steiner Press, 1964.

The Occult Movement in the Nineteenth Century and its Relation to Modern Culture. London: Rudolf Steiner Press, 1973.

Outline of Esoteric Science. Hudson, NY: Anthroposophic Press, 1998.

Theosophy. Hudson, NY: Anthroposophic Press, 1994.

Theosophy of the Rosicrucian. London: Rudolf Steiner Press, 1975.

GENERAL BACKGROUND READING

Autobiography: Chapters in the Course of My Life, 1861–1907. Hudson, NY: Anthroposophic Press, 1999.

Christianity as Mystical Fact. Hudson, NY: Anthroposophic Press, 1997.

Cosmic Memory. Blauvelt, NY: Garber Communications, 1998.

The Essential Steiner, Robert McDermott (ed.). San Francisco: Harper SanFrancisco, 1984.

Intuitive Thinking as a Spiritual Path. Hudson, NY: Anthroposophic Press, 1994.

Spiritual Beings in the Heavenly Bodies and in the Kingdoms of Nature. Hudson, NY: Anthroposophic Press, 1992.

The Spiritual Guidance of the Individual and Humanity. Hudson, NY: Anthroposophic Press, 1992.

The Spiritual Hierarchies and the Physical World: Reality and Illusion. Hudson, NY: Anthroposophic Press, 1996.

ON RUDOLF STEINER

Barnes, Henry. *A Life for the Spirit: Rudolf Steiner in the Crosscurrents of Our Time*. Hudson, NY: Anthroposophic Press, 1997.

Rudolf Steiner (1861-1925) became a respected and well-published scientific, literary, and philosophical scholar, particularly known for his work on Goethe's scientific writings. He developed his early philosophical principles into an approach to methodical research of psychological and spiritual phenomena that has led to innovative and holistic approaches in medicine, philosophy, religion, education, science, agriculture, and the arts. He founded the General Anthroposophical Society, which has branches throughout the world.